A GUILDSMAN'S INTERPRETATION
OF HISTORY

OLD WORLDS FOR NEW

EXTRACTS FROM REVIEWS

Daily News and Leader :
" It is an important controversial work, representative of
many new and far from negligible tendencies in labour and
other advanced circles."

Athenæum :
" The author deals with a variety of topics, among which may
be mentioned the Mediæval Guild System, large organizations,
the division of labour, machinery and industry, the tyranny
of the middleman, the problem of his elimination, and the
decentralization of industry."

The Scotsman :
" While the papers move over eminently controversial
ground, they are freshly reasoned and suggestive."

Sheffield Independent :
" There are ideas in this book worth more than a king's
ransom."

Church Times :
" The Guild Socialist Movement has its many exponents,
but Mr. Penty contrives at once to be exponent and
critic. . . . There are signs in plenty that Guild Socialism
is the next popular social doctrine with which we have to
reckon."

Mr. G. K. Chesterton in the "New Witness" :
" We wish some of the honest elements roughly covered by
the National Party would read such a book as Mr. A. J.
Penty's ' Old Worlds for New ' ; and they might not talk
so excitedly or at least so exclusively about Maximum
Production. . . . Even the few short words of Mr. Penty's
title contain a wide challenge to the progress of the modern
world ; they are not only a parody on Mr. Wells but a very
valid comment on him."

The Herald
" The book should be read by all who are anxious about
altering the present conditions. It has much of permanent
value, and it is provoking and stimulating. It is a terrible
bore to read a book with which you agree in every detail.
You usually go to sleep. No one will do this, however,
that reads ' Old Worlds for New.' "

Manchester Guardian :
" Mr. Penty has considerable claims to be regarded as the
pioneer of Guild Socialism."

LONDON : GEORGE ALLEN & UNWIN LTD.

A GUILDSMAN'S INTERPRETATION OF HISTORY

BY

ARTHUR J. PENTY

AUTHOR OF "THE RESTORATION OF THE GUILD SYSTEM,"
"OLD WORLDS FOR NEW," "GUILDS AND
THE SOCIAL CRISIS"

LONDON: GEORGE ALLEN & UNWIN LTD.
RUSKIN HOUSE, 40 MUSEUM STREET, W.C.1

First published in May 1920.

PREFACE

THE primary object of this history is to relate the social problem to the experience of the past and so to help bring about a clearer comprehension of its nature. " The reason," says the author of *Erewhon*, " why we cannot see the future as plainly as the past is because we know too little of the actual past and the actual present. The future depends upon the present, and the present depends upon the past, and the past is unalterable." It is by studying the past in the light of the experience of the present and the present in the light of the past that we may attain to a fuller understanding both of the present and the past. Certain aspects of industrialism are new to the world, and the past offers us no ready-made solution for them, but to understand them it is necessary to be familiar with Mediæval principles, for such Mediæval problems as those of law and currency, of the State and the Guilds, lie behind industrialism and have determined its peculiar development. If we were more familiar with history we should see the problems of industrialism in a truer perspective and would have less disposition to evolve social theories from our inner consciousness. This neglect of the experience of the past is no new thing; it is as old as civilization itself. Thus in criticizing some of the fantastic proposals of Plato for the reorganization of Greek society, Aristotle says: " Let us remember that we should not disregard the experience of the ages ; in the multitude of years, these things, if they were good, would certainly not have been unknown : for almost everything has been found out, although sometimes they are not put together; in other cases men do not use the knowledge that they have." It would be a mistake to push this idea too far, and refuse to entertain any proposal which could not claim the authority of history, but it would be just as well before embarking on any new enterprise to inquire if history has anything to say about it. If we did we should find that debatable matter was confined within.very narrow limits, and with minds enriched through the study of history we should not waste so much of our time in fruitless discussion. Above all, we should speedily discover that there is no such thing as a cure-all for social ills. We should become more interested in principles and have less regard for schemes.

Though the Guild theory is ultimately based upon historical considerations, the absence hitherto of a history written from the Guildsman's point of view has been a serious handicap to the movement. Not only has this lack prevented it from giving historical considerations the prominence they deserve, but when Guild ideas are adopted by Socialists who have not been historical students they are apt to be distorted by the materialist conception of history which lies in the background of the minds of so many. Hence it becomes urgent, if the movement is not to be side-tracked, that Guildsmen should have a history of their own which gathers together information of importance to them. In this volume are gathered together such facts from a hundred volumes, and it is hoped by organizing them into a consistent theory to show not only that history is capable of a very different interpretation from the one that materialists affirm but that the Guild Movement has a definite historical significance. Indeed, we are persuaded that the success which has followed its propaganda is ultimately due to the fact that it has such a significance.

That the materialist conception of history is a one-sided and distorted conception, all students of history who are not materialists by temperament are well aware. It is made plausible by isolating a single factor in history and

ignoring other factors. The theory of the Class War is
as grotesque and false an explanation of the history of society
as a history of marriage would be that was built up from
the records of Divorce Courts, which carefully took note
of all the unhappy marriages and denied the existence of
happy ones because they were not supported by documentary
evidence. The heresies of Marx stand on precisely such
a footing. They are false, not because of what they say,
but because of what they leave unsaid. Such theories
gain credence to-day because capitalism has undermined
all the great traditions of the past, and thus emptied life
of its contents. It is true that by the light of the materialist
conception considerable patches of history, including the
history of the present day, may be explained. It is true
of the later history of Greece and Rome as of Europe after
the Reformation ; for in the decline of all civilizations the
material factor comes to predominate. But as an explanation
of history as a whole and of the Mediæval period in particular
it is most demonstrably false, and only ignorance, if not
the deliberate falsification in the past, of Mediæval history
could have made such an explanation plausible. It is
important that this should be recognized, not merely because
it is an injustice to the past to have its reality distorted,
but because of its reaction upon the mind of to-day. It
makes all the difference to our thinking about the problems
of the present day whether we believe modern society has
developed from a social system which was inhuman and
based upon class tyranny, in which ignorance and superstition prevailed, or from one which enjoyed freedom and
understood the nature of liberty in its widest and most
philosophic sense. If a man believes that society in the
past was based upon class tyranny he will see everything
in an inverted perspective, he will be predisposed to support
all the forces of social disintegration which masquerade
under the name of " progress " because he will view with
suspicion all traditions which have survived from the past

and have a prejudice against all normal forms of social organization. If it be true that the Middle Ages was a time of tyranny, ignorance and superstition, then to a logically minded person it naturally follows that the emancipation of the people is bound up with the destruction of such traditions as have survived, for to such a mind tradition and tyranny become synonymous terms. But if, on the contrary, he knows that such was not the case, that the Middle Ages was an age of real enlightenment, he will not be so readily deceived. He will know how to estimate at their proper value the movements he sees around him, and not be so disposed to place his faith in quack remedies, for he will know that for the masses the transition from the Middle Ages has not been one from bondage to freedom, from poverty to well-being, but from security to insecurity, from status to wage-slavery, from well-being to poverty. He will know, moreover, that the Servile State is not a new menace, but that it has been extending its tentacles ever since the days when Roman Law was revived.

Looked at from this point of view, the materialist conception of history, with its prejudice against Mediævalism, is a useful doctrine for the purposes of destroying existing society, but must prevent the arrival of a new one. I feel fairly safe in affirming this, because Marx's forecasts of the future are in these days being falsified. Up to a certain point Marx was right. He foresaw that the trend of things would be for industry to get into fewer and fewer hands, but it cannot be claimed that the deductions he made from this forecast are proving to be correct, for he did not foresee this war. The circumstance that Marx gave it as his opinion that the annexation of Alsace and Lorraine by Germany would lead in fifty years' time to a great European war does not acquit him, since the war that he foresaw was a war of revenge in which France was to be the aggressor and had nothing whatsoever to do with industrial development, which this one certainly had. Not having foreseen this war, Marx did not foresee the anti-climax in which the present system seems destined to end. And this is fatal to the whole social theory, because it brings to the light of day a weakness which runs through all his theory— his inability to understand the moral factor and hence to make allowances for it in his theories. Marx saw the material forces at work in society up to a certain point very clearly, and from this point of view he is worthy of study. But he never understood that this was only one half of the problem and finally the less important half. For along with all material change there go psychological changes ; and these he entirely ignores. In the case in question Marx failed to foresee that the growth of the pressure of competition would be accompanied by an increase in national jealousies. On the contrary, he tells us in the *Communist Manifesto* (written in 1847) that national antagonisms are steadily to diminish. But if he misjudged national—I might almost say industrial—psychology on this most fundamental point, it demonstrates that for practical purposes Marx and his materialist conception of history are anything but an infallible guide. And so we are led to inquire whether, if Marx, owing to his neglect of psychology, proved to be wrong on this issue, he may not be equally untrustworthy in other directions ; whether, in fact, the anti-climax which has overtaken national relationships may not likewise take place in industry ; whether the process of industrial central- ization which Marx foresaw is not being accompanied by internal disintegration, and whether the issue of it all is to be his proletarian industralized State or a relapse into social anarchy. Such, indeed, does appear to me to be the normal trend of economic development ; for when everything but economic considerations have been excluded from life—and the development of industrialism tends to exclude everything else—men tend naturally to quarrel, because there is nothing positive left to bind men together in a communal life. Looking at history from this point of view, it may be said that if Marx's view is correct, and if exploitation has played the part in history which he affirms it has, then, frankly, I do not see how civilization ever came into existence. We know that exploitation is breaking civilisation up ; we may be equally sure it did not create it. Moreover, it leaves us with no hope for the future. For if it be true that the history of civilization is merely the history of class struggles, what reason is there to suppose that with the end of the reign of capitalism class struggle will come to an end ? May it not merely change its form ? The experience of the Bolshevik regime in Russia would appear to suggest such a continuation.

It remains for me to thank Mr. J. Pla, Mr. M. B. Reckitt, Mr. G. R. S. Taylor, Mr. L. Ward and Mr. C. White for the interesting material they so generously placed at my disposal, and the Editor of the *New Age* for permission to reprint such chapters and parts of chapters as appeared in his journal.

A. J. P.

66, STRAND ON GREEN. W. 4.
September 1919.

CONTENTS

CHAPTER   PAGE

    I.   GREECE AND ROME 13

   II.   CHRISTIANITY AND THE GUILDS 34

  III.   THE MEDIÆVAL HIERARCHY 47

  IV.   THE REVIVAL OF ROMAN LAW 58

   V.   ROMAN LAW IN ENGLAND 73

  VI.   THE CONSPIRACY AGAINST MEDIÆVALISM . . 85

 VII.   MEDIÆVALISM AND SCIENCE 102

VIII.   THE ARTS OF THE MIDDLE AGES . . . 117

  IX.   THE FRANCISCANS AND THE RENAISSANCE . . 126

   X.   THE REFORMATION IN GERMANY . . . 139

  XI.   THE SUPPRESSION OF THE ENGLISH MONASTERIES . 158

 XII.   THE REFORMATION IN ENGLAND 170

XIII.   THE FRENCH REVOLUTION 189

XIV.   CAPITALISM AND THE GUILDS 214

 XV.   POLITICAL AND ECONOMIC THOUGHT AFTER THE
        REFORMATION 224

XVI.   THE INDUSTRIAL REVOLUTION 237

XVII.   PARLIAMENTARIANISM AND THE NINETEENTH CENTURY 246

XVIII.   ON LIMITED LIABILITY COMPANIES . . . 259

XIX.   THE WAR AND THE AFTERMATH 271

XX.   BOLSHEVISM AND THE CLASS WAR . . 285

XXI.   THE PATH TO THE GUILDS 298

      INDEX 317

A Guildsman's Interpretation
of History

CHAPTER I

GREECE AND ROME

THE first fact in history which has significance for Guildsmen
is that of the introduction of currency, which took place
in the seventh century before Christ when the Lydian kings
introduced stamped metal bars of fixed weight as a medium
of exchange. In the course of a generation or two this
uniform measure entirely replaced the bars of unfixed weight
which the Greeks had made use of when exchange was not
by barter. It was a simple device from which no social
change was expected, but the development which followed
upon it was simply stupendous. Civilization—that is,
the development of the material accessories of life, may
be said to date from that simple invention, for by facilitating
exchange it made foreign trade, differentiation of occupation
and specialization on the crafts and arts possible. But
along with the undoubted advantages which a fixed currency
brought with it there came an evil unknown to primitive
society—the economic problem; for the introduction of
currency created an economic revolution, comparable only
to that which followed the invention of the steam engine
in more recent times, by completely undermining the communist base of the Mediterranean societies. "We can
watch it in Greece, in Palestine and in Italy, and see the
temper of the sufferers reflected in Hesiod and Theognis,
Amos and Hosea, and in the legends of early Rome."
The progress of economic individualism soon divided

Greek society into two distinct and hostile classes—the prosperous landowners, the merchants and money-lending class on the one hand, and the peasantry and the debt-slaves on the other. Hitherto no one had ever thought of elaiming private property in land. It had never been treated as a commodity to be bought and sold. The man who tilled the soil thought of it as belonging to the family, to his ancestors and descendants as much as to himself. But within a generation or two after the introduction of currency the peasantry everywhere began to find themselves in need of money, and they found that it could be borrowed by pledging their holdings as security for loans. It was thus that private property in land first came into existence. Land tended to pass into the hands of the Eupatrid by default. For lean years have a way of running in cycles, and at such times the "haves" can take advantage of the necessities of the "have-nots." [1]

The reason for these developments is not far to seek. So long as exchange was carried on by barter, a natural limit was placed to the development of trade, because people would only exchange for their own personel use. Exchange would only be possible when each party to the bargain possessed articles which the other wanted. But with the introduction of currency this limitation was removed, and for the first time in history there came into existence a class of men who bought and sold entirely for the purposes of gain. These middlemen or merchants became specialists in finance. They knew better than the peasantry the market value of things, and so found little difficulty in taking advantage of them. Little by little they became wealthy and the peasantry their debtors. It is the same story wherever currency is unregulated—the distributor enslaves the producer. So it is not surprising that the Greeks always maintained a certain prejudice against all occupations connected with buying and selling, which they held were of a degrading nature. For though it is manifest that society cannot get along without traders, it is imperative for the well-being of society that they do not exercise too much power. The Greeks found by experience that such

[1] See *The Greek Commonwealth*, by Alfred Zimmern, pp. 110–14.

men were no better than they ought to be and that the association of trading with money-making reflected itself in their outlook on life, leading them eventually to suppose that everything could be bought and that there was nothing too great to be expressed in terms of money.[1]

Though the Greeks thought much about the problem which had followed the introduction of currency, to the end it eluded the efforts of their lawgivers and statesmen to solve it, and mankind had to wait until the coming of Mediævalism before a solution was forthcoming. Then the Guilds solved the problem by restricting currency to its legitimate use as a medium of exchange by means of fixing prices. Plato, it is true, anticipated the Mediæval solution. In *Laws* (917) he actually forbids bargaining and insists upon fixed prices. But nothing came of his suggestion. Perhaps it was too late in the day to give practical application to such a principle. For Plato wrote in the period following the Peloponnesian War when profiteering was rampant, and a restoration of the communal spirit to society, such as followed the rise of Christianity, was necessary before such a measure could be applied. Hence it was that Aristotle reverted to the principle of Solon that the cultivation of good habits must accompany the promulgation of good laws.

All the early Greek lawgivers who attempted to solve the economic problem which currency had introduced sought the solution not along Guild lines, by seeking to restrict currency to its legitimate use as a medium of exchange, but by restricting the use of wealth. Lycurgus preserves the communal life of Sparta for centuries against disruption on the one hand by inducing his fellow-citizens to resume the habits of their forefathers, to sacrifice all artificial distinctions, under the rigid but equal discipline of a camp which included among other things the taking of meals in common, and on the other by enforcing a division of the lands equally among the families and by the institution of a currency deliberately created to restrict business operations within the narrowest limits. It took the form of bundles of iron bars, and it appears to have answered the

[1] See *The Greek Commonwealth*, by Alfred Zimmern, p. 274.

purpose for which it was designed very well, for the Spartans never became a commercial nation.

This state of things continued down to the Peloponnesian War, when the Spartans, finding themselves at a disadvantage with Athens, inasmuch as without coined money they could have no fleet, departed from the law of Lycurgus. About the same time they threw over their system of land tenure. Continual warfare reduced the number of Spartans, and the accumulation of several estates in one family created disproportionate wealth, a tendency which was facilitated by a law promoted by the Ephor Epitadeus who granted liberty to bequeath property. Thus it came to pass that instead of the 9,000 property-owning Spartans mentioned in the regislation of Lycurgus, their numbers were reduced to 600, of whom only 100 were in full enjoyment of all civil rights. Naturally such economic inequalities broke up the communal life. The poorer citizens found themselves excluded from the active exercise of their civil rights, and could not keep pace with the rich in their mode of living, nor fulfil the indispensable conditions which had been imposed by Lycurgus upon every Spartan citizen.

In Attica the problem was faced in a different way. Lycurgus' solution consisted not merely in putting the clock back, as such measures would be called in these days, but by causing the clock to stand still. His solution was a democratic one in so far as democracy is possible among a slave-owning people. But Solon in Attica sought a remedy along different lines. He accepted currency and the social changes which came with it, and substituted property for birth as the standard for determining the rights and duties of the citizens. He divided them into four classes, which were distinguished from each other by their mode of military service and the proportion of their incomes which was paid in taxation. The lowest class paid no taxes at all, were excluded from public offices, but were allowed to take part in the popular assembly as well as in the courts in which justice was administered by the people. Like Lycurgus, he sought to redress the inequalities of wealth, but, unlike him, he sought a solution, not in the enforcement of a rigid discipline upon the citizens, but by removing the temptation

to accumulate wealth. This was the object of his sumptuary
laws, which were designed to make the rich and poor look
as much alike as possible, in order to promote a democracy
of personal habits if not of income. But though he did
not put the clock back as far as Lycurgus,· he did put it
back to the extent of giving things in many directions a
fresh start. It was for this purpose that he cancelled the
debts of the peasantry and effected a redistribution of
property, re-establishing the farmers on their ancestral
holdings. Though he failed to restrain usury, he sought
to mitigate to some extent its hardships by forbidding men
to borrow money on the security of their persons, while he
took steps to redeem those defaulting debtors who had been
sold into slavery by their creditors, using any public
or private funds he could secure for the purpose ; while,
further, he allowed the Athenians to leave their money to
whom they liked provided there were no legitimate male
heirs. These reforms, together with certain changes in
the juridical administration, were the most important of
Solon's laws. He refused the supreme position in the State,
and after making his laws he went abroad for ten years
to give his constitution a fair trial. When he returned
he found his juridical reforms were very successful, but the
economic troubles, though they had been allayed, had not
been eradicated. The peasants had been put back on their
holdings, but they had no capital and could not borrow money.
They did not blame Solon for his laws, but the magistrates
for the way they were administered. The State became
divided into three hostile parties—the men of the Shore,
of the Plain, and of the Mountains—each prepared to fight
for its own economic and territorial interests.

Fortunately at this crisis a man arose capable of handling
the situation. Pisistratus, who led the mountaineers, was
not only a man of statesmanlike qualities, but a noted soldier
and a man of large private means, and after some vicissitudes
he succeeded in making himself absolute master of the country.
When in power he found a remedy for the shortage of capital
among the peasants, which was the source of their economic
difficulty, by advancing to them capital out of his own private
fortune. This provided them with a nest-egg which enabled

2

them to tide over the lean years, or while their trees were growing to maturity. Their troubles were now at an end, and we hear no more about the land question until the Spartans, towards the close of the Peloponnesian War, came and ruined the cultivation.

Meanwhile, as a consequence of the development of foreign trade, Athens became a maritime, commercial and industrial city in which stock-jobbing, lending at usury, and every form of financial speculation broke loose. This led to the division of the social body into two distinct and hostile factions—a minority which possessed most of the capital and whose chief concern was its increase, and a mass of proletarians who were filled with enmity towards this aristocracy of finance, which began to monopolize all political power. It was thus that the religious aristocracy which for so long a period had governed Greece was superseded by a plutocracy whose triumph Solon had unconsciously prepared when he took income as a basis for the division of the classes. During the Peloponnesian War the plutocracy became very unpopular—presumably for profiteering, to which wars give every opportunity—and in Samos, Messenia and Megara the people, tired of economic subjection, revolted, slew the rich, did away with all taxes, and confiscated and divided landed property. The war entirely undermined all stability in the Greek States, leaving behind it as a heritage an unemployed class of soldiers and rowers which the social system was powerless to absorb. They became a constant source of trouble, and from the Peloponnesian War until the Roman Conquest " the cities of Greece wavered between two revolutions ; one that despoiled the rich, and another that reinstated them in the possession of their fortunes." It was in order to find a solution for this unemployed problem that Alexander the Great, at the recommendation of Isocrates, undertook the conquest of Asia and planted unemployed farm colonies of Greeks as far East as Cabul.[1]

Reading Greek history reminds us of the fact that the Class War is not a doctrine peculiar to the present age. But it is interesting to observe that it entirely failed to effect a solution of the economic problem which distracted Greece.

[1] Zimmern, p. 263.

Unregulated currency having given rise to economic individualism and destroyed the common ownership of property,
the solidarity of society slowly fell to pieces. It had undermined alike the independence of the peasantry and the
old religious aristocracy which had hitherto governed Greece,
and had concentrated power entirely in the hands of a
plutocracy which, like all plutocracies, was blind to everything
except its own immediate interests. It was thus that
Greek society, from being united, became div led into two
distinct and hostile classes in which the possibility of revolution became an ever-present contingency. The frequent
revolutions excited by the abuse of power of the plutocracy
led to the thinning of the agricultural population and the
misery of the inhabitants, and prepared the people to suffer
without resistance—nay, perhaps to welcome the Roman
invasion and conquest.

Uncontrolled currency brought the same evils into
existence in Rome, where the concentration of capital in
the hands of a few and its accompanying abuses developed
to a greater extent and far more rapidly than in Greece,
once they got under way. That they developed much
more slowly in the first instance was perhaps due to the
fact that whereas capitalism in Athens was a consequence
of foreign trade, in Rome it was intimately connected with
the growth of militarism. This difference is in all respects
parallel to the difference in modern times between capitalist
development in England and Germany. For while in
Greece, as in England, the development of capitalism was
a private affair due to the initiative and enterprise of
individual traders, in Rome, as in Germany, it was closely
associated with the policy of the Government.

Rome was originally a small agricultural state governed
by an aristocracy in which the Patrons and Clients, as the
two classes of society were called, bore much the same
relation to each other as the lord and serf of feudal times.
The Patrons or Patricians, as they were called at a later
date, were expected by law and custom to defend the Clients
from all wrong or oppression on the part of others, while
the Clients were bound to render certain services to the
Patrons. Just as the spread of currency undermined the

personal relationship existing between the lord and the serf in the Middle Ages, substituting money payments for payments in kind, so it may be assumed that the relationship of the Patrons and Clients in the early days of Rome was transformed by means of the same agency, for it was about the time of the spread of currency among the Mediterranean communities that a new order of things began to come into existence, when the hitherto harmonious relationship existing between the Patrons and Clients was replaced by one of personal bitterness. The bone of contention was the severity of the law against debtors whereby the defaulting debtor became the slave of the creditor, and as the debtor in nearly all cases was a Client, it created bad feeling between the two classes.

The unpopularity of this law against debtors led to its abolition after the fall of the Decemvirate in the fifth century before Christ. Interest on loans was limited to 10 per cent. and later to 5 per cent., while an attempt was made to abolish usury altogether. But the laws to abolish it proved ineffectual. Needy borrowers resorted to usurious lenders, who took good care that repayment was made one way or another. The Patricians appear to have become very grasping and tyrannical, for we read of a series of social disturbances between them and the peasantry over the question of debts and the unwillingness of the Patricians to allow the peasantry to have small holdings of their own. These disturbances were at length brought to an end in the year 286 B.C., when the poorer citizens left Rome in a body, out of protest, and encamped in an oak wood upon the Janiculum. To appease this secession they were granted 14 jugera (about 9 acres) of land each and their debts reduced. For a hundred and fifty years from this date until the appearance of the Gracchi we hear no more of civil dissensions in Rome.

The great change which transformed Rome from an aristocratic and agricultural society into a capitalistic and military one came about as a result of the Punic Wars. Italy was left in a state of economic distress and confusion, and the Romans were led to embark on a career of conquest abroad in order to avoid troubles at home. Moreover, the Punic Wars completely transformed the Roman character. From being a community of hardy, thrifty, self-denying and religious people they became avaricious, spendthrift and licentious. The immediate effect of these wars was to depopulate rural Italy, for the substantial burgesses of the towns and the stout yeomen of the country fell in great numbers during these wars. To this evil must be added the further one that when the campaigns were over and the soldiers returned home they had often contracted licentious tastes and formed irregular habits which were ill suited to the frugal life of the Italian husbandman. So it came about that many who possessed small estates were eager to sell them in order that they might enjoy the irregular pleasures of the city, while those who possessed nothing also tended to gravitate there. Thus a flood of emigration took place from the country to the towns. The countryside became more and more depopulated, while the towns, and Rome most of all, swarmed with needy and reckless men ready for any outrage.

These small estates and holdings passed into the hands of the great Senatorial families, who were every day growing richer by the acquisition of commands and administrative posts which were multiplied by every successive war. They cultivated them by means of slaves, which as a result of the wars now came on to the market in vast numbers, and were sold by public auction to the highest bidders. The cheapness of slave labour reacted to destroy the prosperity of such small free cultivators as had remained on the land. These privately owned large estates in turn tended to be replaced by enormous ones, administered by joint-stock companies which Pliny believed to be the real cause of the depopulation and decay of Italy. All the Public Lands of certain provinces belonged at one time to a few families, and the Roman dominions in Africa, comprising a great part of the north of that continent, belonged to six persons only, whom Nero, later on, thought well to put to death.

The growth of these joint-stock companies which made themselves the masters of the commercial movement is to be traced to a law, passed just before the second Punic War, which made it illegal for Senators to engage in any commercial venture. In order, therefore, to furnish supplies for the army and navy it became necessary to form companies with sufficient capital to undertake the contracts, and in these companies all the wealthy Romans, as well as officers of State, soldiers and politicians, held shares. The Patrician families were no exception to this rule, though they preferred to hold their shares in secret, not caring to be compromised in the eyes of the public, or to show that they were in any way indebted to the bankers and publicani (tax-gatherers), who were at the head of the commercial movement and until the fall of the Republic were the greatest power in Rome. Well has it been said that " the history of Roman Property Law is the history of the assimilation of *res mancipi* to *res nec mancipi* ; [1] in other words, the assimilation of real estate to movable property, of land to currency, of aristocracy to plutocracy.

It was thus in Rome, as in Greece, that uncontrolled currency replaced the class divisions based upon differences of function by class divisions based upon differences of wealth. Financial companies invaded all the conquered nations. There were companies for Sicily, for Asia, for Greece, Macedonia, Africa, Bithynia, Cilicia, Syria, Judea, Spain and Gaul. They had their headquarters at Rome, and the Forum became a kind of stock-exchange in which the buying or selling of shares was always going on and where every man was trying to outwit his neighbour. These companies speculated in everything : in land, building, mines, transport and supplies for the army and navy, and in the customs. This latter was the central source of corruption. Every five years the taxes of the provinces were put up to public auction, and that company which made the highest bid secured the contract if proper security could be given. When the contract was secured the successful company paid into the Imperial Treasury the amount of their bid and made what profit they could out of the transaction. All they collected over and above the amount of their contract they kept for themselves. Naturally the system led to extortion, since the more money the companies could extort from the taxpayers the greater was their profit. The

[1] Sir Henry Maine, *Ancient Law*, p. 283.

extortions incident to this iniquitous system form a principal topic in the provincial history of Rome, for the Roman Governors found it to their interest to support the tax-gatherers on condition of sharing in the plunder. It has been said that a Roman Governor needed to make three fortunes. The first was to provide him with the means of buying the suffrages of the people or of discharging the debts incurred in buying them ; the second was to keep for himself ; and the third was to provide him with the wherewithal to fight the actions in the courts which were certain to be brought against him when he relinquished office.

It goes without saying that a system so corrupt could not but react to corrupt Rome itself. The frequent laws against bribery at elections which may be dated from the year 181 B.C. testify to the change that was taking place. While money was extorted from the provincials, Rome itself escaped taxation altogether, and this reacted to render the Senate an entirely irresponsible body, for when they had now no longer any need to ask the people for money they were subject to no real control and no obstacle stood in the way of their acting as best suited their own personal interest. All lucrative employments were seized by members of the great Senatorial families, while a family that had once been ennobled by office had so many opportunities for making money that it became more difficult every day for a new man to make his way to the Consulship or even into the Senate, which was fast becoming a hereditary body of legislators. It was only when difficult military services were required that they called in the services of independent men.

Now that successful warfare had proved itself so profitable to the Senatorial families and the people had entirely lost control over them, the lust for conquest became general. Wars were now no longer defensive, even in pretence. Like the Germans, who appear to have copied the methods of the Romans, the Senate resorted to the most detestable practices in order to create internal dissensions in other countries. They were determined to have a voice in all matters within their sphere of interest, to make every possible excuse for Roman interference. Senatorial commissions were continually being despatched to arrange the affairs of other nations, for the Roman Senator had no doubt whatsoever in his mind that his people were the strongest and most competent to rule the world. And in the furtherance of their aims they were entirely unscrupulous. The arrogance and brutality of this new aristocracy of wealth knew no limits. They destroyed Carthage and Corinth out of commercial rivalry, while Cicero relates that the Senate caused the vineyards and olive-groves of Gaul to be destroyed, in order to avoid a damaging competition with the rich Roman landlords,[1] just as the Germans for similar reasons sought to destroy the towns and industries of Belgium and Northern France.

This period of Roman history should be particularly interesting to us, as it presents so many striking analogies to the present day. Just as the war promoted by the militarist capitalism of Germany has brought in its train Bolshevism and the Class War, so the militarist capitalism of Rome bore fruit in the slave revolts. As early as 181 B.C. 7,000 slaves in Apulia were condemned to death for brigandage, where travelling had become dangerous without an armed retinue. From attacking travellers they had begun to plunder the smaller country houses, and all except the very rich were obliged to leave the country. But there was not any general revolt until 133 B.C., when the slaves of Sicily revolted. The Romans there were now to feel the vengeance of men brutalized by oppression. Clad in skins, and armed with stakes and reaping-hooks, they broke into the houses and massacred all persons of free condition, from the old man and matron to the infant in arms. Once the standard of revolt was raised, thousands joined in, while the insurrection not only spread over the whole of the island, but broke out in various parts of the Empire. No one could tell where it would stop. For a time they met with success, and defeated an army of 8,000 Romans, but in the end the revolt was suppressed with great cruelty, though it took two years to effect it. A second Slave War broke out in Sicily thirty years later, and a third after the

[1] Cicero, *De Republica*, III. 6.

lapse of another thirty years, the latter being led by a gladiator named Spartacus, after whom the German Bolsheviks named their secret organization. Both of these revolts were suppressed like the first one, and when at length slavery came to an end it was not due to a successful revolt but to a changed attitude of the Roman citizen towards the institution of slavery. " During the first century of the Empire, chiefly under the influence of the Stoic philosophy, as later under that of Christianity, there had been growing up a feeling that a slave was, after all, a human being, and had some claim to be treated as such under the Roman law. Antoninus followed out this idea both in legislation and in his private life, as did his successor also, who adored his memory. They limited the right of a master over his slaves in several ways ; ordaining that if cruelty were proved against a master, he should be compelled to sell the slave he had ill-treated." [1] By such means slavery gradually gives way to Feudalism, which we shall consider in a later chapter.

Though these revolts were successfully suppressed, they shook the complacency of the Romans. A force was set in motion which by a natural sequence led to the Civil Wars and eventually to the Dictatorship and the Empire. Before the Slave War actually broke out it was becoming evident to thinking men that things could not go on in the way they were going and that reform was becoming a matter of urgency. Tiberius Gracchus, who now came to the front as a reformer, was the son of one of the few Romans in whom any public spirit had survived. When travelling through Etruria he had noted her broad lands tilled, not by free yeoman as of old, but by slaves. Soon after this the Slave War broke out, and as he had previously spoken his mind freely on this matter, public opinion in Rome fastened on him as the man to undertake the work of reform. After being elected a Tribune, he proposed to revive the Licinian Law of 364 B.C. by which it was enacted that no head of a family could hold more than 500 jugera (nearly 320 acres) of the Public Land, modifying it only to the extent that permission was to be given to every son to hold half that quantity in addition

---

[1] *Rome*, by W. Warde Fowler, p. 244.

on becoming his own master. It should be explained that by Public Land was meant land owned by the Roman State of which there was much ; for the Senate had retained its hold on a large part of the land of Italy acquired by Rome, though it was mostly leased to the great proprietors. To propose, therefore, that no one should hold more than 500 jugera was to attack the great landholders and companies who administered the vast estates, worked by slave labour, and to seek to replace them by a free yeomanry. Those who gave up possession were to receive compensation for improvements they had effected.

After some difficulty Gracchus succeeded in getting his bill carried by acclamation by the Assembly of Tribes. Within certain limits it was put into operation, and there is reason to believe that it did some good in regard both to depopulation and agriculture. But in order to get it carried during his year of office—and if he could not manage it then he would have to give it up for some time—he deliberately broke with law and usage by carrying a bill deposing the Tribune who acted for the Senate and was opposed to him. This violent and irregular procedure provoked a resistance which cost him his life. He had laid himself open to the charge of attempting to make himself master of the State, and as it was a maxim of Roman Law that the man who aimed at tyranny might be slain by any one, his enemies were not slow to take advantage of his imprudence. He and many of his supporters were killed on the Capitol when he had been Tribune for seven months, and the populace of Rome made no attempt to save him. Nine years later his brother Caius Gracchus was elected Tribune and took up his work, but he and his supporters were likewise slain by their political enemies.

Whatever the Gracchi failed to do, they certainly shook the power and prestige of the Senate. They gave it a blow from which it never recovered. The cruel times that followed made the best men of both parties regret the untimely end of those who had sacrificed wealth, rank and tranquillity in the hope of reforming the State by peaceful methods. But it was not to be done. The path to reform was blocked by the forms of a constitution which had served their purpose while Rome was a small City State, but became an anachronism when Rome became a world-wide Empire ; by the narrow spirit of the oligarchical faction, which was opposed to all change from self-interested reasons ; and lastly by the mean and fickle temper of the mongrel population of Rome whose power was sovereign in legislation and elections. These three factors in the situation reacted upon each other, and finally precipitated political chaos. The refusal of the Senate to face boldly the situation which was developing and their resolve to keep power entirely in their own hands ended by bringing them into contempt. They refused to listen to the Gracchi ; they had to listen to Marius. It was a true epigram that ran " the blood of Gracchus was the seed sown and Marius was the fruit." For there is a definite connection between the two. It was precisely because the Senate refused the legitimate demands of reform that a situation developed which mastered them. The Senate, like our own Government, being entirely under the control of capitalist influences, developed that same total incapacity to act except when pressure was brought to bear upon it. And so it happened that a time came when un-scrupulous adventurers rose to power who understood the art of exploiting their stupidity. While the oligarchy controlling the Senate found themselves able to suppress revolts against their power from below, they found them-selves powerless to control the growing power of their own generals, the jealousies between whom became a constant source of danger and anxiety to the State, whose interests they were supposed to serve, and led eventually to the civil wars which in the last century before Christ brought the whole Roman system to the very brink of ruin.

The reason for these troubles is not far to seek. When Tiberius Gracchus said, " The wild animals of Italy have their dens and lairs ; the men who have fought for Italy have light and air and nothing more. They are styled the masters of the world, though they have not a clod of earth they can call their own," he put his finger on the central weakness of the Roman policy of warfare which created in Italy a landless proletariat of desperate men. It became clearer to the people every day that the governing class expected them to do the fighting while they themselves were to take all the plunder. This realization led to the growth of dissatisfaction which broke loose when the governing class, by opposing the reforms of Gracchus, destroyed the confidence of the people in their good intentions. The consequence was that as nobody felt any loyalty to the Government, the instinct of loyalty which is natural to the vast majority of men was transferred from the Republic to individual generals, whom they regarded as their patrons. The Roman armies, which were such excellent fighting machines, were composed of the soldiers of Marius, of Sulla, of Pompey or of Cæsar. Their swords were at the command of any leader who offered a chance of booty. This new state of things, which reached its height during the civil wars, took its origin with the great Scipio. He had been refused levies by the Senate which he deemed necessary for the invasion of Africa, and he raised volunteers on his own credit, rewarding them with grants of land in Southern Italy. Marius and Sulla held out prospects of booty to the men who served under them, and so on until the fall of the Empire—the loyalty of the soldiers had to be bought. It was the natural and inevitable consequence of the destruction of a free yeomanry in Italy and the rise of a professional soldier class. It is thus to be seen that there is a very definite connection between the attitude of the governing class to the reforms of Gracchus and the civil wars that followed forty-five years later and which were finally brought to an end by the triumph of Augustus.

With the advent of Augustus a new chapter in Roman history is opened. The Republic gives way to the Empire, Roman society takes a new lease of life ; order begins to get the upper hand of anarchy. The immediate cause of the change was that the Senate and Roman people, after bitter experience became at last reconciled to the idea of despotism. They no longer claimed the exclusive right to deal with the ever-increasing administrative business of the Empire, and allowed Augustus a free hand to deal with the chaos which had overtaken it as best he could. This he did in the only way it is possible for a despot to govern— by means of a highly centralized bureaucracy, which he superimposed over popular institutions, many of which he restored, in form at least, where they had fallen into decay. This may not have been an ideal solution of the problems of the Roman Empire, but it was eminently practical. It preserved Roman civilization for centuries from the fear of invasion from without and from disruption from within. Augustus curbed the power of the capitalists and placed the taxation of the Empire on a new basis by the preparation of a Survey in which every house, field and wood was duly valued by responsible officials, thus getting rid once and for all of the system of extortion which was the central source of political corruption. With his capable and loyal helper Agrippa, he travelled over the whole Empire working hard at making settlements of all kinds, and carrying on military operations where they were absolutely necessary. Augustus found the Empire in a state of chaos, he left it a strongly compacted union of provinces and dependent kingdoms.

But Augustus was too clear-headed a man to trust entirely to the machinery of State. He understood that the satisfactory working of any system of government depended ultimately on the character of the people, and so he sought to promote a revival of the old Roman spirit. He called the poets to his aid, and is said to have suggested to Virgil the subject of the *Æneid*, which came to be looked upon as almost a sacred book, loved and honoured as much by Christian Fathers as by Pagan scholars. He saw that if his government was to be stable, Rome and Italy must be loyal, contented and at peace ; and this he secured by what in these days is called welfare work. " The city of Rome, with a population of perhaps half a million, of all races and degrees, had been a constant anxiety to Augustus so far, and had exercised far more power in the Empire than such a mixed and idle population was entitled to. He saw that this population must be well policed, and induced to keep itself in order as far as possible ; that it must be made quite comfortable, run no risk of starvation, have confidence in the goodwill of the gods, and enjoy plenty of amusements. Above all, it must believe in himself, in order to be loyal to his policy. When he returned to Rome after crushing Antony and Cleopatra, the Romans were already disposed to believe in him, and he did all he could to make them permanently and freely loyal. He divided the city into new sections for police purposes, and recruited corps of watchmen from the free population; he restored temples and priesthoods, erected many pleasant and convenient public buildings (this incidentally giving plenty of employment), organized the supply of corn and of water, and encouraged public amusements by his own presence at them. He took care that no one should starve, or become so uncomfortable as to murmur or rebel. On the other hand, he did not mean this motley population to continue to have undue influence on the affairs of the Empire. True, he gave them back their Free State, and you might see magistrates, Senate and assemblies in the city, just as under the Republic. But the people of the city henceforth had little political power. The consuls and Senate, indeed, were far from idle, but the assemblies for election and legislation soon ceased to be realities. In elections no money was now to be gained by a vote, and in legislation the people were quite content with sanctioning the wisdom of Augustus and his advisers." [1]

Though the reforms of Augustus preserved the Empire for centuries, they preserved it at the expense of its vitality, for what Augustus introduced was essentially what in these days we call the Servile State. He maintained order by undermining the independence and initiative of the citizens. This weakness gradually made itself felt, for as time wore on the Roman Empire became increasingly an automatic movement of machinery dependent entirely on the Cæsar of Rome. The great extension of governmental control led eventually to the incorporation of the Collegia as subordinate adjuncts of the State. Exactly what these Collegia originally were or eventually became we are not quite sure, for our information about them is very scanty, and it is therefore unwise to call them Guilds. It is probable they were originally friendly societies, and we know that in the early days of the Empire they began to undertake public duties. The Collegia of the building trade, for instance, began to undertake the duties of a fire-brigade in Roman

[1] *Rome*, by W. Warde Fowler, pp. 196–7.

towns, and this system of delegating functions to organized groups of workers led to the formation of Collegia in different trades. The Government having assumed responsibility for the provision of an adequate food supply, privileges were granted to bakers, corn merchants and shippers in the provinces. This happened at least as early as the reign of Antoninus Pius. In the year A.D. 271 all the incorporated Collegia were pressed into public service by Aurelian in order to fortify Rome, and this appears to have been the beginning of a closer association between the Collegia and the State. Severus Alexander, we are told, " pursued the old policy of stimulating enterprise by bounties," and incorporated " all industries whatsoever " in Guilds and regulated their status in the eyes of the law, which was doubtless a step in the direction of finally converting them into the strictly hereditary castes whose existence is pre-supposed by the legislation of the Constantinian epoch. Though the whole subject is one of great uncertainty, it does appear that efforts were made in Rome to balance the centralizing movement by decentralization as much as possible, and that group organization began to come into existence.[1]

The great defect in the constitution of the Empire was that as the position of Emperor was elective the succession was never guaranteed, and in the third century after Christ this led to serious disorders, which, lasting for a hundred years, were finally brought to a close by the Emperor Diocletian. But these things were only incidents in a decline in which a certain demoralization overtook everything. The provincial cities lost their initiative and energy. They became too dependent upon the centralized Government which daily became more paternal. The old virtues of courage and sacrifice vanished before the growth of pessimism in which the populations, enervated by luxury and sensuality, became feebler and feebler, until finally they were unable any longer to offer effective resistance to the inroads of the barbarians.

We may be sure then that Roman civilization would

[1] See *The Roman Empire*, by H. Stuart Jones, pp. 272-3. Also *Two Thousand Years of Guild Life*, by J. M. Lambert, pp. 22-31.

not have fallen had not Roman society suffered from internal
decay. The reforms of Augustus merely delayed the final
catastrophe ; they could not prevent it, for Roman civilization for centuries before, as we have seen, had been rotten
at the core. Successful warfare had made Rome wealthy,
but it left the increased wealth of the community entirely
at the mercy of the jugglers of finance, who were destitute
of patriotism except in so far as its claims coincided with
the protection of ·their interests. It was to protect the
interests of these economic vampires that the *enlightened*
system of Roman Law was formulated. So often have
we been reminded of the gift that Roman Law is to civilization
that most people have accepted it without question, little
suspecting the iniquity that reigns at its heart. For the
aim of Roman Law, unlike Greek Law, was not to secure
justice but to bolster up a corrupt society in the interests
of public order. Uncontrolled currency having led to
capitalism and capitalism having given rise to social disorders,
Roman Law stepped into the breach and sought by legalizing
injustices to preserve order. It was not concerned with
moral principles. Its aim was not, like Mediæval Law, *to
enable good men to live among bad* [1] but *to enable rich men
to live among poor*. This it did by following the line of
least resistance, which was to give legal sanction to social
injustices once established. Hence the infamous Statute
of Limitations, by which, after the expiration of a certain
period, the actual holder of an estate could no longer be
compelled to restore it to the true owner, unless the latter
should be able to show that within the prescribed time he
had demanded restitution with all the prescribed formalities.
Well did Heine say of this last condition that it " opened
wide the door of chicanery, particularly in a state where
despotism and jurisprudence were at their zenith, and where
the unjust possessor had at command all means of intimida-
tion, especially against the poor who might be unable to defray

[1] " This is the reason why the law was made, that the wickedness of man
should be restrained through fear of it, and that good men could safely live
among bad men ; and that bad men should be punished and cease to do evil
for fear of the punishment." (From the Fuero Juzgo, a collection of laws,
Gothic and Roman in origin, made by the Hispano-Gothic King Chindavinto,
A.D. 640. In the National Library of Spain, Madrid.)

the cost of litigation. The Roman was both soldier and lawyer, and that which he conquered with the strong arm he knew how to defend by the tricks of law. Only a nation of robbers and casuists could have invented the Law of Prescription, the Statute of Limitations, and consecrated it in that detestable book which may be called the bible of the Devil—I mean the codex of Roman Civil Law." [1]

But the evil does not end here. Not only did the revived study of Roman Law during the Middle Ages operate to undermine the communal relations of society and re-establish private property, but in more recent times it has brought confusion into thought about social questions by diverting attention from the primary issue of currency and its regulation to concentrate it upon the relatively secondary issue of property. We shall see its sinister influence at work corrupting the thought of the French Revolution as indeed of the Socialist Movement to-day.

[1] *Confessions*, by Heinrich Heine.

CHAPTER II

CHRISTIANITY AND THE GUILDS

THE underlying cause of the failure of Greece and Rome to grapple with the economic problems which followed the introduction of currency is to be found in the Pagan philosophy of life. That philosophy was one of self-sufficiency and self-assertiveness on a basis of senuous enjoyment, and as such was incapable of exercising a restraining influence upon men when and where foreign trade and successful warfare brought great wealth within their reach. The worship of materialism had ended in leaving society at the mercy of economic problems which eluded the efforts of statesmen and reformers alike. If, therefore, society were ever again to recover its old-time solidarity and be lifted out of the slough of despondency into which it had fallen, it was essential that life and its problems should be faced in a spirit fundamentally different from that of Paganism. This new spirit the world found in Christianity : with the spread of its teachings the tide begins to turn and a new chapter opened in the history of mankind.

In these days we are so accustomed to regard religious faith as something essentially divorced from the ordinary routine of life that it is difficult to realize that Christianity in the Early Church was as much a gospel of social salvation in this world as of happiness in a life to come. The two went hand in hand, and it was this that gave Christianity the wonderful power which made it such a driving force. The Early Church continued the communistic tradition of the Apostles. Thus we read in Acts ii. :—

Then they which gladly received this word were baptized ; and the same day there were added unto them about three thousand souls. And they continued steadfastly in the apostles' doctrine and fellowship, and in breaking of bread, and in prayers. And fear came upon every soul ; and many wonders and signs were done by the apostles. And all that believed were together, and had all things common, and parted them to all men, as every man had need.

And again, at the end of Acts iv. there is to be found another description of their life:—

And the multitude of them that believed were of one heart and of one soul : neither said any of them that aught of the things which he possessed was his own ; but they had all things in common. And with great power gave the apostles witness of the resurrection of the Lord Jesus : and great grace was upon them all. Neither was there any among them that lacked : for as many as were possessors of lands or houses sold them, and brought the price of the things that were sold, and laid them down at the apostles' feet : and distribution was made unto every man according as he had need. And Joses, who by the apostles was surnamed Barnabas (which is, being interpreted, the son of consolation), a Levite, and of the country of Cyprus, having land, sold it, and brought the money, and laid it at the apostles' feet.

Looking at Christianity in the light of these texts, we find ourselves in the presence of a creed whose aim it was to promote communal relationships in society, for it is manifest that in the mind of the Early Christians the Fatherhood of God involved the Brotherhood of man, and *vice versa*. If men and women were to live together as equals, if they were to share a common life and hold goods in common, they must have in common ideas as well as goods, or there would be no cement to bind them together. In order that common ideas might prevail amongst them, they must acknowledge some supreme authority, some principle of conduct which was above and beyond personal opinion. Above all, they must be fortified in spirit against any temptation to private gain. If wealth was not to obtain a hold upon them they must cultivate an attitude of indifference towards riches. This was the gospel of Christ in its social aspect. It taught men not to despise the world but to renounce it, in order that they might acquire the strength to conquer. In teaching this gospel Christianity introduced the world to a new moral principle. Hitherto the world was divided between two opposed theories of life or moral principles—Paganism and Buddhism. The gospel of Paganism had been to urge men to conquer the world, and it found an end in despondency. Buddhism, realizing the moral failure which must necessarily follow the pursuit of purely material aims, sought to solve the problem by teaching men to renounce the world, which it taught was illusion. Such an attitude towards life is repugnant to healthy-minded men, as being merely an evasion of the whole problem of life. Nevertheless, the choice was ultimately between Paganism and Buddhism—for all religions clove to one or the other idea, until Christianity appeared in the world, when by teaching men to renounce the world in order that they might conquer it, it fused the two apparently contradictory moral principles. It sought, as it were, by a strong appeal to what was centripetal in his nature, to counteract the natural centrifugal tendencies in man. It was through this new moral principle that Christianity triumphed, for it proved itself to be a principle of great dynamic power, capable of bracing up the moral fibre, and inspiring heroism and a great awakening of human forces. The founders of Christianity conclude by an earnest invocation of the end of the world—i.e. the end of the existing social order, and not of the earth, as is generally supposed—and strange to say, their invocation was realized. The lowly quiet man not desirous of riches came into his own. He began to be respected, and was no longer treated with scorn, as he had been under Paganism. From this point of view, the triumph of Christianity may justly be regarded as a triumph of democracy. " In the fourth century the Council of Constantinople was composed of bishops who were ploughmen, weavers, tanners, blacksmiths, and the like." [1]

Although pure communism survives to-day in the monastic orders of the Roman Church, the communism of laymen did not last very long. Exactly how long we are not quite sure, but it is generally assumed that it did not survive apostolic days for any lengthy period. The reason does not seem far to seek. Experience proves that communism in household possessions is not compatible with family life, and it is to be assumed that the Early Christians were not long in finding this out. But the communal ownership of land is a different matter, and the effect of the Christian

---

[1] *The Church and Democracy*, pamphlet by Charles Marston, quoted in *Socialism in Church History*, by Conrad Noel.

teaching was undoubtedly to preserve for centuries the communal system of land ownership of the barbarian tribes who overran the Empire in the west, as it doubtless restored communal ownership in places where it had disappeared. That confusion should exist in regard to the attitude of Christianity and the Mediæval world towards property is, I am persuaded, due to the fact that St. Thomas Aquinas is regarded as representative of the Mediæval point of view. It is insufficiently realized that his teaching about property was of the nature of a compromise intended to reconcile stubborn facts with the communistic teaching of the Gospel. In the thirteenth century, when he wrote, the Church was already defeated. It had failed in the attempt to suppress the revival of Roman Law, and the practical consequence of the failure was that landlordism was beginning to supplant communal ownership. To attack the institution of property as such was difficult, for the Church itself was implicated. It was already immensely rich. It is said it was in possession of a third of the land. In such circumstance, Aquinas apparently thought the only practicable thing to do was to seek to moralize property. Hence his endorsement of Aristotle's dictum " private property and common use." Possession was not to be considered absolute, but conditional upon the fulfilment of duties. A man might not hold more property than that for which he had personal need. Although certain forms of private property might be held, it must be administered in accordance with the necessities of the holder's own position. Superfluity was common, and the right and property of the poor. In certain cases of necessity " all things became common."

It was the communistic spirit of Christianity that gave rise to the Guilds. They were called into existence by the needs of protection and mutual aid. The earliest Guilds, as might be expected, were religious Guilds, and were voluntary associations. Their purposes were what we would call social, as well as religious ; their funds being expended on feasts, masses for the dead, the Church burial fees, charitable aid, and the like. Brentano tells us that the Guilds had a dual origin, and resulted from the amalgamation of the sacrificial societies of the barbarians with the religious

societies of Christendom ; he tells us that the word Guild
meant originally a festival or sacrificial feast, and was applied
subsequently to the company who thus feasted together.[1]
The Guilds probably had historical continuity with the
Roman *Collegia*, some of which were partly craft and partly
religious, others entirely religious.

With the dissolution of the Roman Empire it was natural
that associations should be formed for the purposes of
defence.   Such were the Frith Guilds, which were compulsory
associations, each with a corporate responsibility for the
conduct of its members.   They provided also for common
aid in legal matters, such as defence against false accusation.
These Guilds, however, need not detain us any more than
the great number of other Guilds which existed for particular
purposes, such as hunting and fishing, for the repairing of
the highways and bridges, and for various other objects.
We must pass on to the Middle Ages, when the Guilds
definitely became economic organizations, under the protection of patron saints, for it is with economic Guilds that
we are specially concerned.

" The primary purpose of the craft Guild was to establish
a complete system of industrial control over all who were
associated together in the pursuit of a common calling.
It enveloped the life of the Mediæval craftsman in a network
of restrictions which bound him hand and foot.   It did
not suffer the minutest detail to escape its rigid scrutiny
and observation.   It embodied in its regulations a whole
social system, into which the individual was completely
absorbed by the force of public opinion and the pressure
of moral and social conventions.   It embraced within its
scope not only the strictly technical, but also the religious,
the artistic, and the economic activities of Mediæval society.
It was first and foremost undoubtedly an industrial organization, but the altar and the pageant, the care for the poor
and the education of the young, were no less part of its
functions than the regulation of wages and hours and all
the numerous concerns of economic life." [2]

---

[1] *History and Development of Guilds,* by L. Brentano.
[2] *An Introduction to the Economic History of England,* by E. Lipson,
pp. 295–6.

There can be little doubt that it was because the Guilds of the Middle Ages were pervaded by religious sentiment that they were so successful as economic organizations, for we must not forget that the sense of brotherhood and human solidarity was restored to the world by Christianity after it had been broken up by the growth of capitalism under the Roman Empire. This sense of the brotherhood of mankind made possible the Just Price which was the central economic idea of the Middle Ages. It was an idea unthinkable in Rome, where conquest and exploitation seemed but the natural order of the universe. The Just Price left no room for the growth of capitalism by the manipulation of exchange, for it demanded that currency should be restricted to its primary and proper use as a medium of exchange.

It was this Mediæval conception of the Just Price that, for the first time in history, made the regulation of currency possible, and it is only by relating all the Guild regulations to this central idea that so many of them become intelligible. The Just Price is necessarily a fixed price, and, in order to maintain it, the Guilds had to be privileged bodies having an entire monopoly of their respective trades over the area of a particular town or city ; for it was only by monopoly that a fixed price could be maintained, as society found to its cost when the Guilds were no longer able to exercise this function. Only through the exercise of authority over its individual members could the Guild prevent profiteering, in its forms of forestalling, regrating, engrossing, and adulteration. Trade abuses of this kind were ruthlessly suppressed in the Middle Ages. For the first offence a member was fined ; the most severe penalty was expulsion from the Guild, which meant that a man lost the privilege of practising his craft in his native town.

But a Just and Fixed Price cannot be maintained by moral action alone. If prices are to be fixed throughout production, it can be done only on the assumption that a standard of quality can be upheld. As a standard of quality cannot finally be defined in the terms of law, it is necessary, for the maintenance of a standard, to place authority in the hands of craftmasters, a consensus of whose opinion constitutes the final court of appeal. In order to ensure a supply of masters it is necessary to train apprentices, to regulate the size of the workshop, the hours of labour, the volume of production, and the like ; for only when attention is given to such matters are workshop conditions created which are favourable to the production of masters. It is thus that we see all the regulations—as, indeed, the whole hierarchy of the Guild—arising out of the primary necessity of maintaining the Just Price.[1]

The elaborate organizations of the Guilds did not spring full-grown, but were evolved gradually, as a result of experience in the light of the central idea of the Just Price. Support is given to the thesis that, as economic organizations, the Guilds grew up around the idea of the Just Price, by the fact that when Guilds first made their appearance they were not differentiated into separate trades. The first Guilds which assumed economic functions were the Guilds Merchant,[2] which the various charters acknowledged as the ruling power within cities, and upon which they confer not only the right of regulating trade, but the right of municipal self-government. Being mixed organizations, they would naturally be concerned primarily with the maintenance of a standard of morality in commercial transactions. In the eleventh century, when the first of these charters in this country was granted by the sovereign, the towns were small, the largest not containing more than seven or eight thousand inhabitants. Agriculture was still one of the main occupations of the burgesses, and its produce one of the principal elements of their trade. It was, perhaps, the smallness of the towns that accounts for the fact that at that date craftsmen did not organize themselves separately but became members of the Guilds Merchant, or, in other words, of the municipality, for in those days the two

[1] Apprenticeship became an integral element in the constitution of the Craft Guild because in no other way was it possible to ensure the permanency of practice and the continuity of tradition whereby alone the regulation of the Guild for honourable dealing and sound workmanship could be carried on from generation to generation ; or to raise up, as one Guild expresses it, " honest and virtuous masters to succeed us in the worshipful fellowship for the maintenance of the feats of merchandise " (Lipson, pp. 282–3).

[2] The earliest known reference to the Guilds Merchant is in a charter to the town of Burford, 1087–1107 (ibid., p. 240).

were identical. All concerned in industry, in whatsoever capacity, joined the same organization. A comparatively small town would contain merchants enough—each of them trading in several commodities—to form a Guild Merchant, and at that time anybody who bought and sold anything beyond provisions for daily use ranked as a merchant. The population, indeed, would need to be much greater before separate trades could support organizations of their own. This point of development was reached about a hundred years later, when the Craft Guilds, after making their separate appearance, finally substituted their collective power for that of the Guilds Merchant, which survived as the municipality controlling the separate Craft Guilds.

The immediate grievance that precipitated the struggle which ended in the establishment of the Craft Guilds was the fact that membership of the Guilds Merchant was confined to such as owned land in the towns. At first there was no objection to this, because in those early days every burgess held land. Gradually, however, a class of craftsmen appeared that did not own land, and as these were excluded from the Guilds Merchant, they rebelled. No doubt the craftsmen who were members of the Guilds Merchant had their own grievances, for in a mixed organization it invariably happens that those things which concern the majority or dominant party receive attention, while the interests of the minority are neglected. As, a century after the formation of the Guilds Merchant, the craftsmen everywhere were in revolt, it is a fair assumption that it was because they found their particular interests neglected. Anyway, it is interesting to observe that the craftsmen who were the first to rebel —the weavers and fullers—were those who did not produce exclusively for a local market, and who would consequently be the first to feel the tyranny of the middleman. When all circumstances are taken into account, this explanation of the rebellion of the craftsmen seems to me to be the only probable one. The explanation generally given by economic historians, that the quarrel between the weavers and the Guilds Merchant was due to the fact that as the Flemings had originally introduced the weaving industry into England a certain proportion of the men engaged in that craft would be of alien ancestry, and the Guild merchants would in consequence be inclined to act unfavourably towards them, has been disposed of by Mr. Lipson,[1] who contends that it was not that the Guilds Merchant desired to exclude the weavers, but that the weavers declined to be brought within the jurisdiction of the Guilds Merchant. It seems to me, however, that he errs when he offers as an explanation of their refusal the purely selfish one that, having secured special royal charters for themselves, the weavers strove to evade the control of the Guilds Merchant in order to avoid the payment of taxes, because it is reasonable to assume that special royal charters would not have been granted unless the weavers could show due cause why they should be accorded exceptional treatment, which suggests the existence of a real grievance against the Guilds Merchant. If the motive had been such as Mr. Lipson suggests, it is certain that all other crafts would have supported the endeavour of the Guilds Merchant to bring the weavers into line. The fact that the submission of weavers in the year 1300 was speedily followed by the formation of separate Guilds for other crafts clearly demonstrates that there was some general economic cause at work, and this, I submit, was the grievance under which the producer has at all times laboured—the tendency to fall under the domination of the middleman. On the Continent these struggles between the Guilds Merchant and the craftsmen developed into fierce civil wars, but in England the struggle was not so violent. In both cases, however, the end was the same. Political equality was secured, and political power in the municipality passed out of the hands of the merchants into those of the craftsmen, who organized separate Craft Guilds for each trade, these Guilds henceforth buying the raw materials for their members and, in certain cases, marketing their goods. The services of the merchants were now dispensed with. What became of the merchants we hardly know, but probably the Merchant Adventurers about whom we read later are a revival of them. The whole subject, however, is obscure.

Within a century of the general establishment of Craft

[1] Lipson, pp. 323–7.

Guilds we find that monopolies began to appear among them, and are followed by struggles between the journeymen and the masters. Hitherto it had been possible for every craftsman who had attained to " sufficient cunning and understanding in the exercise of his craft " to look forward to a day when he would be able to set up in business on his own account, and to qualify as a master of his Guild, and in this connection it must be understood that the Mediæval Guild was not an organization which sought to supplant the private individual producer by a system of co-operative production. The Guild did not seek to organize self-governing workshops, but to regulate industry in such a way as to ensure equality of opportunity for all who entered it. About the middle of the fifteenth century, however, a time came when this ideal could be upheld only with increasing difficulty, for a class of skilled craftsmen came into existence who had no other prospect beyond remaining as journeymen all their lives. When once the permanent nature of these decayed circumstances had become recognized, the journeymen began to organize themselves into societies which are called by Brentano " Journeymen Fraternities," and in Mr. Lipson's recent work " Yeomen's Guilds " which, while accepting an inferior status as unalterable, sought to improve the position of their members as wage-earners. There were strikes for higher wages, sometimes with success. These fraternities, in other cases, acted merely as defensive organizations, to combat a tendency towards a lowering of the standard of living which seems to have made its appearance about that time, and which was due to the same group of economic causes which precipitated the Peasants' Revolt. The Peasants' Revolt will be dealt with in a later chapter.

It is interesting to observe that in the formation and organization of the journeymen societies the Friars played an important part, as they did in the organization of the Peasant's Revolt, a circumstance which probably accounts for the fact that these fraternities were in the first place formed as religious ones. The Master Saddlers of London complained that "under a feigned colour of sanctity the journeymen formed 'covins' to raise wages greatly in excess."[1]

[1] Lipson, p. 357.

From the outset the London Guilds adopted a policy of
repression towards them, but in other towns—as at Northamp-
ton and at Oxford—a spirit of compromise prevailed. At
Chester the bitterness became so intense that the quarrel
was fought in quite a Continental style, the Master Weavers
attacking the journeymen with pole-axes, baslards, and
iron-pointed poles. Generally speaking, no solution of
the difficulty was arrived at. The journeymen waged a
kind of guerilla warfare against the masters, much as trade
unions do against capitalists to-day. In 1548 an Act of
Parliament forbade the formation of unions for improving
conditions of labour, but this was when the Guilds had for
all practical purposes ceased to exist as organizations regulating the conditions of production.

Critics of the Guilds are accustomed to point to these
struggles as testifying to the prevalence of a tyrannical
spirit within the Guilds, but such, however, is to misjudge
the situation. It becomes abundantly clear from a wider
survey of the economic conditions of the later Middle Ages
—as we shall discover when we consider the defeat of the
Guilds in a later chapter—that, whatever evils the Guilds may
have developed, the changes which overtook them came about
as the result of external influences operating upon them
from without, rather than through defects which were
inherent in their structure from the beginning. It cannot
be said of them that they carried within themselves the
seeds of their own destruction, as will readily be understood
when it is remembered that, as Mr. Lipson has said, " their
underlying principle was order rather than progress, stability
rather than expansion " ; or, as I would prefer to put it,
order rather than expansion, stability rather than mobility.
While it is clear that in the fourteenth and fifteenth centuries
the masters endeavoured, by making their admission fees pro-
hibitive, to exclude others from their ranks, it is manifest that
this policy was dictated by the instinct of self-preservation,
when they were beginning to feel the pressure of the competition of capitalist manufacture. This spirit of exclusive-
ness did not actuate the Guilds in their early days. The
problem then was not how to keep people out of the Guilds,
but how to get them in. The Guilds Merchant were willing

at the start to extend privileges to all who agreed to abide by the Just Price. When the Guilds changed, it was because they had failed in their original aim of making the Just Price co-extensive with industry, and were suffering from the consequence of their failure. Looked at from this point of view, the internal quarrels of the Guilds appear as the dissentions not of victorious but of defeated men, not of the spirit which created the Guilds, but of the spirit that destroyed them.

Even if this interpretation be not accepted, it would be irrational to condemn the Guilds because they laboured under internal dissensions, for on such grounds every human organization which existed in the past or exists to-day stands condemned within certain limits, such dissensions being in the nature of things. The experience of history teaches us that all organizations need readjustment from time to time : the growth of population alone is sufficient to cause this. Moreover, every social organization tends to develop little oligarchies within itself. Mr. Chesterton has well said that " there happen to be some sins that go with power and prosperity, while it is certain that whoever holds power will have some motive for abusing it." From this point of view, the test of righteousness in social con-stitutions is not that they do not develop oligarchies and tyrannies, for all institutions tend to do this. Rather let us ask what resistance may be organized against any such encroachments on popular liberty, and it is the eternal glory of the Guild system that such rebellion was always possible. The motto of the old Liberals, that " the price of liberty is eternal vigilance," is, says Mr. de Maeztu, no more than the organization of this jealousy of the Guilds." [1] I would respectfully recommend this idea to the considera-tion of the Fabian and the Marxian alike, for it is the failure to perceive this central truth of the Guilds that leads the one to place faith in a soul-destroying bureaucracy, and the other in class war. These ideas are but different aspects of the same error—a complete inability to understand what is the norm in social relationships. Shrinking from the very thought of rebellion, the Fabian seeks the creation

[1] *Authority, Liberty, and Function*, by Ramiro de Maeztu, p. 198.

of a Leviathan against which rebellion would be in vain ;
while, with an outlook equally perverted, the Marxian
imagines that the social struggle which is inherent in any
healthy society, and is necessary to effect periodic readjust-
ments, can, by a grand supreme effort be abolished once and
for ever.

CHAPTER III

THE MEDIÆVAL HIERARCHY

" HEAVY laborious work," says Heinrich von Langenstein, the Mediæval economist, " is the inevitable yoke of punishment which according to God's righteous verdict has been laid on all the sons of Adam. But many of Adam's descendants seek in all sorts of cunning ways to escape from this yoke and live in idleness without labour, and at the same time to have a superfluity of useful and necessary things ; some by robbery and plunder, some by usurious dealings, others by lying, deceit, and the countless forms of dishonest and fraudulent gain by which men are for ever seeking to get riches and abundance without toil." [1]

It is because in every society a minority of men have always been, and probably always will be, actuated by such anti-social motives that government all at times is necessary. They bring to naught the dreams of the philosophic anarchist and other kinds of social idealists the moment any attempt is made to give practical effect to their theories. As it was understood in the Middle Ages, the function of government was to give protection to the community by keeping this type of man—the man of prey—in a strict subjection. By insisting upon the maintenance of a Just and Fixed Price, the Guilds were able to keep him under in the towns where their jurisdiction obtained. It is for this reason that the Guilds are to be regarded as the normal form of social organization in the Middle Ages, for as the Mediæval idea was that man should live by the sweat of his brow, no other form of organization would have been necessary, had all men been actuated by the best intentions. Outside

[1] *History of the German People at the Close of the Middle Ages,* by Johannes Janssen, vol. ii. p. 94.

the towns, however, such economic control·had not been established, because a precedent condition of such control was never attained.   In rural areas the man of prey had never been brought entirely under military and civil control, and it was the attempt to subjugate him that brought into existence the Feudal System.   The primary necessity of self-defence was its *raison d'être*.

Such appears to be the probable explanation of the phenomenon of Feudalism, for exactly how it came into existence is largely a matter of conjecture.   After the break-up of the Roman Empire, when Europe was overrun by barbarian tribes and orderly government had broken down, the man of prey found himself at large.   Robber knights (or brigands, as they would be termed in those days) made their appearance everywhere in Western Europe, and preyed upon the industrious part of the population.   Divided into groups or clans, these people would find it expedient to be permanently organized for the purposes of self-defence, ready always to repel the raider whenever he chanced to make his appearance. It would be necessary in such communities to carry on the dual vocations of agriculture and defence.   The clan would be divided into two sections, the more adventurous spirits taking upon themselves the responsibility of military defence, while the rest would agree to feed them : out of such an arrangement it can be seen that the Feudal manor might gradually arise.   The fighting-men would tend to become a class apart, and would claim rights and privileges over the non-combatant section of the community.   The chieftain of the fighting-men would become the lord, and the fighting-men would be his retainers.   This system would be imposed upon other clans by means of conquest.   The successful chief would divide the conquered territory among his followers, and compel the conquered peoples to become their serfs. In other cases, the Feudal relationship would be established because some group of people sought the protection of a superior lord.

Looking at Feudalism from this point of view, it may be said that while its existence was due to the depredations of the robber knights, and though these knights would have certain groups of workers at their mercy, there would be other knights, or lords, who came into being as protectors of the communal rights of the people. Such were the chivalrous knights of romance and legend. By reason of the different circumstances which had created the various Feudal groups —in fact, according to whether they owed their existence to depredation or defence—a different social life would obtain within the group. The serfs would enjoy varying degrees of liberty. The serfs of the robber knights would be tyrannized over, because the robber knights would never feel their position to be secure ; but the serfs of the chivalrous knights would enjoy all the advantages of a communal life, for the chivalrous knights, owing their position to popular election, would have no desire to tyrannize. After the lapse of centuries and the changes inevitable in an hereditary in-stitution, the original character of the groups, influenced by the changing personalities of the lords, would tend to become modified.

Anyway, although William the Conqueror is popularly supposed to have introduced the Feudal System into England, it is nowadays admitted that it existed here long before the Norman Conquest, that much of it was not developed until after the Norman period, and that at no time was Feudalism a uniform and logical system, outside of historical and legal textbooks. Feudal land was held in various ways and on various terms by the villains, the cottiers, and the serfs. According to Domesday Book, the last mentioned did not exceed more than 16 per cent. of the whole population. In addition to these, however, there were the free tenants, who did no regular work for the manor, but whose services were requisitioned at certain periods—such as harvest-time —when labour was required.

The principle governing the Feudal System was that of reciprocal rights and duties, for lord and serf alike were tied to the soil. Although the serf had to give half of his labour to his lord, it was not exploitation, as we understand the term ; for in return for his labour, which went to support the lord and his retainers, military protection was given to the serf. The amount of labour which a lord could exact was a definite and fixed quantity, and was not determined merely by the greed of the lord. The class division was

primarily a difference of function rather than a difference
of wealth. The baron did not own the land, but held it
from the king on definite terms, such as furnishing him with
men in times of war, and of administering justice within
his domains. But in this country the baron rarely possessed
that criminal jurisdiction in matters of life and death which
was common in continental feudalism. He assisted at the
King's Council Board, when requested. To suit their own
convenience, the barons divided up these territories among
their retainers, on terms corresponding to those on which
they held their own. It was thus that the whole organization outside of the towns was graduated from the king,
through the greater barons, to tenants who held their possessions from a superior lord to whom they owed allegiance.

Such was the principle of the Feudal System. Although
the system was in no way uniform in the majority of cases,
it probably worked fairly well, for the relation between the
lords and the serfs was an essentially human one. Based
upon recognized services and rights, it was not a barrier
to good understanding and fellowship. In countries where
semi-feudal relationships still exist—as on many of the
large estates in these countries—in Cuba and Mexico, there
is no feeling of personal inferiority between master and man.
A traveller from these parts tells me that in Cuba it is the
custom for owners of big plantations to breakfast with
their men. The owner sits at the head of the table with
his overseers, friends, and guests, and below the "salt" sit
the workmen, according to rank and seniority, down to
the newest black boy. Meeting on the plantation, the
owner exchanges cigarettes with his men, and they discuss
with animation politics, cock-fighting, or the prospects of
the crop. Feudal England, I imagine, was something
like this, and not the horrible nightmare conjured up by
lying historians, interested in painting the past as black
as possible, in order to make modern conditions appear
tolerable by comparison. Where there was a good lord life
would be pleasant, for the serf lived in rude plenty. The
defect of the system would be the defect of all aristocracies
—that where there was a bad lord redress would be difficult
to obtain. For though a lord might, in theory, be deprived

of his fief for abuse of power, the abuse would have to be very gross before such a thing could happen. We are safe, I think, in concluding that where the lord was inclined to be arbitrary it would be difficult to restrain him, though, of course, as the people would in those days have the Church on their side, their action would tend to modify the original proposition.

The Feudal System was essentially a form of organization adapted to a stage of transition with no finality about it. As the relationships existing between the lords and the serfs were dictated primarily by military necessity and based upon payment in kind, they were bound to have been disintegrated by the growth of orderly government on the one hand and the spread of the currency on the other. There was, nevertheless, nothing in the nature of things why when Feudal society did disintegrate it should have been transformed into landlordism and capitalism, for as the old Feudal order was dissolved by the spread of currency the agricultural population might just as conceivably have been organized into Guilds. Moreover, I believe they would have been, but for a change in the legal system which entirely undermined the old communal relationships of the Feudal groups ; or, to be precise, if the Communal Law which had hitherto sustained Mediæval society had not been displaced by the revival of Roman Law. This issue we shall have to consider in the next chapter.

Whatever misgivings Mediævalists may have had respecting the institution of Feudalism, they had none respecting the institution of Monarchy. Feudalism they might regard as a thing of transition which was bound to pass away, but the institution of Monarchy they contemplated on quite a different plane. It was a part of the natural order of things, and almost with one voice Mediæval publicists declared monarchy to be the best form of government. St. Thomas Aquinas defends the institution of monarchy entirely on the grounds of practical expediency. One man must be set apart to rule, because " where there are many men and each one provides whatever he likes for himself, the energies of the multitude are dissipated unless there is, also, some who has the care of that which is for the benefit of the multitude." [1]　"A power that is united is more efficacious in producing its effect than a dispersed or divided power." [2]　"The rule of the many nearly always ended in tyranny, as clearly appears in the Roman Republic, which, while for some time the magistracy was exercised by many enmities, dissensions, and civil wars, fell into the hands of the most cruel tyrants." [3]

There is here no suggestion of the Divine Right of Kings. That was a post-Reformation idea and the invention of James I.　The doctrine of the unconditional duty of obedience to monarchs was wholly foreign to the Mediæval mind. Monarchs were instituted for the sake of the people, not the people for the sake of the monarchs.　"As a rule, each prince on his accession was obliged to swear fidelity to all written and traditional customs, and it was only after he had conferred a charter of rights that fealty was pledged to him.　Thus, Duke Albert IV of Bavaria directed that every prince's son or heir should, on receiving the vow of fealty, secure to the State deputies of the prelates, nobles, and cities, their freedom, ancient customs, and respected rights ;　and pledge himself not to interfere with them in any way.　The formal clause, ' The land and each inhabitant of it shall be undisturbed in his rights and customs,' was a sure guarantee against the arbitrary legislature of the princes without counsel, knowledge, or will of the Estate-General." [4]

According, then, to the Mediæval view, the king was not so much the ruler as the first guardian of the State ; not so much the owner of the realm as the principal administrator of its powers and interests.　His power was not absolute, but limited within certain bounds.　The principle involved is the one which runs through all Mediæval polity of reciprocal rights and duties.　All public authority was looked upon as a responsibility conferred by a higher power, but the duty of obedience was conditioned by the rightfulness of the command.　"The Mediæval doctrine taught that every command which exceeded the limits of the ruler's authority

[1] *New Things and Old in St. Thomas Aquinas*, edited by H. C. O'Neill, pp. 222–3.　[2] Ibid., pp. 226.　[3] Ibid., pp. 227.
[4] Janssen, vol. ii. pp. 131–2.

was a mere nullity, and obliged none to obedience. And then, again, it proclaimed the right of resistance, and even armed resistance, against the compulsory enforcement of any unrighteous and tyrannical measure, such enforcement being regarded as an act of violence. Nay, more, it taught (though some men with an enlightened sense of law might always deny this) that tyrannicide was justified, or, at least, excusable." [1]   Manegold of Lautenbach teaches that the king who has become a tyrant should be expelled like an unfaithful shepherd. Similar revolutionary doctrines are frequently maintained by the Papal party against the wielders of State power.   John of Salisbury emphatically recommends the slaughter of a tyrant, for a tyranny is nothing less than an abuse of power granted by God to man. He vouches Biblical and classical examples, and rejects the use of poison, breach of trust, breach of oath. [2]   St. Thomas Aquinas is against tyrannicide, but is in favour of active resistance against tyrants, though he recommends that " if the tyranny is not excessive it is better to bear it for a time than, by acting against the tyrant, to be involved in many perils that are worse than tyranny." [3]

The paradox of the position was that it was precisely in the Middle Ages, when there was nothing sacrosanct about the institution of monarchy, that kings were popular and their lives were very much safer than they are to-day. They were supposed to act impartially, to protect the people against oppression by the nobles, and to be the impersonation of justice, mercy, generosity, and greatness ; and it is to be presumed that it was because they did to some extent fulfil such expectations that monarchy was popular. It was an ancient and generally entertained opinion that the will of the people was the source of all temporal power ; but, while kings owed their authority immediately to the goodwill of the people, it was felt that, ultimately, it was derived from God. Which belief is an entirely rational one, for, considering that all legitimate monarchies are hereditary, if God does not choose the actual successor to

[1] *Political Theories of the Middle Ages,* by Dr. Otto Gierke, p. 35.
[2] Ibid., p. 143.
[3] *New Things and Old in St. Thomas Aquinas,* pp. 227-8.

the throne, then no one does. To accept God as the ultimate source of authority was to the Mediæval mind a much more satisfactory explanation than the legal fictions with which moderns seek to escape from the dilemma.

All earthly lordship is, however, limited by its nature. It is limited by human and geographical considerations. Hence, in this world there are many temporal powers. But the universe is one. If human intercourse is to be possible, if temporal powers are to prevail, there must be certain common standards of morals, of thought and of culture. If these are to be upheld in the world, they must rest on certain fixed and unalterable dogmas. There must be the recognition of an ultimate good, a true and a beautiful. But men, owing to their limitations, are incapable of determining the nature of these. Left to themselves, they tend to emphasize their points of difference and to lose what they have in common. They will worship material things, and, like the builders of Babel, end in a confusion of tongues, no man knowing what to or what not to believe. Hence the need of Divine interposition to reveal to the world the nature of the truth by which alone mankind can live, and to secure its recognition among men. Hence, also, the Christian Church, which exists to uphold in the world the revealed truth which otherwise would be forgotten, and to transmit the truth, pure and undefiled, from generation to generation. And hence, again, the priority of the Spiritual over the Temporal Power, of the Church over the State. For the State, being of its nature earthly, maintains itself by considerations of expediency, and, apart from the daily reminder of permanent truth which the existence of a spiritual power gives, would place its reliance entirely in the sufficiency of material things.

Such was the Mediæval conception of the social order. It rested upon the constitutive principle of unity underlying and comprehending the world's plurality. The Mediævalists reconciled the philosophical contradiction implied in the simultaneous existence of the one and the many by accepting in the visible world a plurality of temporal powers, supported and sustained by the indivisible unity of the spiritual power. Along with this idea, however, came the necessity of the division of the community between two organized orders of life, the spiritual and the temporal ; for it was maintained that the care of the spiritual and moral life of the community —the whole-hearted pursuit of wisdom—was incompatible with political administrative work. Granting certain pre-supposed conditions, Church and State were the two necessary embodiments of one and the same human society, the State taking charge of the temporal requirements, and the Church of the spiritual and supernatural. Hence the Holy Roman Empire, the Mediæval conception of which was that of two swords to protect Christianity, the spiritual belonging to the Pope and the temporal to the Emperor. Although it claimed continuity with the Roman Empire, it was in no sense an attempt to revive the idea of universal monarchy, since it was laid down that the Emperor, though he was the first and august monarch—the highest of Papal vassals— was not to aim at the establishment of a universal monarchy, the destruction of nationalities, or the subjection of other nations to his personal rule. On the contrary, it was the mission of the Church to achieve an ideal union of mankind by changing the heart and the mind of man. What was required of the Emperor was that, in the first place, he should seek to establish amongst the nations a system of organization —a League of Nations, as it were—which should arbitrate on international questions, in order that war among Christian nations might be brought to an end. In the next, it was to be his duty to lead the Christian princes in defence of the Faith against all unbelievers.[1] This Mediæval Empire, which dates from the year 800, when Charlemagne was crowned Emperor of the West by Pope Leo III, continued to exist until the end of the eighteenth century, when what remained of it fell finally before the armies of Napoleon ; but until the thirteenth century, when its decline definitely set in, it was the centre of European national life and as a matter of fact it did succeed in preserving peace in Central Europe for centuries. It is of more than passing interest to note that the sinister influence which undermined its

[1] At the beginning the object of the Empire could have had nothing to do with the suppression of heresy, for though a popular movement against heresy existed at an earlier date, it was not until the latter half of the twelfth century that its suppression was countenanced by the Church.

power was precisely the same one which corrupted Mediæval civilization, and has led to the anarchy and confusion of the modern world.

Modern historians are accustomed to look upon the inauguration of the Holy Roman Empire as the great mistake of the Middle Ages, inasmuch as, by giving rise to a long succession of quarrels between the two heads of Christendom it led to a spirit of religious and political intolerance. Such a judgment is perhaps a superficial one, for there was nothing in the original conception of the Empire which would necessarily have produced such results. At the time of its first promotion a strong case was to be made in its favour. Christendom was then in great danger of being overthrown by the Saracens, while the Papacy lived in fear of the Lombards. The Church was sorely in need of a temporal defender. Twice did Charlemagne cross the Alps to rescue the Papacy from the clutches of the Lombards, thus bringing temporal security to it. The great quarrel between the Popes and the Emperors over the Right of Investiture, which terminated early in the twelfth century, defined the respective spheres of influence of the Spiritual and the Temporal Powers. Once this source of difficulty had been removed, there is no reason to suppose that, in the ordinary course of things, the doctrine as taught by Pope Gelasius in the fifteenth century, that " Christian princes are to respect the priest in things which relate to the soul, while the priests in their turn are to obey the laws made for the preservation of order in worldly matters, so that the soldier of God should not mix in temporal affairs and the worldly authorities have naught to say in spiritual things," [1] which was accepted prior to the quarrel over Investiture, might not have been resumed when the quarrel was ended. Unfortunately for the success of the Empire, an indirect consequence of the quarrel was the revival of Roman Law, and this, by raising issues of such a nature as to make compromise impossible, destroyed for ever the possibility of co-operation between Church and State. After this revival, the issue was no longer one of defining the respective spheres of influence between the two authorities, but the more fundamental one of whether considerations

[1] Janssen, vol. ii. p. 111.

of principle or of expediency should take precedence; whether, in fact, there was a higher law which earthly monarchs should obey, or whether law should be dependent entirely upon the personal will of princes. This issue was fundamental, and, as I have already said, it made compromise impossible. As compromise was impossible, co-operation was impossible. It became a question of who should rule ; whether the Church would consent to make herself subservient to the ambitions of princes, or whether political arrangements were to be regarded as part and parcel of the ecclesiastical organization. As the Emperors sought to encroach upon the prerogatives of the Church, the Popes strove to attain temporal power, and the struggle resulted in corrupting both Church and State, and in breaking up the Mediæval social order. In proportion as the Holy See succeeded in this aim it became increasingly secularized, its territorial possessions leading it to subordinate spiritual duties to acquisitive ambition. When, after the Great Schism in the earlier part of the fifteenth century, the Popes succeeded in asserting their final and triumphant absolutism, they became to all intents and purposes mere secular princes, by whom religion was used as an instrument for the furtherance of political ambitions. Their enormous revenues were spent upon the maintenance of Papal armies and fleets and a court unrivalled in its magnificence and corruption. This state of things continued until the Reformation came upon the Church as a scourge from God and paved the way for the counter-Reformation, when the Church, after the loss of her temporal authority, found recompense in a renewal of her spiritual vitality.

CHAPTER IV

THE REVIVAL OF ROMAN LAW

MENTION was made in the preceding chapter of the revival
of Roman Law, which was incidental to the quarrels between
the Popes and the Emperors, and eventually broke up
Mediæval society and inaugurated the modern world. The
importance of this revival demands that more should be
said about it.

To understand exactly what is meant by the revival
of Roman Law it is first of all necessary to realize that though,
as a completely codified system resting upon the will of the
Emperor, Roman Law had fallen largely into desuetude,
it did not disappear entirely from the world after the fall
of the Roman Empire. While retaining their own laws and
customs, which were communal in character, the barbarian
tribes that had invaded the Empire and settled within its
borders, incorporated in their tribal codes certain of the
Roman laws that did not clash with their communal arrangements. Definite information upon this period is lacking,
but it is to be assumed that the Roman laws which they
adopted were of the nature of rules and regulations rather
than such as were concerned with conduct. It is natural
to make this assumption ; because, in the first place, of the
existence of a large body of law, best described as regulations, which has to do with public convenience, and is
not to be directly deduced from moral considerations (the
rule of the road is a well-known example of this kind
of law), might be readily adopted by peoples possessing
a social and economic life entirely different from the Roman
one ; and in the next because, as the Roman method
is essentially adapted to the needs of a personal ruler, it
would be natural that the chiefs of the tribes would avail

themselves of the decisions on delicate points of law which had been arrived at by the Roman jurists. It was for this reason that the study of Roman Law had never been entirely abandoned, and the Visigothic compilation became the standard source of Roman Law throughout Western Europe during the first half of the Middle Ages. Together with the Canon Law of the Church, Roman Civil Law was studied at the ecclesiastical faculties of jurisprudence, for learning during the so-called Dark Ages meant little more than the salvage of such fragments of ancient knowledge as had survived the wreck of Roman civilization.[1]

Though parts of the Roman Code which were concerned with matters of convenience became incorporated in the tribal law of the barbarians, Roman Law in its fundamental and philosophic sense had been abandoned in favour of the Canon Law of the Church. The latter, which consists of the body of laws and regulations made or adopted by ecclesiastical authority for the government of the Christian organization and its members, differs as a judicial science from Roman Law and Civil Law, inasmuch as it is primarily concerned with the conduct of another society, the Kingdom of God upon Earth. As such, its ultimate source is God. It consists of Apostolic letters, ordinances of the Councils, and Papal Bulls, briefs, or decretals. It was not yet, however, a definitely codified system, and did not become one until the twelfth century, when Gratian gave it a systematic form. Prior to the time of Gratian, the Canon Law took the form of decisions pronounced in cases submitted to the Pope from all parts of Christendom. By such means the Christian rule was brought into relation with the communal life of the tribes, and a body of law was coming into existence capable of maintaining the communal life of the people along with a higher and more complex civilization. But the promise of a society which might have realized the Kingdom of God upon Earth was never fulfilled, and it was not fulfilled because of the sinister influence of Roman Law, which was resurrected to break up the unity of Christendom.

The circumstances that led to the revival of Roman Law are immediately connected with the great quarrel over the

[1] Cf. *Roman Law in Mediæval Europe*, by Sir Paul Vinogradoff, pp. 4–7.

Right of Investiture which became such a burning issue
during the pontificate of Gregory VII. The organization
of the Church had been a haphazard growth. The Church
shared in feudal land-holding ; in addition to the tithes,
immense estates had come into her possession, by bequests
from the faithful, or through the labours of the monastic
orders, who had reclaimed vast tracts of waste land. For
the defence of her property the Church resorted to secular
means. Bishops and abbots, confiding their domains to
laymen, on condition of assistance with the sword in case
of need, became Temporal Lords—with vassals to fight for
them, and with courts of justice—exercising all the privileges
common to lay lords. On the other hand, there were bishop-
dukes, bishop-counts, and the like, who were vassals of
other lords, and especially of the king, from whom they
received the investiture of their temporalities. In some
cases, abbeys and churches had been founded by the faithful
on condition that the right of patronage—that is, the choice
of beneficiaries—should be reserved for them and their heirs.
Thus in various ways ecclesiastical benefices were gradually
transformed into fiefs, and lay suzerains claimed the same
rights over ecclesiastics as over other vassals from whom
they received homage and invested them with the emblems
of their spiritual offices.

Had this system not been grossly abused, it might have
continued indefinitely. During the vacancy of a bishopric
or abbey, its revenues went to fill the royal treasury, and
when short of money, monarchs everywhere took advantage
of their positions as patrons and allowed benefices to remain
without pastors for long periods. The Emperor Otto II
was charged with having practised simony in this connection ;
while under Conrad II the abuse became prevalent. At
the close of the reign of William Rufus, one archbishopric,
four bishoprics, and eleven abbeys in England were found
to be without pastors. At a Synod of Reims in 1049 the
Bishops of Nevers and Coutances affirmed that they bought
their bishoprics. The system led, moreover, to favouritism.
Lay authorities interfered in favour of those in whom they
were interested, so that, in one way and another, the system
became a crying scandal and Gregory VII resolved to put

a stop to it. He considered, too, that it was intolerable that a layman, whether emperor, king, or baron, should invest ecclesiastics with the emblems of spiritual office—ecclesiastical investiture should come only from ecclesiastics. It was this that led to the great struggle over the Right of Investiture. To the Emperor Henry IV it was highly undesirable that the advantages and revenues accruing from lay investiture should be surrendered; it was reasonable, he thought, that ecclesiastics should receive investiture of temporalities from their temporal protectors and suzerains. After a bitter struggle, which was carried on all over Christendom, a compromise was agreed upon and ratified at the Diet of Worms in 1122. The Emperor, on the one hand, preserved his suzerainty over ecclesiastical benefices; but, on the other hand, he ceased to confer the ring and crozier, and thereby not only lost the right of refusing the election on the grounds of unworthiness, but was deprived also of an efficacious means of maintaining vacancies in ecclesiastical offices.

Meanwhile, the dispute led to the establishment at Ravenna of a faculty of jurisprudence, under the patronage of the Emperor, which had important consequences. Countess Matilda of Tuscany—a staunch supporter of Gregory VII—in 1084 sought to counteract the influence of this Imperialistic school by the creation of a centre for the study of Roman Law that would act on the Papal behalf; and it was in connection with this school at Bologna that Irnerius, who had already taught didactics and rhetoric, began to devote himself to the study of jurisprudence. Prior to this date the study of Roman Law had been traditional rather than scholarly. Exponents of the law did not go back to the original sources of legal science, but took the law very much as they found it—as a thing of custom or tradition, whose credentials they had no reason to suspect. Irnerius, however, abandoned this more or less casual method study in favour of a return to the original sources of Roman Law, taking the Justinian Code as a guide. It is from this new departure that the revival of Roman Law is to be dated.[1] The researches

[1] As to the exact contribution of Irnerius to the revival, the following passage of the chronicler, Richard of Ursperg, supplies us with an important

undertaken in the first instance to strengthen the Papal case against the Emperor had results very different from what had been intended. They resulted in the revival of a theory of law which was favourable to the Emperor rather than to the Pope, and which immediately caused the struggle between them to be embittered, by raising in an acute form the question of supremacy, and eventually undermining Mediæval civilization by dethroning the Canon Law in favour of the Roman Code.

That the Glossators, as the pioneers of this revival were called, did not foresee the consequences of their work—that they did not see that they were seeking the promotion of a system of law antipathetic to everything that Christianity stood for—is probably true. At the same time, there is no reason to doubt that it was the superficial brilliance of the Roman Code which led them astray. They were infatuated by its beauty, its searching analyses, its logical deductions, and brilliant explanations. It had such a simple and plausible way of dealing with immediately practical issues that they came to regard it as the very embodiment of common sense, and deemed it to be entitled to the same universality of application as the laws of mathematics and logic, little suspecting the iniquity that reigned at its heart. It was, as we saw in the first chapter, originally formulated for the purpose of preserving a capitalistic and corrupt society from premature dissolution, and we shall see that its revival, by seeking always the promotion of individual and private interests at the expense of communal and public ones, operated to introduce into Mediæval society the same evil elements as had corrupted Rome. Unable to conceive the practical possibility of realizing justice in a society whose communal ties had been dissolved by an unregulated currency, Roman Law had addressed itself to the more immediately practicable though less ambitious task of maintaining order. This it achieved by disregarding

clue. It reads : " Dominus Irnerius, at the request of the Countess Matilda, renewed the books of the laws, which had long been neglected ; and, in accordance with the manner in which they had been compiled by the Emperor Justinian of divine memory, arranged them in divisions, adding, perchance, a few words here and there " (*The Universities of Europe in the Middle Ages*, by Hastings Rashdall, vol. i, pp. 116).

moral issues, by inculcating the policy of following always the line of least resistance (thus exalting momentary expediency above considerations of right), by giving legal security and sanction to private property (no matter by what means it had been obtained) as the easiest way of avoiding continual strife among neighbours. It was, in fact, a system of law designed primarily for the purpose of enabling rich men to live among bad, as emphatically as the Canon Law was designed to enable good men to live among bad; for while the Canon Law based its authority upon the claim of right, the ultimate appeal of Roman Law was to might rather than to right, since, according to it, right and wrong are not eternally fixed and immutable principles—not something above and beyond personal predilections—but are dictated entirely by considerations of expediency and convenience. In a word, the Roman Law does not conceive of law as a higher authority over men— as a development of the moral law—but postulates the existence of a divorce between law and morality as two entirely incompatible and opposed principles.

Naturally, systems of law differing so fundamentally as the Roman and the Canon Laws sought the support of different sanctions. The Canon Law, as we saw, rested on the assumption that there was a higher law of the universe, and that all justice proceeds from God. Accordingly, it happened under Canon Law that the ruler was merely a functionary—the agent or director of right—exercising power conditionally upon the fulfilment of duties which were enjoined upon him. On the contrary, Roman Law, substituting order for justice as the aim of law, sought its ultimate sanction in the will of the Emperor, whom it invested with sovereign power, declaring him to be the source of all law, which could only be altered by his own arbitrary decree, in general as in individual cases. This was a natural and inevitable deduction from the Roman theory. Making no claim to supernatural revelation, it was driven by this self-imposed limitation to search for authority not in the ascendancy of truth, of ideas, or of things, but in the authority of persons, finally in one person—the Roman Emperor. Hence it is that Roman Law is by nature opposed to demo-

cratic ideals. For whereas, under Canon Law, it can be
maintained that if the ruler is merely a functionary exercising
powers conditionally upon the fulfilment of certain duties he
may be challenged if he fail in them, there can be no appeal
on a basis of principle or right against the kind of authority
exalted by Roman Law, for how can the king do wrong if
the source of law resides in his personal will. In consequence,
rebellion against the abuse of authority in all countries
where Roman Law obtains takes the form of an appeal from
the Divine Right of Kings to the Divine Right of the People ;
that is, from one will to many wills. And this can merely
increase the confusion, since as apart from the recognition of
the existence of an authority which transcends the individual
will no agreement is possible among a multitude of wills,
reaction to the authority of an autocracy can only be a matter
of time. It is a vicious circle from which there is no escape,
as the modern world must discover sooner or later.

The tendency inherent in Roman Law towards autocracy
was not long in manifesting itself. The Commentators,
who succeeded the Glossators, led the way. Perceiving that
their own personal interests were to be served by espousing
the cause of the Emperor rather than that of the Pope,
they declared that the Roman Empire still existed inasmuch
as the Roman Emperors of the German Empire were the
legal successors of the Emperors of Rome, and that, in
consequence, the will of the Emperor was still law and the
Justinian Code binding. This speciousness is, however, to
be regarded as the merest camouflage. In the first place,
because subsequent developments suggest that this dogma
of continuity was advanced only because the lawyers found
in it a convenient fiction whereby the rule of the lawyers
might be substituted for the rule of Emperor and Pope alike ;
and in the next place, because it so happened that while,
in theory, what was received was the law of Justinian's
books, in practice what was received was the system which
the Italian Commentators had long been elaborating, and, as
Gierke insists, this was an important difference. The system
which the Commentators advanced was a thing of compromise
between the old Roman Law and the existing German Law.
It was the thin edge of the wedge ; it was designed to give

immediate practical results, and it was successful. A start was made, and as time wore on the system became more and more Roman, and less and less German, until, eventually, it became almost purely Roman.[1] The Hohenstaufen family fell into the trap which the Commentators had so carefully prepared for them. They accepted the decision of the Commentators as a justification of their absolutism, and henceforth did all in their power to secure the acceptance of the new code. Frederick Barbarossa at once claimed for himself all the rights which the Cæsars had exercised, and Roman Law was used by the Emperors as a weapon against Canon Law in ecclesiastical-political disputes. These new developments aroused the opposition of the Church, which set itself against the spread of Roman Law. In 1180 Pope Alexander III forbade the monks to study the Justinian Code. In 1219 Honorius III extended this prohibition to all priests, and in the following year he forbade laymen, under pain of excommunication, to give or listen to lectures on the Justinian Code in the University of Paris. In 1254 Innocent IV extended this last prohibition to France, England, Scotland, Spain, and Hungary. But such prohibitions were of no avail. Roman Law found support among the secular princes, and it was proving itself too profitable to those who followed it to be easily suppressed under such circumstances. It is said that so eager were students to acquire a knowledge of it that at one time the study of theology was almost abandoned.

Meanwhile, efforts were made to meet the danger by more positive measures. In 1151 Gratian published the *Decretum*, in which the materials collected by a succession of Canonists were re-edited and arranged with a superior completeness. His labours paved the way for the first official code of Canon Law which was promulgated by Gregory IX in 1234. It was hoped that the publication of this Papal law-book would, by defining the issues, settle the dispute once and for all ; but, unfortunately, it did nothing of the kind. The struggle between Church and State increased in intensity and bitterness. In the year 1302 Boniface VIII promulgated his famous

[1] Cf. *Introduction to Gierke's Political Theories of the Middle Ages*, by F. W. Maitland, p. xv.

5

Bull, *Unam Sanctum*, in which the case for Papal supremacy was set forth. Its main propositions were drawn from the writings of St. Bernard, Hugh of St. Victor, St. Thomas Aquinas, and the letters of Innocent III. As such, it summarizes the conclusions of thirteenth-century thinkers on the relations of Church and State. The claim for supremacy rests on the affirmation that the spiritual authority is higher than the temporal authority, that the Church, as the guardian of the Christian law of morals, has the right to establish and guide the secular power, and to judge it when it does not act rightly.[1] It was the last desperate attempt which the Papacy made to save Christian morals from corruption at the hands of the Roman lawyers. It did not have the desired effect, for the secular authorities treated with scorn the idea that they should surrender unconditionally to the Pope. It was a situation that would never have arisen but for the revival of Roman Law. The Popes found themselves in a difficult position. The choice, as they saw it, was between allowing the whole fabric of Mediæval civilization to be undermined by the worst of Pagan influences, or of asserting the supremacy of the Papacy in secular affairs. It was a desperate remedy to seek, and one conceivably worse than the disease. It was an attempt to seek to effect by external means a change that can come only from within. Experience teaches us that reform cannot be imposed from without in that kind of way. But what is so easy for us, with the experience of attempted reform behind us, to see to-day was not so easy to see in the Middle Ages, when methods were still untried, and in justice to the Mediæval Papacy we

---

[1] The chief passage of *Unam Sanctum* should be quoted. It reads : " There are two swords, the spiritual and the temporal ; our Lord said not of these two swords, ' it is too much,' but ' it is enough.' Both are in the power of the Church ; the one spiritual, to be used by the Church ; the other material, for the Church ; the former that of priests, the latter that of kings and soldiers, to be wielded at the command and by the sufferance of the priest. One sword must be under the other, the temporal under the spiritual. . . . The spiritual instituted the temporal power, and judges whether that power is well exercised. The eternal verse of Jeremiah is adduced. ' If the temporal power errs, it is judged by the spiritual.' To deny this is to assert with the heretical Manicheans two co-equal principles. We therefore assert, define, and pronounce that it is necessary to salvation to believe that every human being is subject to the Pontiff of Rome " (Milman's *History of Latin Christianity*, vol. vii. p. 125).

ought at least to acknowledge that, whatever motives may have actuated it, whatever mistakes it may have made, it fought, at any rate, on the right side. It did not allow civilization to become corrupted, exploitation to be legalized, without first making desperate efforts to prevent it; and, though the Church itself in turn became corrupted by the evil influences which had been let loose upon the world, it resolutely fought them so long as the issue was doubtful.

Although the Roman lawyers had been encouraged and patronized by the Emperors, it was not until the fourteenth century, when Charles IV assigned to jurists of the Roman School positions in the Imperial chancery, placing them on a par with the lower nobility, that Roman Law began to exercise much influence in Germany. Henceforth the Roman lawyers used all their influence and energy in securing recognition of the Roman Code as the one most fit for universal application. In 1495 the " Reichskammergericht "—the central Imperial Court—deliberately adopted Roman Law for its guidance as the common law of the Empire. In 1534 and 1537 the principalities of Julick and Berg (in the Rhine province)resolved to remodel their laws on the Roman pattern, in order to avoid clashing with the central Imperial Court. Under the influence of such considerations the movement towards the codification of local laws, on the basis of their reformation and of the reception of Roman doctrine, sweeps over Germany. The towns of Worms and Nüremberg (1479) were among the first to carry through such reformations. Most of the monarchically organized principalities followed suit, with the notable exception of some of the North German States, which remained faithful to the jurisprudence of the Sachenspeigel [1]—of which we shall speak hereafter. Hitherto faculties of jurisprudence, consisting mainly of experts in the Canon Law, had been complements of the theological faculties. Now, however, foundations were made in the German universities for the teaching of Roman Law as a secular study.

The reception of Roman Law appears mainly as a movement of the upper classes and of the political authorities connected with them. Once it had succeeded in establishing itself

[1] Cf. Vinogradoff, pp. 127-8.

at the top, dependent bodies found it to their advantage
to come into line. Its rapid spread in the German towns
in the early sixteenth century was due primarily to the
rapid expansion of German commerce about that time,
which created a demand for a uniform system of law. Mediæval Law, where it was not of Canonical origin (that is, the
law of tribal origin), was a local affair. As a unity, German
Law did not exist at the close of the Middle Ages. It was
broken up into countless local customs, which, for this very
reason, were unable to tackle the wider problems of civil
intercourse consequent upon the expansion of trade. The
fundamental principle of German Customary Law amounted
to a recognition of the right of each group of citizens to apply
its own customary ideas to the dealings of members with one
another. The law of knights and of fees was differentiated
not only from the law of the country in general but also from
municipal law, guild law, and peasant law ; while, further,
there was the great cleavage between the lay and the ecclesiastical courts. The laws of these different groups remained
in close touch with popular conceptions, and sometimes
attained considerable eminence in their treatment of legal
problems, but they were not connected with any legal system
and lacked precision in details. Most legal questions had
to be settled finally by unwritten or unenacted law, which
had to be " found " for the purpose. Thus it came about
that at the very moment when in Germany the social and
economic unit was changing from a local to a national one,
when German society was enjoying a kind of hothouse
prosperity, resulting from its commercial relations with
Italy and the Levant on one side and with the Scandinavian
North, Poland, and Russia on the other, German Customary
Law was crippled by the absence of a common code of laws
and a lack of professional learning. Further progress was
possible only through providing a remedy for these defects,
and this the Roman lawyers were able to do. They triumphed
because at this critical period they were able to supply a
felt need for a uniform system of law. Mediæval Customary
Law went down not because it was not good law, not because
it was by its nature unfitted for grappling with the problems
of a wider social intercourse, but because its systematic

study had been too long neglected and it was unable to offer effective resistance to the disciplined enemy.[1]

Although Mediæval Customary Law was defeated, it put up a good fight towards the finish. In the same way that scholars set to work to codify the Canon Law when its position was threatened by the spread of Roman Law, so the Customary Law found scholars anxious to save it. Many authoritative treatises on Customary Law now made their appearance. The most remarkable and influential of these was compiled by Eike von Repgow on the law of the Saxons. It provided the courts of Saxon Germany with a firm basis in jurisprudence, which was widely accepted and maintained. The Northern Territories, armed with this jurisprudence of the " Sachenspeigel," opposed a stubborn resistance to the encroachments of Roman Law. Commenting on this fact, Sir Paul Vinogradoff says : " This proves that the wholesale reception of Roman rules is not to be accounted for by any inherent incompetence in German Law, since where, as in Saxon lands, excessive particularism and uncertainty were counteracted, German Law proved quite able to stand its ground."[2]

This admission from such a high authority on Roman Law is important, and it becomes doubly important when considered in connection with another passage, in which he expresses his opinion as to the motives which led to the reception of Roman Law. " It is evident," he says, " that the reception of Roman Law depended on political causes : the legal system was subordinated to the idea of the State towering over individuals and classes, and free from the intermixture of feudalism. It was bound to appeal to the minds of all the pioneers of the State conception, to ambitious Emperors, grasping territorial princes, reforming legists, and even clerical representatives of law and order. Coming as it did from an age of highly developed social intercourse, Roman Law satisfied in many respects the requirements of economic development."[3] In other words, Roman Law succeeded because it gave support to the individual who pursued his own private interests without regard to the commonweal, without concern even whether others were

---

[1] Cf. Vinogradoff, pp. 109–11.   [2] Ibid., p. 113.   [3] Ibid., p. 130–1.

thereby ruined. Hence it was that the introduction of the Roman Code created unspeakable confusion in every grade of society. Exactly in proportion as it grew and prevailed, freedom and liberty went to the wall. The lawyers invested avaricious and ambitious princes and landlords with legal authority not only to deprive the peasants of their communal rights, but to evict them from their life-lease possessions and to increase their taxes. Such immoral procedure destroyed the feeling of brotherhood in communities and encouraged enormously the spirit of avarice. The vocation of law degenerated everywhere into a vulgar moneymaking trade. On every side it sowed the seeds of discord, and the people lost their confidence in the sanctity and impartiality of the law.

There is an amusing story of a French lady who, visiting Orleans and seeing so many law students, exclaimed : " Oh, woe, woe ! In our neighbourhood there is but one attorney, and he keeps the whole country in litigation. What mischief will not this horde make."[1] Everywhere the lawyers excite the indignation of public-spirited men. The charge is brought against them that they create rights and discover wrongs where none exist, that they encourage greed in the merchants, that they disgust men with public life by complicating matters with interminable formalities and tiresome trifles. Old customs and unwritten laws lose their force ; the lawyers regard as valid nothing that cannot be sustained by documentary evidence. In a sermon preached in Germany in 1515 we find the following : " When I warn you to beware of usurers and of those who would plunder you, I also warn you to beware of advocates, who now prevail. For the last twenty or thirty years they have increased like poison-weeds and are worse than usurers, for they take away not only your money but your rights and your honour. They have substituted a foreign code for the national one, and questions that used to be settled in two or three days now take as many months and years. What a pity people cannot get justice as they did before they knew these liars and deceivers whom no one wanted."[2]

If there be any comfort to be got from this painful story

[1] Janssen, vol. ii. p. 173.   [2] Ibid., vol. ii. p. 175.

it is that in the long run the Emperors whose ambitions first let this evil loose upon the world got nothing out of it for themselves. They were, as much as the peasantry, a part of the Mediæval order of society, and the spread of Roman Law undermined their power as effectively as it destroyed the prosperity of the peasantry. The system of private warfare which existed in pre-Christian times had never been abolished within the Empire, but it had been kept within certain bounds. It was permissible only under certain circumstances, when authorities refused or had not the power to interfere. Certain formalities were to be observed. Combatants were not to attack an enemy before giving him three days' notice. Hostilities were to be suspended on certain days, called " The truce of God." Certain persons, such as clergymen, pilgrims, labourers, and vine-tenders, and certain places, such as churches and cemeteries, were to be respected. But in later times, as a consequence of the corrupting influence of Roman Law, which spread broadcast the seeds of discord and increased greed and avarice among the princes, this spirit of chivalry disappeared, and the mighty availed themselves of every opportunity to oppress the weak. Every description of violence and outrage went unpunished, and the Empire was a prey to anarchy and confusion. Hence it was that for once ecclesiastics and lawyers came together in face of a common peril, and the doctrine was taught that social salvation could be found only by the Emperor asserting his ancient authority. Cardinal Nicholas of Cusa, the great ecclesiastical and secular reformer of the fifteenth century, voiced the popular sentiment when he blamed the Emperors for believing that a remedy could be found by gentle means. " What but ruin," he says, " is to be expected when each one thinks of himself ? If the sovereign hand has lost its power to quell interior dissensions, avarice and greed will prevail, war and private quarrels will increase, the dismembered Empire will go to ruin, and what has unjustly been acquired will be squandered. Let not the princes imagine that they will long retain what they have plundered from the Empire ; when they have broken all the ties that bind the States, and mangled the head and the limbs, there must be an end of all authority ; there is none left to whom to turn for help—and where there is no order there is anarchy, there is no more safety for any one.   While the princes are fighting among themselves a class will arise who will know no right but the force of arms, and as the princes have destroyed the Empire they in their turn will be destroyed by the rabble.   Men will seek for the German Empire and not find it.   Strangers will divide our lands and we shall be subject to foreign powers." [1]   But the Emperor was powerless.   His Empire had been disintegrated by Roman Law.

[1] Janssen, vol. ii. pp. 149-50.

CHAPTER V

ROMAN LAW IN ENGLAND

PASSING on from a consideration of the reception of Roman Law in Germany to a consideration of its influence in England it will be necessary in the first place to challenge the opinion of the legal profession that law in this country is English and not Roman.

In the sense in which the legal profession use the word Roman, no doubt their judgment is well-founded. The legal mind is fond of hair-splitting technicalities and differences, and without doubt they have their reasons for believing that English Law differs from Roman Law, though I have not succeeded in discovering what they are. But any decision in this matter must depend upon how Roman Law is defined. If emphasis is to be given to secondary details, then it may be that experts could bring sufficient evidence to show that English and Roman law are very different. But if we take our stand upon broad, fundamental propositions, this is clearly not the case. One does not need to be a legal expert to understand that English Law to-day is in all its essentials a law designed to enable rich men to live among poor as emphatically as Mediæval Law was designed to enable good men to live among bad, and that this different moral aim separates it from English Mediæval Law as completely as it identifies it with the Roman Code. English Law to-day may have historical continuity with the Common Law of the earlier Middle Ages, but in its informing spirit, its broad, basic principles and framework, there is no denying it is Roman through and through. The writers of legal textbooks such as Bracton based their ideas upon Roman Law, and it was always in the minds of lawyers for guidance and comparison if it was not actually quoted from the bench. Every-

where English Law, like Roman, exalts private interests at
the expense of communal ones, and in consequence conceives
of the State as an instrument for the maintenance of order
rather than the enforcement of justice. For a law which
exalts private interests is essentially an instrument of anarchy,
and maintains order only for the purpose of putting off the
evil day.[1]

In England, as on the Continent, the principles of Roman
Law were imposed from above, and got a footing by appealing
to the immediate self-interest of the monarchy. Henry II
saw their value as a means of increasing his personal power
at the expense of his barons, and it was in his reign that the
process which culminated in the highly centralized monarchy
of the Tudors began to make headway. Henry had destroyed
the military independence of the barons by instituting scutage,
whereby the barons agreed to a money payment in lieu of
their obligation to provide him with men-at-arms in time of
war. He now set to work with the help of his legal advisers
to undermine their power in their own domains. The
manorial courts of the barons had been partly shorn of their
powers by the judicial reforms of Henry I. Henry II sought
to carry this work further by developing the *curia regis* or
Royal Court of Justice. That court had originally been the
court of the king's barons, corresponding to the court of
his tenants, which every feudal lord possessed. From this
central court, Henry sent out justices on circuit, and so brought
the king's law into touch with all parts of the kingdom,
breaking open the enclosed spheres of influence of the manorial
courts by emptying them of their more serious cases, and
it may be that at the start these justices dispensed a law which
was cheaper, more expeditious, and more expert than that
of the manor and scarcely different in intention. It was by
such means that the idea was gradually promoted that the
king's law and the king's right took precedence over those
of other individuals and groups, and the people were induced
to acquiesce in a change, the ultimate consequences of which
they were unable to foresee.

At first sight these changes have all the appearance of
a change in the right direction. Feudalism rested on local

[1] Cf. Ashley's *Economic History*, vol. i. part i. p. 131.

isolation, on the severance of kingdom from kingdom, and barony from barony, on the distinction of race and blood, on local military independence, on an allegiance determined by accidents of birth and social position. It might appear, therefore, that now, when the circumstances which had created feudalism were disappearing, when the spread of currency was undermining its integrity, that the new developments that aimed at breaking down this isolation, destroyed the military independence of the barons, took the administration of the law out of the hands of men without a legal training, and placed it in the hands of experts, who brought order and uniformity into it, was a change in the right direction. And so it might have been, had not the justices whose decisions were to leave a lasting impression on the law of the land been men who despised the common and traditional law. Their minds had been trained upon Roman Law, and they set to work to remodel the common law in such a way as to undermine the basis of Mediæval institutions and popular liberty. In the long run, much the same kind of thing happened in England as in Germany, though the English lawyers were perhaps more subtle in their methods. They did not advocate a revival of the Justinian Code ; perhaps because the fiction of continuity could not very well be applied in this country, but they introduced the changes piecemeal. Bracton, the great jurist of the time, upon whose writings our knowledge of the period is largely based, sought to accomplish this end by fitting English facts into a framework of Roman Law.[1] Such is the English Common Law.

The contrast between the old Mediæval Law and the new Anglicized Roman Law is most strikingly illustrated by the new legal attitude towards the question of private property, and in the treatment of the law of persons. A suspicion gains ground that a consequence of the introduction of Roman ideas of law was an attempt in the thirteenth century to transform feudalism into slavery. Nothing was sacred to the lawyers that could not be supported by documentary evidence. The rights and customs of the people they looked upon as nominal and revocable. " In Anglo-Saxon times, the predecessor of the villain, the ceorl, was not a slave at

[1] Cf. Vinogradoff, p. 97.

all, but had a standing against his lord in the court of law."[1]
But the Roman Code made no provision for the rights of
different social classes. It recognized only autocrats and
slaves. Hence it was that, when confronted with Feudalism
an institution in which the lords were not autocrats but
functionaries, and the villains not slaves but dependents,
the lawyers were at a loss as to how to apply the Roman
rule. They appear to have vacillated for some time, but
" after some contradictory decisions the court ended by
applying strictly the rule that villains have no claim
against their lords and that in law what is held by the
villain is owned by the lord."[2]   Bracton follows Azo as
to the very important generalization " all men are born
either free or slaves."[3] There is no getting round these
facts. That a decision on this issue had to be made
suggests that, prior to the introduction of Roman ideas of
law, the right of the villain to appeal against his lord was
presumed, and that the courts wavered some time between
contradictory opinions, because things were happening behind
the scenes which had to be taken into consideration, or, in
other words, that their final decision was governed by considerations of political expediency. We saw that, by means
of scutage, the military power of the barons had been
destroyed. The Royal Courts of Justice were now engaged
in the task of destroying their judicial power, and it is not
unreasonable to suppose that a time came when the lords
began to ask the question, " Where do we come in ? " under
the new order the king and his lawyers were seeking to
establish. It would become daily clearer to the lawyers that
if the development of the Royal Courts of Justice was to
continue and to expand, the lords would have to be brought
to terms. If they were to acquiesce in the change, their
status would have to be guaranteed in some new way. And I
suggest that a bargain was struck. The Crown was to be
allowed to absorb the judicial functions, and the lords were
to be allowed to enslave their serfs.

But the change could not stop here. If the lord was to
be given absolute control over his serfs, he must be made
absolute owner of the land, for the spread of currency into

----

[1] C. Vinogradoff, p. 100.   [2] Ibid., p. 100.   [3] Ibid., p. 98.

rural areas by substituting money payments for payment in kind was disintegrating the old feudal order. Hence it came about that the lawyers revived the Roman individualistic theory of property. The lord was to be acknowledged no longer as a functionary who held his land conditionally upon the fulfilment of certain specific duties towards his serfs and tenants, but was to be recognized as the absolute owner of the land, while, moreover, he was to be given certain privileges over the common lands. The foundation of the law on this subject is in the " Statute of Merton " of 1235, which laid down that lords might " make their profit " of their ," wastes, woods and pastures," in spite of the complaints of " knights and freeholders " whom they had " infeoffed of small tenements in their manors," so long as these feoffees had a sufficient pasture so much as belongeth to their tenements."[1] This was the thin end of the wedge. Like all the law on the subject, it is delightfully and intentionally vague, in order that the lawyers might twist and twine its meaning, and the lords bully their dependents as best suited their ends. The question, of course, arises how much is " sufficient pasture." This is obviously a matter of opinion, and as the burden of proof lay upon the tenant, who, if he objected to enclosures, had to prove that he could not find sufficient pasture, the statute in effect granted the lords the right to enclose the common lands to their hearts' content, and allowed the peasantry no redress against injustice, as the courts were in conspiracy against them.

Before the lawyers came along with their Roman Law, Feudalism was a defensible if not an ideal form of organization. But the lawyers poisoned the whole system. They became the stewards of the lords and instructed their noble patrons " in all the legal methods of taming down the peasants so that they might not shoot up too high." They put them up to all the little dodges by means of which the common lands might be enclosed, and how, by attacking things piecemeal, they might encroach upon the communal rights of the people. They were behind the evictions which the new commercial lords undertook, in order that tillage might be turned into

[1] *An Introduction to English Economic History and Theory*, by W. J. Ashley, vol. i. part ii. p. 271.

pasture, when sheep-farming became so profitable. By such means funds were secured to feed the ever-increasing taste of the upper classes for luxury and display, and by such means the unrest was created which led to the Peasants' Revolt of 1381, when the lawyers got all they were looking for. Every one of them who fell into the hands of the rebels was put to death; " not until all these were killed would the land enjoy its *old freedom* again " the peasants shouted as they fired the houses of the stewards and flung the records of the manor courts into the flames. When they entered London they set ablaze the new inn of the lawyers at the Temple together with the stately palace of John of Gaunt and the houses of the foreign merchants, against whom also they had grievances. Whoever may have had doubts as to the source of the mischief, the peasants, who were led by the friars, had their minds made up. It was not a rising against Feudalism as it had existed a couple of centuries earlier, but a rising against a corrupted Feudalism in general and the lawyers in particular, whom the peasants rightly believed had corrupted it as they believed they were corrupting the mind of the young sovereign. For one object of their rising was to free him from evil counsellors whom they believed abused his youth.

The Peasants' Revolt is the turning-point in English history, as similar revolts on the Continent in the latter half of the fourteenth century are the turning-point in the history of Continental nations. To ascribe the break-up of Mediæval society to the economic changes which followed the Black Death is to draw a smoke-screen across history. It is to attribute to a general and indefinable cause social phenomena which can be most explicitly traced to a very definite and particular one, since the economic confusion which followed the Black Death would not have come about had not the communal relations which held society together a couple of centuries earlier been disintegrated by the machinations of the lawyers. The peasants, therefore, in seeking the destruction of the lawyers put their finger rightly on the primary cause of the dissolution of the old Mediæval order. To this extent their instincts were true. But unfortunately while they were right as to the cause of the evils from which they were suffering they were wrong in regard to their general economic policy. Quite apart from the lawyers, the old feudal order based upon payment in kind was being disintegrated by the spread of currency into rural areas which was substituting money payments for services, and it was urgent, if economic difficulties were not to follow upon this change, that currency should be regulated in rural areas by Guilds. But this aspect of the problem they appear to have overlooked entirely, for instead of demanding charters from their sovereign for organization of agricultural Guilds along with their demand for the abolition of serfdom, they demanded liberty to buy and sell. This mistake was a fatal one, since if they had demanded charters for Guilds the whole course of English history would have been different. For then the Guilds would have covered the whole area of production, and as capitalism would not then have been able to get a foothold, the position of the Guilds in the towns would not have been undermined in the sixteenth century by the pressure of the competition of capitalist industry. After a time such Agricultural Guilds would have been sufficiently wealthy to buy out the landlords in the same way that the plutocracy of Rome came to dispossess the landed aristocracy, or they would have acquired sufficient power to confiscate the lands if this policy had recommended itself. But this great opportunity of recovering the land of England for the people was lost because the peasants at the time saw only their immediate interests. Profiting by a rising market, they did not understand the dangers to which an unregulated currency exposed them. But when at last in the sixteenth century they did become cognizant of the evil, it was too late. The Guilds in the town had been defeated and capitalism was already triumphant. It is strange how history repeats itself. As in Rome we saw that an unregulated currency gave rise to Roman Law, so in the Middle Ages we see the revival of Roman Law being accompanied by the spread of an unregulated currency. There is a definite connection between these two phenomena. The Roman theory postulating an individualistic society was not only opposed to all organizations within the State, because in the time of the Republic such organizations had been used as a basis of conspiracy but to the maintenance of the Just Price as well, for a right to buy in the cheapest

market and sell in the dearest was admitted in the Justinian
Code. There can therefore be no doubt whatsoever that the
influence of the lawyers would be opposed to the spread of
Guild organization in rural areas.

In spite of the popular feeling against the lawyers which
the Peasants' Revolt evinced, the legal profession steadily
strengthened its grip on the government of the country.
By the reign of Elizabeth the lawyers had not only concentrated
all judicial functions into their own hands, but Parliament
itself had become an assembly of lawyers. Bacon, though
himself a lawyer, had a great contempt for the profession.
No amount of legal knowledge, he believed, would make a
statesman or equip a man to deal with matters of high policy.
" The wisdom of a lawyer," he said, " is one, that of a lawmaker
another. Judges ought to remember that their office is to
interpret law, and not to make law or give law." And so
he viewed with alarm the growing influence of Parliament,
as it implied the growing influence of lawyers. " Without
the lawyers," he said, " the country gentlemen would be
leaderless." He had no objection to Parliament so long as
they did not attempt to control the Government, but he
clearly foresaw the paralysis that would overtake State policy
if ever the lawyers got the upper hand. For though later
the Revolution taught men that lawyers prefer some form
of monarchy, it is a nominal or limited monarchy in which
they believe. Their ambition is not to occupy the throne but
to be the power behind the throne, and it is this ambition
that makes them at once so powerful and so irresponsible,
which enables them at once to commit injustice and to visit
others with the consequences.

As against the idea of a sovereign assembly, Bacon exalted
the Crown. The royal prerogative represented in his mind
the case of enterprise and initiative as against pedantry and
routine. But monarchy in his day was beginning to find its
position difficult in the new order which it had been one of
the chief means of promoting. Monarchy, as I insisted
earlier, was essentially a Mediæval institution. The monarchs
were the highest of temporal authorities, but they were
subject to the spiritual authority of the Popes. Monarchs
did not care very much about this. They were restive under

it even when they acquiesced. They wanted their rule to be absolute, and it was this that led them to give support to the Roman lawyers, who made law depend upon the monarchs' will and not ultimately upon a higher and external authority. After quarrelling with the Popes for centuries the monarchs succeeded in countries where Protestanism had triumphed in emancipating themselves from the control of the Popes. But things did not then work out exactly as they expected. When the Popes were gone the religious sanction was gone, and monarchs began to find that instead of contending against the Popes they had to contend against their own peoples, who now began to question their authority. Hence the doctrine of the Divine Right of Kings by which James I sought to rehabilitate monarchy. He wrote two treatises on the subject in which he expounded his views. In one of these, *A King's Duty in his Office,* he distinguished the lawful ruler from the tyrant by the fact that the former feels responsibility towards God, while the latter does not. Hence the lawful ruler claims unconditional obedience from his subjects and was answerable to God alone, but the people owe no allegiance to the tyrant. But in the other one, *Basilicon Doron,* which was prepared for his eldest son Henry and was not written for publication, he maintains that a king was to be obeyed whether he ruled justly or unjustly. In the first place because in abolishing monarchy the State, instead of relieving, would double its distress, for a king can never be so monstrously vicious that he will not generally favour justice and maintain order ; and in the next, because a wicked king is sent by God as a plague on people's sins, and it is unlawful to shake off the burden which God has laid upon them. " Patience, earnest prayer and amendment of their lives are the only lawful means to move God to relieve them of that heavy curse." [1] It was essentially the philosophy of Protestantism and Roman Law which treats all rights as subjective as opposed to the doctrine of objective rights postulated by Mediævalism.[2]

So far from settling matters, the system of government

[1] See *Political Thought in England from Bacon to Halifax,* by G. P. Gooch, pp. 7–22.

[2] See *Authority, Liberty and Function,* by Ramiro de Maeztu.

6

by prerogative as preached and practised by James only made matters worse. It brought him into collision with the lawyers and the Puritans, who shattered the power of the Stuarts. The opposition which James had to face came from the lawyers, and particularly from Edward Coke, who was their leader. He had served successively under Elizabeth as Speaker and Attorney-General, and in these positions he appeared mainly as a defender of the Crown against the dangers of conspiracy. But on being appointed Chief Justice of Common Pleas his attitude towards the king changed, and he now began to play the rôle of champion of the courts against the encroachments of the king. He was the greatest legal scholar of his age, and being a conservative by temperament, he came to exalt the common law above king and Parliament. It was the sovereign, and supreme over both of them. His position was altogether too paradoxical to become a constitutional theory, for the rule of the law, according to his interpretation, would mean not merely the rule of the lawyers but finally the rule of the pedant and antiquarian. To Coke, law was an end in itself, and he believed just as much in the Divine Right of Law as James believed in the Divine Right of Kings, and so a collision became inevitable. Through the patronage of kings, the Roman lawyers had been gradually raised to positions of highest authority in the land. Now the time came when the law, which was mainly their own creation, was to be used as a weapon with which to challenge the royal authority.

Though Coke's idea of the sovereignty of law as an esoteric science interpreted by professional jurists died with its author, it is customary to regard him as one of the founders of constitutional government. The contest between King and Parliament continued for nearly a century and was only finally brought to an end by deposing the last of the Stuarts, which was followed by the enactment of the Bill of Rights passed in 1689 which put an end for ever in England to all claim to Divine Right or hereditary right independent of the law. It was, among other things, a great victory for the lawyers. Henceforth an English monarch became just as much the creature of an Act of Parliament as any member of the Civil Service. Parliament also secured absolute control over taxation and the Army, which incidentally owed its existence as a permanent institution to the fact that after the Revolution the Army of Cromwell refused to be disbanded, regarding itself as the defender of the liberties of the people against landlords, royalists and Catholics. With Parliament supreme the triumph of the lawyers was assured. Little by little, as their ally, Capitalism, whom they had succeeded in emancipating from the "fetters of the Middle Ages," undermined in the economic world what was left of the old social order, the control of government passed into their hands until, in our day, they are supreme. But what kind of government is it?

> Parliaments built of paper
> And the soft swords of gold,
> That twist like a waxen taper
> In the weak aggressor's hold.

Such is Mr. Chesterton's description of a government of lawyers. Experience is teaching us that Bacon was right in holding that no amount of legal knowledge will equip a man for the high policy of State. Roman Law, being divorced from morals, tends to corrupt the minds, where it does not corrupt the morals of those who study it. And it comes about this way : without a base in morality, law inevitably becomes increasingly complicated, for its framework can only be maintained amid such circumstances by defining precisely every detail. Instead, therefore, of the mind of the student being directed towards a comprehension of the broad, basic facts of life, it is directed towards the study of subtle controversies and hair-splitting differences which befog the intelligence. As success in the legal profession follows preoccupation with such trivialities, a government composed of lawyers is necessarily a weak government that waits upon events because it is incapable of decision on vital issues. But while on the one hand Roman Law reduces its devotees to impotence so far as constructive statesmanship is concerned, on the other the very complexity of the law paralyses the efforts of men without legal training to secure reform. Hence it is, while parties have changed and battles have been fought over burning political issues, nothing can get done. And because reform becomes impossible, anarchy grows apace, which in turn encourages the growth of legalism in vain attempts to put a boundary to the growth of disorder. It is thus the modern world has entered a vicious circle in which anarchy begets legalism and legalism begets anarchy and from which there can be no escape so long as the principles of Roman Law remain unchallenged.

Considering the iniquity that has been associated with Roman Law almost from the days of its revival, it is extraordinary that it should still command respect. But what is more extraordinary still is that while it succeeded in corrupting Mediæval society it has not only succeeded in escaping censure itself, but has managed to transfer the odium which belongs to itself to the institutions which it was the means of corrupting. The Church, the Monarchy, Feudalism and the Guilds each in turn suffered at its hands. Each and all of them in turn have been condemned as intolerable tyrannies because each of them in some measure stood for the communal idea of society, and as such at different times have offered resistance to the growth of a system of law whose aim it has been to dissolve all personal and human ties and to replace them by the impersonal activity of the State. If Capitalism to-day is our active enemy, let us clearly recognize that Roman Law is the power behind the throne.

CHAPTER VI

THE CONSPIRACY AGAINST MEDIÆVALISM

AN appreciation of the part which Roman Law played in the corruption of Mediæval society and in the creation of modern thought and civilization should go a long way towards the removal of the prejudice which prevails to-day against most things Mediæval, and which distorts out of its proper perspective everything which then existed. This prejudice has many roots, and therefore it becomes necessary, ere proceeding with our story, to seek the removal of the prejudice by explaining its origin. I hope to show that though to-day this prejudice may be little more than a misunderstanding, it did not begin as such, but as a conspiracy.

We need not go far to find evidence in support of this contention. Consider, for one moment, the utterly irresponsible way in which the word Mediæval is thrown about in the daily Press. Among a certain class of writers it is the custom to designate as Mediæval anything which they do not understand or of which they do not approve, quite regardless of the issue as to whether it actually existed in the Middle Ages or not. During the war, for instance, how often did we read of Mediæval Junkerdom, notwithstanding the fact that the Middle Ages was the age of chivalry, and that, as a matter of fact, the spirit of German militarism approximates very nearly to that of the military capitalism of Ancient Rome. For the Romans, like the Germans, did not hesitate to destroy the towns and industries of their rivals. It was, as I have already pointed out, for commercial reasons that they burnt Carthage and Corinth, and caused the vineyards and olive-groves of Gaul to be destroyed, in order to avoid a damaging competition with the rich Roman landlords. Or, again, when anything goes wrong in a government department, for reasons not apparent on the surface, the shortcoming will be described as Mediæval regardless of the fact that bureaucracy is a peculiarly Roman institution and scarcely existed in the Middle Ages. There is no need to multiply instances, as they are to be met with in the Press daily. But the result is tragic. An all-pervading prejudice is created, which militates against clear thinking on social and political questions, for a prejudice against Mediævalism is a prejudice against all normal forms of social organization ; it is a prejudice which may spell Bolshevism in the days to come ; for, after all, Bolshevism is itself nothing more than modern prejudices and historical falsehoods carried to their logical conclusions.

Now, it stands to reason that this gross solecism is not without a cause. Nobody on the Press ever speaks of Rome or Greece in this irresponsible way, and the question needs to be answered : Why is the Middle Ages the only period in history singled out for such thoughtless misrepresentation ? The answer is, that at one time this indiscriminate mud-slinging had a motive behind it—a motive, however, that has since disappeared. Cobbett, I think, got at the bottom of it when, a hundred years ago, he pointed out that Protestant historians had wilfully misrepresented the Middle Ages because there were so many people living on the plunder of the monasteries and the Guilds, and consequently interested in maintaining a prejudice against the Middle Ages, as the easiest way of covering their tracks. It was not for nothing that Cobbett's *History of the Reformation*[1] was burnt by the public hangman. It was burnt because it was more than a history—because it exposed a conspiracy. But the prejudice exists ; it has other roots which require to be attacked.

We need not pause to consider how the prejudices of freethinkers have militated against an understanding of the Middle Ages, as the free thinking of freethinkers is no longer above suspicion. In so far as their prejudices are in these days a force to be reckoned with, it is as a part of the Marxian or Bolshevik gospel. The rise to popularity of the Marxian creed has given the anti-Mediæval prejudice a new lease

[1] *A History of the Protestant Reformation in England and Ireland*, by William Cobbett. (Reprint by Washbourne & Co., 1s. 6d.)

of life, by refusing in the first place to admit that any but material forces have ever played more than a secondary part in the shaping of history, and what naturally follows from it, distorting or ignoring such facts as do not happen to fit in with the materialist conception. How gross are the prejudices which have been impressed upon the minds of the workers may be understood by any one who will take the trouble to read such a book as that produced by one of the Neo-Marxians, *A Worker Looks at History*, by Mr. Mark Starr. It is an important book because of the wide circulation it has amongst the workers. Popular misconceptions and prejudices are exaggerated. In the chapter entitled " The Renaissance from the Mediæval Night " the author, after referring to the schools of Alexandria, says : " Christianity proscribed philosophy, abolished the schools, and plunged the world into an abyss of darkness from which it only emerged after twelve hundred years." Mr. Starr is indignant at this. But it never occurs to him to enquire what these schools taught ; and this is important. He assumes that they taught what he admires in the Pagan philosophers, for whom I have as much regard as has Mr. Starr. But these schools of the Neo-Platonists were degenerate institutions. They taught everything that Mr. Starr would hate. Their teaching was eclectic—a blending of Christian and Platonic ideas with Oriental mysticism. They believed in magic. Their reasoning was audacious and ingenious, but it was intellectual slush without any definite form or structure. Above all, it encouraged a detachment from the practical affairs of life, and thus became an obstruction to real enlightenment. It was well that these schools were suppressed ; they needed suppressing, for no good can come of such misdirection of intellectual activities, and I doubt not had Mr. Starr been then alive he would have risen in his wrath against their unreality. The Early Church was opposed to these degenerate intellectuals, because, while the Church desired to establish the Kingdom of God upon Earth, they were content for it to remain in heaven. But Mr. Starr has been so prejudiced against Mediævalism that he attributes to the Church all the vices which it sought to suppress.

Though the Early Church closed the schools of the Neo-Platonists, it did not suppress philosophy. On the contrary, Greek culture was preserved at Constantinople, while much of Greek philosophy was absorbed in Christian theology. Before the close of the New Testament Canon, Greek philosophy had begun to colour the expression of Christian doctrine; in the hands of the Fathers of the Church it entered into its very substance. The logos of Plato reappears as the doctrine of the Trinity, which, incidentally, is not an explanation of the universe, but " a fence to guard a mystery."[1] It reappears, however, not as an intellectual abstraction, but as a concrete reality, and, as such, possesses a dynamic power capable of changing the world. It was this burning desire to change the world which made the Early Christians so impatient with the Neo-Platonists, who made speculation an excuse for inaction, as it makes the Neo-Marxians to-day rightly impatient with a certain type of Socialist intellectual. Moreover, it was this insistence upon practical activity which made Christianity so dogmatic in its theology. Marxians at any rate ought to realize that strenuous activity must rest upon dogmas. On the other hand, the weakness of Pagan philosophy was that it was powerless to influence life. " Cicero, the well-paid advocate of the publicani and bankers, whom he frequently calls in the most idyllic style *ornamentum civitatis, firmamentum rei publicæ flos equitum* while philosophizing on virtue, despoiled with violence the inhabitants of the province he administered, realizing, *salvis legibus*, two million two hundred thousand sestercia in less than two months. Honest Brutus invested his capital at Cyprus at 48 per cent.; Verres in Sicily at 24 per cent. Much later, when the economic dissolution of the Republic had led to the establishing of the Empire, Seneca, who, in his philosophical writings, preached contempt of riches, despoiled Britain by his usury." [2]

While the prejudice against Mediævalism doubtless had its origin in malice and forethought, it is encouraged by the fallacious division of Mediæval history into the Middle Ages

[1] *Essays in Orthodoxy*, by Oliver Chase Quick.
[2] A. Deloume, *Les Manieurs d'Argent à Rome*, quoted in Nitti's *Catholic Socialism*.

and the Dark Ages.   By means of this artificial and arbitrary division the popular mind has been led to suppose that mankind was plunged into darkness and ignorance after the decline of Roman civilization, while it is generally inferred that this was due to the spread of Christianity, which it is supposed exhibited a spirit hostile to learning and enlightenment rather than to the inroads of the barbarian tribes. A grosser travesty of historic truth was never perpetrated. But the travesty is made plausible by the custom which many historians have of detailing the history of a particular geographical area, instead of making history continuous with the traditions of thought and action, the geographical centres of which change from time to time.   Treating the history of Western Europe according to the former method, the period of Roman occupation is followed by one of barbarism, in which almost every trace of civilization disappears for a time, and no doubt the people who dwelt in this part of Europe did live through a period of darkness.   That, however, was the case with the Western Empire only.   The Eastern Empire was never overrun by the barbarians.   On the contrary, its capital, Constantinople, maintained during all this period a high state of civilization, and was the artistic and cultural centre of the world.   While the barbarian hordes were overrunning the Western Empire, the Eastern Church preserved the traditions of Greek culture, which, as order became restored in the West, gradually filtered through Venice until the fall of Constantinople in 1453.   The subsequent emigration of Greek scholars and artists to Italy removed the last barrier between the culture of Eastern and Western Europe.

It was at Constantinople, during the sixth century, that the Code of Justinian was made.   It is painful for me to have to record this fact, seeing that it led, unfortunately, to the revival of Roman Law, and it is mentioned here not as a recommendation, but merely as testimony to the existence of intellectual activity during the so-called Dark Ages.   The task of extracting a code from the six camel-loads of law-book certainly testifies to the existence of learning. Moreover, it was during this period that the Byzantine school of architecture flourished.   The reputation of the cathedral

church of Santa Sophia, built in the sixth century, was so
great that the twelfth-century William of Malmesbury knew
of it " as surpassing every other edifice in the world." Of
this architecture Professor Lethaby writes :—

" The debt of universal architecture to the early Christian
and Byzantine schools of builders is very great. They
evolved the church types ; they carried far the exploration
of domical construction, and made wonderful balanced
compositions of vaults and domes over complex plans.
They formed the belfry from the Pharos and fortification
towers. We owe to them the idea of the vaulted basilican
church, which, spreading westward over Europe, made our
great vaulted cathedrals possible. They entirely recast
the secondary forms of architecture ; the column was taught
to carry the arch, the capital was reconsidered as a bearing
block and became a feature of extraordinary beauty. The
art of building was made free from formulæ, and architecture
became an adventure in building once more. We owe
to them a new type of moulding, the germ of the Gothic
system, by the introduction of the roll-moulding and their
application of it to ' strings ' and the margins of doors.
The first arch known to me which has a series of roll-mouldings
is in the palace of Inshatta. The tendency to cast windows
into groups, the ultimate source of tracery and the foiling
of arches is to be mentioned. We owe to these Christian
artists the introduction of delightfully fresh ornamentation,
crisp foliage, and interlaces, and the whole scheme of Christian
iconography." [1]

This is no small achievement. Only an age as indifferent
to the claims of architecture as our own could underrate
its magnitude. To the average historian, however, this
period of history is a blank, because he lacks the kind of
knowledge and sympathy necessary to assess its achievements
at their proper value. To his mind, enlightenment and
criticism are synonymous ; and, finding no criticism, he
assumes there was no enlightenment, not understanding that
criticism is the mark of reflective rather than of creative
epochs. For, though at times they appear contemporaneously,
they have different roots, and the critical spirit soon destroys

[1] *Architecture*, by Professor W. R. Lethaby.

the creative, as we shall see when we come to consider the Renaissance. How false such standards of judgment are may be understood by comparing the Dark Ages with our own. In those days there was plenty of architecture, but little, if any, architectural literature. To-day the volume of architectural literature and criticism is prodigious, but there is precious little architecture.

While the traditions of culture all through this period were preserved and developed in the Eastern Church with its centre at Constantinople, the task which fell to the Western, or Roman, Church was of a different order. Upon it was thrust the task of civilizing the barbarian races of the West which had overthrown the Roman Empire, and it is to the credit of the Early Church that it succeeded where the Romans had failed. Success was achieved through different methods. Roman civilization had been imposed by violence and maintained by compulsion : it was always an exotic affair, and it fell to pieces when the force of the barbarians became at last more powerful than that of the Roman Empire. The success of Christianity is attributable to the fact that it effected a change in the spirit of the peoples. This great achievement was the work of the early Monastic Orders, whose missionary zeal was destined to spread Christianity throughout Europe.

The early Christian monks had been characterized by a decided Oriental tendency to self-contemplation and abstraction, and in their missionary enterprises their inter-course with the rude populations was limited to instructing them in the homilies and creeds of Christ. Augustine and his forty companions, who were sent forth by Gregory the Great to convert Britain (A.D. 596), " acted on a very different principle, for in addition to the orthodox weapons of attack and persuasion which they employed against their opponents, they made use of other, but equally powerful, methods of subjugation, by teaching the people many useful arts that were alike beneficial to their bodies and their minds. As soon as they settled in Kent, and had begun to spread themselves towards the north and west, they built barns and sheds for their cattle side by side with their newly erected churches, and opened schools in the immediate neighbourhood of the house of God, where the youth of the nominally converted population were now for the first time instructed in reading, and in the formulæ of their faith and where those who were intended 'for a monastic life or for the priesthood, received the more advanced instruction necessary to their earnest calling." [1]

We read that the Benedictines of Abingdon, in Berkshire, were required by their canonized founder to perform a daily portion of field labour, in addition to the prescribed services of the Church. "In their mode of cultivating the soil they followed the practices adopted in the warmer and more systematically tilled lands of the south. They soon engaged the services of the natives in the vicinity and repaid their labours with a portion of the fruits of their toil, and in proportion as the woods and thickets were cleared, and the swamps and morasses disappeared, the soil yielded a more plentiful return ; while the land, being leased or sub-let, became the means of placing the monastery, which was, in fact, the central point of the entire system, in the position of a rich proprietor. From such centres as these the beams of a new and hopeful life radiated in every direction." [2]

"The requirements of the monks, and the instruction they were able to impart around them, soon led to the establishment in their immediate neighbourhood of the first settlement of artificers and retail dealers, while the excess of their crops, flocks and herds, gave rise to the first markets, which were, as a rule, originally held before the gate of the abbey church. Thus hamlets and towns were formed, which became the centres of trade and general intercourse, and thus originated the market tolls, and the jurisdiction of these spiritual lords. The beneficial influences of the English monasteries in all departments of education and mental culture expanded still further, even in the early times of the Anglo-Saxons, for they had already then become conspicuous for the proficiency which many of their members had attained in painting and music, sculpture and architecture. The study of the sciences, which had been greatly advanced through the exertions of Bede, was the means of introducing

[1] *Pictures of Old England*, by Dr. Reinhold Pauli, chap. ii.   [2] Ibid.

one of his most celebrated followers, Alcuin of York, to the court of Charlemagne, for the purpose of establishing schools and learning in the German Empire. And although every monastery did not contribute in an equal degree to all these beneficial results, all aided to the best of their power and opportunities in bringing about that special state of cultivation which characterised the Middle Ages." [1]

So much for the Dark Ages and the malicious libel which insinuates that the Mediæval world was opposed to learning. So far from such insinuations being true, every Monastic Order, for whatever purpose originally founded, ended in becoming a learned order. It was the recognition of this fact that led St. Francis, who was a genuinely practical man, to insist that his followers should not become learned or seek their pleasures in books, " for I am afraid," he says, " that the doctors will be the destruction of my vineyard." And here is found the paradox of the situation : so long as learning was in the hands of men who valued it as such it made little headway, but when at length the new impulse did come, it came in no small measure from the Franciscans, from the men who had the courage to renounce learning and to lead a life of poverty, for in the course of time the Franciscans became learned, as had done the other orders. Thus we see that the central idea of Christianity—to renounce the world in order to conquer it—bears fruit not only in the moral but in the intellectual universe.

Sufficient has now been said to refute the charge that the Mediæval Church was opposed to learning. The case of the Franciscans in decrying learning is the only one known to me, and their action, as we shall see in a later chapter, turned out to be a blessing in disguise. What the Mediæval Church was against was heresy, which was often associated with learning, but the suppression of heresy is a thing fundamentally different from opposition to learning, and there is nothing peculiarly Mediæval about it. The Greeks condemned Socrates to death for seeking to discredit the gods, while Plato himself came finally to the conclusion that in his ideal State to doubt the gods would be punishable by death. The Roman Emperors persecuted the Christians

[1] Ibid.

for refusing observance to the gods, Marcus Aurelius himself being no exception to this rule, while we ourselves show equal readiness to persecute heresy against the State, as in the case of the pacifist conscientious objectors. And so it will always be when great issues are at stake. A people with a firm grip on fundamental truth attacks heresy at its roots in ideas. A people like ourselves, that has lost its grip on primary truth, waits until it begins to influence action, but once the heresy is recognized, all peoples in all times have sought its suppression.

Before going further, let us be clear in our minds as to what we mean by heresy. At different times it has meant different things, but, in general, it might be defined as the advocacy of ideas which, at a given time in a given place, are considered by those in power as subversive to the social order, and the instinct of self-preservation has impelled all peoples in all times to suppress such ideas. In the Mediæval period such persecutions were associated with religion, because in that era all ideas, social and political, were discussed under a theological aspect. The position is simple. If it be affirmed that every social system rests finally upon the common acceptance of certain beliefs, any attempt to alter beliefs will tend, therefore, in due course to affect the social system. Plato carried this idea much farther than the question of religious beliefs. In the *Republic* he says : " The introduction of a new style of music must be shunned as imperilling the whole State ; since styles of music are never disturbed without affecting the most important political institutions." " The new style," he continues, " gradually gaining a lodgment, quietly insinuates itself into manners and customs ; and from these it issues in greater force, and makes its way into mutual compacts ; and from making compacts it goes on to attack laws and constitutions, displaying the utmost impudence until it ends by overturning everything, both in public and in private." Plato here recognizes that if communal relations in society are to be maintained and men are to share common life, it can be only on the assumption that they share common ideas and tastes. From this it follows that the nearer a society approaches the communal ideal the more it will insist upon unity of faith, because the more conscious it will be of ideas that are subversive of the social order.

The heretic was the man who challenged this community of beliefs, and it was for this reason that he was looked upon as a traitor to society. In the Middle Ages a man was not originally interfered with because he held unorthodox views. He was interfered with because he sought by every means in his power to spread such views among the people, and he met with much stronger opposition from the public themselves than from ecclesiastic authority. The ideas for which the heretics were persecuted were individualist notions disguised in a communist form. The heretics had no " sense of the large proportion of things." They were not catholic-minded in the widest meaning of the term. They had no sense of reality, and if they had been allowed to have their own way they would have precipitated social chaos by preaching impossible ideals.

The position will be better understood if we translate the problem into the terms of the present day. Suppose the Socialists succeeded in abolishing capitalism and established their ideal State, and then suppose a man came along preaching individualist ideas, attempting to bring back capitalism in some underhand way by the popularization of a theory the implications of which the average man did not understand. At first, I imagine, he would not be interfered with. If he began to make converts, however, a time would come when Socialists would either have to consent to the overthrow of their society in the interests of capitalism or take measures against him. If ever they were faced with this dilemma there can be little doubt how they would act. The Mediævalist attitude towards the heretic was precisely what the Socialist attitude would be towards such a man. The controversies over the Manichean, Arian, and Nestorian heresies raged for centuries, and no action was taken against them until it became clear what were the issues involved, when the Church, through its Councils, made definite pronouncements and the heresies were suppressed. They were suppressed because men had instinctively come to feel that they imperilled not only the unity of the Faith but the unity of the social order as well.

Historical evidence suggests that this is the right avenue of approach, since the persecution of heretics began with secular and not with ecclesiastical authority. During the first three centuries of the Early Church there was no persecution of heretics. All the influential ecclesiastics then agreed that the civil arm might be employed to deal with them, by prohibiting assemblies and in other ways preventing them from spreading their views, but that the death penalty was contrary to the spirit of the Gospel. For centuries such was the ecclesiastical attitude, in both theory and practice. This attitude did not recommend itself to the successors of Constantine, however, who, continuing in the persuasion of the Roman Emperors that the first concern of the imperial authority was the protection of religion, persecuted men for not being Christians, in the same spirit that their predecessors had persecuted men because they were Christians. At a later date—somewhere about the year 1000—when Manicheans expelled from Bulgaria spread themselves over Italy, Spain, France, and Germany, the people, thinking that the clergy were supine in the suppression of heresy, took the law into their own hands and publicly burnt the heretics. Thus it is recorded that in 1114, when the Bishop of Soissons, who had sundry heretics in durance in his episcopal city, went to Beauvais to ask advice of the bishops assembled there for a synod, the " believing folk," fearing the habitual soft-heartedness of the ecclesiastics, stormed the prison, took the accused out of the town and burnt them. Such incidents, which suggest the Lynch law of America, were not uncommon in the early Middle Ages, when the persecution of heretics was due to the fanatical outbursts of an over-zealous populace or to the arbitrary action of individual rulers, but never to ecclesiastical authority.

It was not until the latter half of the twelfth century that the attitude of the Church changed, owing to the rise of the Catharists, better known to history as the Albigenses, so called from the town of Albi (in South-west France), where a council was held against them. The Albigenses taught a creed that carried the Manichean heresy to its logical conclusion. The Manicheans had identified good and evil with spirit and matter. According to them, spirit was good and matter was evil. Hence their contempt of the body, and hence, too, the Christian dogma of the Resurrection of the Body, whereby it was sought to combat the evils consequent upon such a perverted attitude towards life by affirming " that in any final consummation the bodily life of man must find a place no less than the spiritual." [1] The Manichean heresy had been taught by the Gnostic sects in the early days of Christianity. It had been suppressed but had reappeared again from time to time in its old form. Now, however, it was to receive a new development. If spirit were good and matter evil, if the bodily life of man on earth were to be regarded as a form of penance to which man was condemned because of evil deeds in former lives, then the sooner he could by self-effacement and rigid discipline pay the penalty of his misdeeds (that is, to work off the bad karma, as Theosophists would say) the better it would be for him. Hence it was that the ascetic rigorists among the Albigenses preached a doctrine which was tantamount to the advocacy of suicide—they sought to escape this life by slow starvation. Although such extremists were at all times few in number, they were the objects of an adoring reverence from the people, which led to the rapid spread of such teachings in Germany, France, and Spain. About the same time, and mixed up with the Albigenses to some extent, there occurred an outburst of witchcraft, magic, and sorcery—the old religion, as the Italians call it—and the Church was at last roused to action. Terribly afraid of this new spirit, which she considered menaced not only her own existence but the very foundations of society as well, the Church in the end shrank from no cruelty that she might be rid of it for ever. The action of the Church was rather the result of panic produced by suspicions in the minds of normal men than an outburst of primitive savagery. In the South of France the Albigenses were very powerful, for not only were they very zealous, but the nobility, for reasons of their own, supported them, a circumstance which imparted to the Albigenses the aspect of a powerful political party, in addition to that of an heretical sect. They were

[1] *Essays in Orthodoxy*, by Oliver Chase Quick.

7

condemned at various Councils, including the Lateran Council of 1179, but these condemnations merely increased the opposition of the Albigenses. Pope Innocent III, whose juristic mind identified heresy with high treason, resolved to extirpate the heresy, and in 1198 he sent two Cistercian monks to try pacific measures. These failing, he began his serious and deliberate policy of extermination. He ordered a crusade to be preached against the Albigenses. Indulgences were promised to all who took part in this holy war, and soon afterwards Simon de Montfort (father of the founder of the English parliament) led a crusade which was carried on until ended politically by the Treaty of Paris in 1229. The Albigenses, as a political party, were now suppressed, and an Inquisition was left behind to uproot any sporadic growth of heresy. The Inquisition then established was a secular and temporary institution. The definite participation of the Church in the administration of the Inquisition dates from 1231, when Gregory IX placed it under ecclesiastical control. Exact information as to the motives which led him to take this action is lacking, but the hypothesis is advanced by the writer of the article on the Inquisition in the *Catholic Encyclopædia* that its introduction might be due to the anxiety of the Pope to forestall the encroachments of the Emperor Frederick II in the strictly ecclesiastical province of doctrine. This hypothesis I am disposed to accept, for it makes intelligible much that would otherwise be obscure, and, if it be correct, means that the establishment of the Inquisition is finally to be attributed to the influence of Roman Law.

It will be remembered that the Commentators won the favour of the Emperors by declaring that, as the successors of the Roman Emperors, their will was law, and that the Hohenstaufen family gladly accepted this decision as a justification of their desire for absolutism. Frederick II, following in the footsteps of his father, Frederick Barbarossa, sought by every means to make his power supreme over Church and State. Bearing this in mind, it is not unreasonable to suppose that the rigorous legislation that he enacted against heretics, and which he unscrupulously made use of to remove any who stood in the path of his ambitions, was not to be attributed to his affected eagerness for the purity of the Faith, but because he saw that the power that persecuted heresy became, *ipso facto*, the final authority in matters of faith, and that with such a weapon in his hands he would be in a position to encroach gradually upon the ecclesiastical province of doctrine, so that finally Church doctrine would come to be as much dependent upon the will of the Emperor as the Civil Law. It is suggested that Gregory perceived whither Frederick's policy was leading, and that he resolved to resist his encroachments in the only way that was open to him. He could not have prevented the persecution of heretics even had he so desired, for, as we have seen, their persecution was rooted in popular feeling. What he could do, however, was, by regularizing the procedure, to prevent Frederick from abusing his power, and Gregory accordingly instituted a tribunal of ecclesiastics that would pronounce judgment on the guilt of those accused of heresy. This action was immediately of service to the heretics, for the regular procedure thus introduced did much to abrogate the arbitrariness, passion, and injustice of the civil courts of the Emperor.

The Church, then, undertook the task of deciding who was and who was not a heretic, and this was as far as interference went. What was to be done with one found guilty of heresy was, as heretofore, left to the civil authorities to decide. Torture had been used in civil courts as a means of extracting evidence, but its use was for long prohibited in the ecclesiastical courts. Its introduction into the latter was due to Pope Clement V, who formulated regulations for its use, but it was to be resorted to only under very exceptional circumstances. Why the Pope should have been led to make this decision—what especial factors should have impelled him to take a step so fatal—is not evident, but we do know that torture was most cruelly used when the Inquisitors were exposed to the pressure of civil authorities, and that in Spain, where the Inquisitors were appointed by the Crown, the Inquisition, under the presidency of Torquemada (1482–94) distinguished itself by its startling and revolting cruelty. Here again, however, as in the case of the Emperor Frederick II, it was used as an instrument to further the political ambitions of the Kings of Spain, who profited by the confiscation of the property of the heretics, which was not inconsiderable, remembering that several hundred thousand Jews at this time quitted Spain to avoid persecution.   Pope Sixtus IV made several attempts to stop the deadly work, but was obliged through pressure from Spain to deny the right of appeal to himself.   The situation had then got quite out of hand.   The persecution of heretics ceased to be a popular movement, and became generally detested.   Its cruel punishments, secret proceedings, and prying methods caused universal alarm, and led not only to uprisings of the people against a tyranny which was regarded by many as " worse than death " but, by investing heretics with the crown of martyrdom, defeated its own ends and brought orthodox Christianity into discredit. After the period of the Reformation the Inquisition relaxed its severity, but it lingered on until it was finally abolished in Spain in 1835.

The passions that are aroused by the very name of the Inquisition make it difficult to judge its work, while an impartial history of it has yet to be written.   From its history, as from that of the persecution of heresy, there clearly emerges the fact that religious persecution was due in the first place to the initiative of the civil authority, that at a later date it became a popular movement, and that for centuries the ecclesiastics resisted the demands of both the civil authorities and the people for persecution. Furthermore, when the attitude of ecclesiastics changed it was owing to the heresy of the Catharists, which threatened at the same time not only the existence of the Church but the very foundations of society ; and that when at last the Papacy did move in the matter it was because of the danger that worse things might happen if the persecution of heretics was to continue independent of ecclesiastical direction. Looking at the dilemma which presented itself to Gregory IX, it is extremely difficult to say which was the less momentous of the two evils between which he had to choose —whether he was to allow ambitious Emperors to persecute heretics as a means of furthering their Imperial desire to control the Church, or whether, by regularizing the procedure, the Church might mitigate the evils of lay prosecution, even though she incurred the odium of tyranny as a consequence. But of this we may be certain, that the tyranny was not only foreign to the spirit of Christianity and ecclesiastical authority, but it was directly attributable· to the spread of Roman Law, which, awakening in the hearts of Emperors and Kings the desire to subordinate religion to State authority, as had been the case in Rome, awakened also the Pagan spirit of religious persecution. The contrary hypothesis generally held, that the religious persecution is due to the intolerance of ecclesiastical authority, is untenable, not only because the facts of history flatly contradict it, but because as compulsion is emphatically an attribute of the State, the ecclesiastical authority is finally powerless to use it to further its ends apart from the co-operation of the State. And the best proof I can bring in support of this contention is that the Church was powerless to suppress Roman Law—the heresy that laid the foundations of materialism and undermined the position not only of the Church but of Christianity itself—because it was supported by the secular authorities.

CHAPTER VII

MEDIÆVALISM AND SCIENCE

EVERYBODY nowadays is willing to grant that the Middle Ages was great in architecture ; though I would remind admirers of Gothic that this appreciation is quite a recent thing. The right to admire Gothic had to be fought for. Less than a hundred years ago Sir Walter Scott thought it necessary to apologize to his readers for his love of it. This change of opinion as to the merits of Gothic is due to the powerful advocacy of Ruskin and to the activities of the architects of the Gothic Revival. We are now beginning to realize that the Mediævalists knew something about economics and social organization. But few people realize that not only was the basis of science laid in the Middle Ages but that its methods remain Mediæval to this day, for in this respect science remained unaffected by the influence of the Renaissance.

That so much ignorance should obtain on this subject is due to the conspiracy about things Mediæval which Cobbett was the first to expose. The popular notion is that during the " long Mediæval night," when the Church held sway over men's minds, education was hampered ; Papal Bulls forbade the study of chemistry and practical anatomy, as dissection of the human body was regarded as an heretical experiment ; all reasoning was deductive, and such experimentalists as there were wasted their time in the search for the philosopher's stone which was to transmute base metal into gold, or for the elixir of life ; whilst the bulk of the people were kept in a state of " grovelling ignorance and superstition." All advance was made by scholars who were persecuted by the Church in order to keep the people in subjection to its tyranny, and the results of their labours have enabled science to confer untold benefits upon civilization. But I will not press this latter point. Poison gas, liquid fire, and bombs from aeroplanes, have brought a doubt into many minds as to the truly beneficial intentions of science, and there are many in these days who incline to the view that the "Mediæval prejudice," so called, was not altogether unjustified after all.

In these circumstances it is somewhat distressing to find that the Mediævalists had no such prejudice. It is possible they might have had, could they have clearly foreseen all the horrors which science has let loose upon the world. But they were not sufficiently far-sighted, and as a matter of fact they applied themselves to the study of science with great avidity. It will clear the air if we begin by bringing evidence to refute these popularly accepted notions. The supposed Papal decree forbidding the study of chemistry turns out on examination to be nothing of the kind. The decretal of John XXII (1316–34) did not aim at the chemist, but at the abuse of chemistry by the alchemist, who incidentally was not the fool he is popularly imagined to be, but a trickster who cast counterfeit money and a fraudent company promoter who got money out of people by getting them to subscribe to schemes for extracting gold from sea-water,[1] and it was on this account that he was condemned. Legitimate science, as we shall see later, was encouraged and subsidized by the Popes. Meanwhile it may be observed that while the Mediævalists distinguished between chemistry and alchemy, no such distinction obtains to-day. Our alchemists do not waste their time in attempting to make gold out of silver ; they have found a much more profitable business in making wool out of cotton, silk out of wood, and leather out of paper ; while these abuses are not in these days forbidden by Papal Bulls but are taught and encouraged at our technical universities.

Now let us turn to the supposed prohibition of dissection which it is popularly taught was regarded as an heretical experiment because it came into collision with the Christian dogma of the Resurrection of the Body. There may, of

[1] The text of this decree is to be found in *The Popes and Science*, by Dr. J. J. Walsh, pp. 125–6.

course, have been ignorant people who objected to it on this score, but such an objection could not have been advanced officially because, as we saw in the last chapter, the dogma does not relate to our existing physical bodies but to the fact " that in any final consummation the bodily life of man must find a place no less than the spiritual." Such being the case, it is not surprising to find that in the Middle Ages no objection was made officially to dissection on religious grounds. The Bull promulgated by Boniface VIII which has so often been interpreted as forbidding dissection had another purpose. Its aim was to stop a barbarous custom which had grown up of boiling the corpses of distinguished people who had died in foreign lands in order to remove the flesh before sending the bones home to be buried. Benedict XIV on being asked as to whether this Bull forbade dissection replied as follows :—

" By the singular beneficence of God the study of medicine flourished in a very wonderful manner in this city (Rome). Its professors are known for their supreme talents to the remotest parts of the earth. There is no doubt that they have greatly benefited by the diligent labour which they have devoted to dissection. From this practice beyond doubt they have gained a profound knowledge of their art and a proficiency that has enabled them to give advice for the benefit of the ailing as well as a skill in the curing of disease. Now such dissection of bodies is in no way contrary to the Bull of Pope Boniface. He indeed imposed the penalty of excommunication, to be remitted only by the Sovereign Pontiff himself, upon all those who would dare to disembowel the body of any dead person and either dismember it or horribly cut it up, separating the flesh from the bones. From the rest of this Bull, however, it is clear that this penalty was only to be inflicted upon those who took bodies already buried out of their graves, and, by an act horrible in itself, cut them in pieces in order that they might carry them elsewhere and place them in another tomb. It is very clear, however, that by this, the dissection of bodies, which has proved so necessary for those exercising the profession of medicine is by no means forbidden." [1] This reply of

[1] *The Popes and Science*, p. 59.

the Pope's ought to settle the question, but if further corrobor-ation is needed it may be mentioned that at this time dis-section was carried on in all the important cities in Italy, at Verona, Pisa, Naples, Bologna, Florence, Padua, Venice, and at the Papal Medical School at Rome.

Let us now pass on to consider the introduction of science into Europe by the Saracens. As a plain statement of fact, Europe in the Middle Ages did get science from the Saracens. This is perfectly true. But the deduction it is usual to make from this fact—namely, that the lower state of Western European civilization at that time was due to the prejudice against science of the Mediæval mind under the influence of Christianity—is most demonstrably false. The difference between the two levels of civilization is to be accounted for by the simple fact that whereas the Saracens established their Empire over communities already civilized in which the traditions of Roman civilization survived, the Mediæ-val Church had the much more difficult task of rebuilding Western civilization from its very foundations after it had been entirely destroyed by the barbarians. Naturally this, in its early stages, was a much slower process. Bearing in mind these circumstances, there is nothing remarkable in the fact that the Saracens knew of Aristotle and the sciences at a time when Western Europeans did not. But that the Mediævalists accepted them from the Saracens is surely evidence of an open-mindedness which did not disdain to learn from a heterodox enemy, rather than of an incurable prejudice against all new kinds of knowledge. How unsub-stantial is this charge against the influence of Christianity becomes apparent when the question is asked, Whence did the Saracens get their knowledge of Aristotle and the sciences ? They could not have got it direct from the Greeks, for Mahomet was not born until the year A.D. 571, and as Christianity had established itself at least two centuries before in the communities around and east of the Mediterranean basin, apart from other evidence it would be a reasonable speculation to assume that they got their knowledge from some Christian source. But it so happens that this is not a matter of speculation but of ascertained historical fact, the Christian sect of Nestorians having been the connecting link by which

Greek science and philosophy were transmitted from the conquered to the conquerors, and it came about this way :

" When the Caliphate was usurped by the Ommiades, the fugitive Abbasid princes, Abbas and Ali, sojourned among the Nestorians of Arabia, Mesopotamia and Western Persia and from them acquired a knowledge and a love of Greek Science and philosophy. Upon the accession of the Abbasid dynasty to the Caliphate in A.D. 750, learned Nestorians were summoned to court. By them Greek books were translated into Arabic from the original or from Syraic translations and the foundations laid of Arabic science and philosophy. In the ninth century the school of Bagdad began to flourish, just when the schools of Christendom were falling into decay in the West and into decrepitude in the East. The newly awakened Moslem intellect busied itself at first chiefly with mathematics and medical science ; afterwards Aristotle threw his spell over it and an immense system of orientalized Aristotelianism was the result. From the East Moslem learning was carried into Spain ; and from Spain Aristotle re-entered Northern Europe once more and revolutionized the intellectual life of Christendom far more completely than he had revolutionized the intellectual life of Islam.

" During the course of the twelfth century a struggle had been going on in the bosom of Islam between the philosophers and the theologians. It was just at the moment when, through the favour of the Caliph Almansur, the theologians had succeeded in crushing the philosophers that the torch of Aristotelian thought was handed on to Christendom. The history of Arabic philosophy, which had never succeeded in touching the religious life of the people or leaving a permanent stamp upon the religion of Mohammed, ends with the death of Averroes in 1198. The history of Christian Aristotelianism and of the new scholastic theology which was based upon it begins just when the history of Arabic Aristotelianism comes abruptly to a close." [1]

Early in the thirteenth century Aristotle made his debut in the University of Paris. But the translations studied

[1] *The Universities of Europe in the Middle Ages*, by Hastings Rashdall, vol. i. pp. 351–2.

were not taken from the Greek but from the Arabic. Thus
Aristotle arrived in an orientalized dress and was accompanied
by commentators and by independent works of Arabian
philosophers, some of which claimed the sanction of Aristotle's
name. This new learning, which brought with it a whole
cargo of heresies, was associated with the name of Averroes
(who incidentally was persecuted by the Saracens as a heretic
during his lifetime and remembered only as a physician
and jurist after his death). " It stirred the mental powers
to recover an earlier and now lost truth sometimes moving
the mind to science, sometimes to strange apocalyptic vision ;
now to a conviction that a fresh outpouring of the Spirit was
impending, now to pantheistic denial of all explicit revelation or positive religion, now to a defiant sectarianism, now
to the wild torture of ascetic individualism." [1] Whatever
the form, all were animated by a genuine hostility to the
powers that were, and Paris was the scene of an outburst
of free thought which at one time promised to pass far
beyond the limits of the schools. This outbreak of heresy
goes far to explain the alarm with which the advent of the
Arabic Aristotle was at first regarded. It was followed by
a persecution of heretics. In 1210 " a batch of persons
infected with heresy—priests and clerks from the neighbouring
Grand-pont—were handed over to the secular arm, some
for the stake, others for perpetual imprisonment. At the
same time the books of Aristotle upon natural philosophy
and his commentators were forbidden to be read at Paris
publicly or privately for a period of three years." [2]

The rapidity with which Aristotle, and even his Arabic
commentators, lived down these suspicions and was transformed into a pillar of orthodoxy is one of the most remarkable
facts in the history of the Middle Ages. The study of Aristotle had been forbidden by the Council of Paris. It was
renewed by Pope Gregory IX in 1231 but with the significant
reservation " until they have been examined and purged
of all heresy." But this ban was soon removed. Copies
of Aristotle in the original Greek were obtained from Constantinople, and with the aid of these the theologians soon

---

[1] *Religious Thought and Heresy in the Middle Ages*, by F. W. Bussell, p. 6.
[2] Rashdall, vol. i. pp. 356–7.

learnt the art of distinguishing the genuine Aristotle from
spurious imitations and assisted greatly in the advancement
and purification of science by the resistance they offered
to the study of alchemy, astrology and magic with which
in those days it was associated. In 1254 nearly the whole
range of Aristotelian writings were prescribed by a statue
of the Faculty of Arts at Paris as textbooks for its masters.

These facts, then, make it clear that there was no opposition
to the study of Aristotle and the sciences as such, but to
the heresies which were associated with them. Experience
proved that so far from this opposition being detrimental
to the cause of science it had the opposite effect of furthering
its interests by cleansing it of falsities. The task of proving
to the world that faith and science might go hand in hand
was the work of the two great monastic orders of St. Dominic
and St. Francis, which came into existence about this time
and immediately owed their existence to the need of defending
Christendom against the new forces of wealth and learning
which threatened it with ruin. The intellectual life of
Europe for the next two centuries is so intimately bound
up with these two great orders that it becomes necessary
to pause to give a brief account of them.

While both of these orders attacked what was ultimately
the same problem, they attacked it in fundamentally different
ways. The problem as St. Francis saw it was that the social
evils and heresies had their root in a corrupted human nature
to which men became increasingly liable as they acquired
wealth and so lost touch with the primary facts of life. St.
Francis was a simple, unintellectual layman, and confronted
with the problems of his age, he turned his back upon the
world with its wealth, its learning and its heresies, which
he regarded as vanities, and taught a gospel of poverty,
work and renunciation. His followers were to renounce
wealth and all intellectual pursuits and seek salvation through
work. They were to labour among the poor, and in order
that they might be of service to them they were to seek
identity with them in position and fortune. In a word,
the Franciscans were the Salvation Army of their day,
differing with them to the extent that they eventually became
one of the great intellectual forces of the age.

St. Dominic approached the problem from the opposite end. It was not with him so much that the heart was going wrong as the head. He accepted civilization and its accompaniments. Science, music, architecture, painting were each to be regarded as a path through which truth could be approached. But he realized clearly as few people to-day did, until quite recently when the war shook us out of our complacency, that knowledge may just as easily be an agent for evil as for good. Nay, more easily ; since left to itself without any central and guiding principle to co-ordinate its activities, it will, instead of serving the common interests of mankind, degenerate into mere pedantry by being exalted as an end in itself, or become a disruptive force by giving rise to heresies, or be used for selfish and personal ends. Hence it was that the Dominicans, like the Franciscans, broke with the monastic tradition of settling in the country and established themselves in the towns, and firstly in those where universities were established— at Paris, Bologna and Oxford—in order to keep themselves informed of all the learning of the day. They realized that though the suppression of heresy might prevent foolish people, who were carried off their feet by the introduction of new ideas, from bringing truth itself into discredit by seeking the popularization of immature thought, yet Mediæval civilization could not be preserved merely by repressive measures and that the only final justification for such repression was as a measure of expediency to gain time for the proper formulation of thought, in order that it might be organized into a constructive force instead of dissipating itself in intellectual subtleties, heresies and disruptive influences. Their method made for thoroughness and was the enemy of superficiality.

The Dominicans were not long in demonstrating to the world the wisdom of their policy. Two great Dominicans, Albertus Magnus and St. Thomas Aquinas, were the means of purging the reputation of Aristotle of ill fame by the development of a great system of orthodox Aristotelianism which drew a clear line between the provinces of science and religion. " The lines laid down by Aquinas as to the attitude of reason towards revelation are, amid all change

of belief as to the actual content of revelation, the lines
in which, as much in the Protestant as in the Mediæval
or Modern Roman Churches, the main current of thought
has moved ever since." [1] It revolutionized theology. One
of their contemporaries insists on the absolute novelty
of their methods, arguments, reasons, objections and replies.
They not only won back the universities to the allegiance
of the Church but secured for science the patronage of the
Church. Henceforth science becomes a recognized faculty
in every Mediæval university, and its study is encouraged
by the Popes. John XXII was a great patron of science,
as indeed was Pius II. An extract from his Bull promulgated
for the University of Basle in 1460 will bear quotation. It
runs : " Among the different blessings which by the grace
of God mortals can attain to in this earthly life, it is not
among the least that, by persevering study, he can make
himself master of the pearls of science and learning which
point the way to a good and useful life. Furthermore,
education brings man to a nearer likeness to God, and enables
him to read clearly the secrets of this universe. True education and learning lift the meanest of earth to a level with
the highest." " For this reason," continues the Pope,
" the Holy See has always encouraged the sciences and
contributed to the establishment of places of learning, in
order that men might be enabled to acquire this precious
treasure and, having acquired it, might spread it among
their fellow-men." It was his ardent desire " that one of
these life-giving fountains should be established at Basle,
so that all who wished might drink their fill at the waters
of learning."[2]

Such words did not fall upon deaf ears. The annals
of the universities show how zealously the clergy acted on
the Pope's exhortation to study science not only by advising
young men to follow such studies but by attending as students
themselves. For in the Mediæval universities men of all
ages and from every class of society mingled together. Young
men of peasant origin were there with men of ripe years and
of established position—abbots, provosts, canons and princes.
Never were there more democratic institutions. The comrade-

---

[1] Rashdall, vol. i. p. 367.   [2] Janssen, vol. i. pp. 88–9.

ship through the university was one in which all who went there met on equal terms. The universities were self-governing corporations, they paid no taxes, and were accorded many privileges as a token of respect to learning. All classes contributed to their support, but the clergy were by far the most generous.

But to return to our subject. Not only did the labours of Albertus Magnus and St. Thomas Aquinas effect a re-conciliation between the Church and science by indicating the spirit in which the new teaching was to be received, but they also wrote upon psychology, metaphysics, physics, physiology, natural history, morals and social science. The former especially was an indefatigable student of nature. His twenty-one folio volumes are considered a perfect ency-clopædia both of the knowledge and polemics of his time, and it is claimed for them that together with the compila-tions of Vincent of Beauvais they laid the basis of the great scientific encyclopædias of our day. Albertus, moreover, applied himself energetically to the experimental sciences. But the credit for this new departure, which revolutionized the method of science, belongs to the Franciscans rather than the Dominicans. " They took up the study of physics and chemistry, not, however, as heretofore, by the path of theoretical speculation, but by the co-operation of experiment —an advance in method they were the first to establish, and by which Roger Bacon arrived at the most remarkable results in almost every branch of physical science." [1]

Now the fact that this new development came through the Franciscans is interesting, and I think it is fair to assume that it was no accident. Immediately it was due to the fact that the care of the sick which was enjoined upon them tended to direct their minds towards the study of medicine and natural history. But there was a deeper reason. The Franciscans had a strong practical bend of mind. Learning being forbidden them by the rule of their order, they naturally acquired the invaluable habit of observing facts for them-selves—a habit which book-learning is very apt to destroy. Men who begin life with much book-knowledge are very apt to look at things from the special angle provided by

[1] *Pictures of Old England*, by Dr. Reinhold Pauli, chap. ii.

the books they have read and to neglect the lessons which
the observation of facts can teach. It was thus that the
Franciscans' renunciation of learning stood them in good
stead ; it proved to be the means whereby a new impulse
was given to the acquisition of knowledge. The central
idea of Christianity—that the world can only be conquered
by those who are first prepared to renounce it—is a principle
of action that holds good just as much in the intellectual
and scientific as in the moral universe, and I might add that
in so far as any progress has in these days been made in the
revival of architecture, the crafts and arts, it has come about
through the actions of men who proceeded upon this principle.
The return to fundamentals always involves renunciation.

While it is to be acknowledged that the foundations
of modern science were laid in the Middle Ages, it is equally
important to recognize that the new impulse which the
Franciscans gave was essentially a Mediæval one, and that
science remains Mediæval in its method to this day. For
when the Franciscans threw over the method of theoretical
speculation in favour of co-operation by experiment, they
gave practical application in the realm of science to the
method of work which in the Middle Ages obtained in the
arts, for, as we shall see in the next chapter, Gothic Art
was the creation of experimental handicraft, and it was
the abandonment of this method owing to Renaissance
influences that finally led to the disappearance of art from
the world. But science never threw over this Mediæval
experimental, craft basis, which is the secret of its progressive development, and it remains Mediæval in method to
this day.

But while science remains Mediæval in its method, it
is no longer Mediæval in its spirit, for it has rejected the
discipline by which the Mediævalists sought to guide it.
The judgment of Albertus Magnus and St. Thomas Aquinas
that there were two orders of science—the natural, comprising everything that can be grasped by reason, and the
supernatural, which comprises all the truth known by revelation—was accepted alike by the Church and the students
of science, and the heretical tendencies which had come
with the Arabic Aristotle dwindled to impotence. Averroistic

beliefs lingered on in a more or less disguised and purely
speculative form, disputants in the Arts avoiding the charge
of heresy by taking cover under the convenient distinction
between philosophical and theological truth, maintaining
that what was true in the one might be false in the other
and *vice versa*. But when in the sixteenth century, owing
to the influence of the Renaissance of which we shall have
something to say hereafter, belief in the absolute truth of
the Christian revelation had come to be widely questioned,
there was a new outburst of pantheism and free thought.

It was because of his advocacy of heresies, and not because
of his scientific opinions, that Bruno was put to death. The
case of Galileo is different, and it is too long a story to be
gone into here. There were faults on both sides, but it
cannot be maintained that the attitude of the Church was
determined by hostility to science, and in this connection
I cannot do better than quote Huxley, who, writing to
Professor Mivart in 1885, said : " I gave some attention
to the case of Galileo when I was in Italy, and I arrived
at the conclusion that the Popes and the College of Cardinals
had rather the best of it." [1]

In judging the attitude of the Church at this period we
must not forget that the Copernican theory had not then
been proved, but was only advanced as a hypothesis and
was violently attacked by scientists at the time. Kepler
and Newton finally proved it. What the Church objected
to was not the theory that the earth was round, but the
entirely illogical deduction which Galileo made from it
that therefore Christianity was false. For Christianity
has nothing to say on the matter at all. It is not a theory
of the universe, but a theory of conduct basing its claim
for acceptance upon Divine sanction. The Church, moreover,
bases its authority upon the Christian tradition, and not
upon the Bible. But the Church was nervous, and justifiably
nervous, at the consequences which might follow the popularization of such a theory, whether it eventually proved to
be true or not, and had no desire to meet trouble half-way.
For the average man does not discriminate very carefully,

[1] *Life and Letters*, vol. ii. p. 424. See also Whetwell's *History of Inductive
Sciences*.

and the fact that the story that Joshua commanded the sun to stand still upon Gibeon is to be found in the Bible is sufficient in the minds of many to discredit the whole Christian theology as a degrading superstition and to release them from all the moral obligations which Christianity sought to impose. And this nervousness was not felt only by the Roman Church. Whereas the Church did its best to handle a difficult situation in a diplomatic way, demanding no more than that scientists should not preach unproven hypotheses as truth, the leaders of Protestantism were violent in their opposition. Luther denounced Copernicus as an arrogant fool who would overthrow all scientific astronomy and contradicted Holy Writ, while Melanchthon wished the promulgation of such pestilent doctrines to be suppressed by the civil power.[1] In the turmoil of the Reformation science and heresy became more closely related though by no means identified, for science was followed and encouraged as much by the post-Reformation Church as by the Mediæval one.

It is to be observed that heresy is not necessarily a belief in something false, but an exaggeration of one aspect of truth insisted upon to the damage or denial of other and equally important truths. The tendency of scientists to exaggerate the importance of the material side of things whilst ignoring as imponderable the spiritual and moral side of life is their peculiar form of heresy. It results in a loss of mental balance, a failure to see life as a whole, in its true proportions. It makes the scientist an untrustworthy guide in the practical affairs of life. The publication of Lord Bacon's *Advancement of Learning* and the *Novum Organum* served only to increase the tendency of the scientific mind towards monomania—a tendency which appears to be the inevitable accompaniment of an exclusive preoccupation with the study of phenomena. The inductive method is the method of reasoning familiar to all who concern themselves with the practical arts, and is invaluable for the attainment of certain immediate and definite ends. But the attempt of Bacon to give it universal validity—for, as Macaulay said, it is ridiculous to suppose he invented

[1] See Prowe, *Nicolaus Copernicus*, vol. i. part ii. p. 232–4.

it—must after the experience of over three centuries of work upon such lines be judged a failure, for science is as far from the truth of things as ever. " After a glorious burst of perhaps fifty years, amid great acclamation and good hopes that the crafty old universe was going to be caught in her careful net, science finds herself in almost every direction in the most hopeless quandaries ; and whether the rib story be true or not, has, at any rate, provided no very satisfactory substitute for it." [1]

The reason for this failure is obvious. There is no such thing as a purely materialist explanation of the universe. Final causation is not to be found in the material world, and scientists, in excluding the spiritual side of things from their calculations as imponderable, exclude the consideration of those things which might offer an explanation. For unity is to be found at the centre of life ; it is not to be deduced merely from a study of phenomena on the circumference. But even if science were to follow the lead given by Sir Oliver Lodge and carried its investigations beyond the material into the realm of psychic phenomena, it could never penetrate the final mystery of life. The moral principles to which religions give sanction are finally commandments and incapable of rationalist explanation, though experience of their working may be able to give them rationalist justification. They are not to be deduced from the study of phenomena, but rest finally on the affirmation of the supernatural.

While it must be admitted that reasoning based exclusively upon phenomena has failed to penetrate the mystery of the universe, the invasion of other departments of inquiry by the inductive method of reasoning, such as that of sociology has been followed by results equally disastrous. It has produced endless confusion. It is possible to deduce secondary truth from primary truth, but not the reverse, which science attempts. I sometimes think that the Devil made his debut in the modern world as the friend of learning, which he had the insight to see might be used for the purpose of banishing wisdom by the simple and apparently innocent device of multiplying knowledge. At any rate, whether the

[1] *Civilization : its Cause and Cure*, by Edward Carpenter.

Devil planned or no, such has been its practical effect. For the multiplication of knowledge has certainly introduced confusion into the popular mind. Thus it has come about that the scientific method of inquiry has had the effect of burying primary truth under an avalanche of secondary half-truths. It has exalted knowledge above wisdom, mechanism above art, science above religion, man above God. In thus reversing the natural order of the moral and intellectual universe, it has led to a general state of mental bewilderment such as was never before witnessed. The ambition of the scientist to comprehend all knowledge has been followed by the unfortunate discovery that knowledge —the things to be known—is bigger than his head, and he gets some inkling of the meaning of the proverb : " A fool's eyes are on the ends of the earth."

Considerations of this kind lead me to the conclusion that civilization has reached a turning-point not only in its political and economic history, but in its very methods and ideas, and that the next development must be away from the universal towards a reassertion of the principle of unity which was the central principle of Mediæval thought. In the new synthesis which will appear, science will not attempt to lead mankind, but will be content with a secondary and subordinate position. Science has terribly misled the world. But it is possible that all its work has not been in vain. For it has explored the universe for us, and as a result of its labours it may be that when the new order does arrive it will rest on much surer foundations than ever did the civilizations of the past. With the knowledge of evil which science let loose upon the world, we know where the pitfalls lie. But we shall never be able to conquer this mass of knowledge which science has given us until we have first the courage to renounce it.

CHAPTER VIII

THE ARTS OF THE MIDDLE AGES

In an earlier chapter I said that the promise of Mediævalism was never entirely fulfilled. That is true of its life and social organization. The sinister influence of Roman Law began to dissolve it before it was as yet firmly established. But it is not true of the Arts, for in them the promise was entirely fulfilled, and for this consummation we are indebted to the two great Mediæval orders—the Dominicans and the Franciscans; the former because of their intellectual orthodoxy, which preserved Mediæval society from disruption at the hands of the heretics, and because of the encouragement and help they gave to the development of the Arts, and the latter because of the new spirit and vitality which they breathed into Mediæval society. It would not be untrue to say that from the beginning of the thirteenth century the Mediæval spirit as it expressed itself in thought and in the Arts was the resultant of the action and interaction of the Dominican and Franciscan minds. The latter, by their emotional temperament and broad democratic sympathies, tended to widen the range of experience, to venture on new experiments and to encourage new developments, while the function of the former was to be for ever gathering up, as it were, to bring unity and order out of the diversity to which the Franciscan spirit ever tended. Yet the more these two orders differed, the more they were alike. They were alike in their absolute belief in Christianity as the truth revealed, and in their detestation of the pantheistic rationalism which began to show its head at the beginning of the thirteenth century, and which they combined to crush.

Gothic Art, which reached its perfection in the thirteenth, fourteenth and fifteenth centuries, was a tree with very deep roots, and its progressive development may be dated from the year A.D. 800, when Charlemagne, after driving the Saracens out of France, consolidated his power and was crowned by the Pope Emperor of the West. For this date is not only a definite landmark in the political history of Europe, but it marks a turning-point in the history of the Arts, for Charlemagne was more than a successful warrior ; he was a great patron of culture, and endeavoured successfully to make the heart of his Empire a centre of culture and learning. The Palatine Church of Aachen (Aix-la-Chapelle), built by him as a national monument, may be said to have set in motion ideas of architecture which affected the whole of · Western Europe. To this Carlovingian centre there came craftsmen from far and wide—from Spain, Lombardy, and the Eastern Empire—for it was the ambition of Charlemagne to gather together such remnants of Roman tradition as had survived the barbarian invasions in order to effect a revival of the Arts. His intention was to revive the Roman Art whose splendid remains then overspread the whole of Gaul. But from this renaissance there arose results far different from what he had anticipated, differing from them, in fact, as widely as his Empire differed from that of the Cæsars. His object of revivifying Art was achieved, but not in the way he proposed, for in the space of three centuries the movement he set on foot led to the creation of an entirely new style, which, though it long bore traces of its origin, was nevertheless, as a whole, unlike anything the world had ever seen before ; in a word, Gothic Art.

The immediate reason for this result, so different from what Charlemagne had anticipated, is to be found in the fact that the craftsmen whom he gathered together were possessed of traditions of design differing widely from those of antiquity. They were, moreover, men of a different order. The Roman workmen executed designs prepared by an architect in much the same way as do the workmen of to-day, but their labour was essentially servile. But these newer craftsmen, however, not only executed work but were themselves individually capable of exercising the function of design. Moreover, they were capable of co-operating together, for they shared a communal tradition of design in the same way that people share a communal tradition of language. Each craftsman worked as a link in this chain of tradition, and this changed method produced a different type of architecture. It was a communal architecture, while that of the Roman was individual. Not individual in the modern sense, for all Roman architects practised the same style, but individual in the sense that a Roman building was the design of one man who directed the workman in regard to the details of his work, and no room was left for the initiative of the individual craftsman.

It is the variety of detail due to the initiative of individuals that lends an interest to Gothic architecture far and away beyond that of the personal architecture of the architect. It has a richer texture. For in a communal art " each product has a substance and content to which the greatest individual artists cannot hope to attain—it is the result of organic processes of thought and work. A great artist might make a little advance, a poor artist might stand a little behind ; but the work, as a whole, was customary, and was shaped and perfected by a life-experience whose span was centuries." [1]

In the Middle Ages every craft possessed such communal traditions of design, and each craftsman produced the designs that he executed. But in the production of architecture there must needs be some one to co-ordinate the efforts of the individual craftsmen. This position in the Mediæval period was occupied by the master mason or master carpenter, as the case might be, who exercised a general control in addition to the ordinary requirements of his craft. He differed from the architect of Roman times to the extent that his function was not to give detailed designs for others to execute, but to co-ordinate the efforts of living units ; it was the custom then for each craft to supply its own details and ornaments.

This different system naturally gave different results. Roman architecture, or, to be more correct, the Greek,

[1] *Mediæval Art*, by W. R. Lethaby.

from which it was derived, was refined and intellectual. It was as Lowell said :—

As unanswerable as Euclid,
The one thing finished in this hasty world.

In other words, it was a kind of æsthetic cul-de-sac from which the only escape was backwards by a return to the crafts : for it is only by and through the actual experiment with material that new ideas in detail can be evolved. A skilful architect may have fine general ideas, but he will have no new ideas of detail. Such details as he does use will be studied from the work done in the past by actual craftsmen, for, as I have already said, it is by actually handling material that new ideas of detail can be evolved. Hence it was that the Mediæval system of building, by giving the master minds opportunities for actually working on their buildings, developed a richness and wealth of detail unknown to Greek or Roman work. And what is of further interest, all the details to which Gothic Art gave rise had a peculiar relation to the material used. Greek and Roman architecture is abstract form which is applied more or less indifferently to any material. But it is one of the aims of Gothic design to bring out the intrinsic qualities of the materials. The details in each case are peculiar to the material used. Thus, in carving any natural object, it would be the aim of the craftsman not merely to suggest the general form of the thing intended, but to suggest, in addition, the qualities of the material in which it is executed. The treatment would, therefore, be conventionalized—a lion would emphatically be a wooden lion, a stone lion or a bronze lion, as the case might be. It would never be a merely naturalistic lion : in each case there would be no mistaking the material of which it was made, for the form would be developed upon lines which the technical production of each most readily suggests. That is the secret of convention.

Now, this change from the Roman to the Gothic method of work is finally to be accounted for by the fact that, since the day when the Roman style was practised, Christianity had triumphed in the world, and with it a new spirit had come into existence. In Greece and Rome the humble worker had been treated with scorn by men of science and philosophers. The ordinary man accepted his inferior status as necessary to the natural order of things. Even slaves did not regard their position as contrary to morality and right. In the thousand revolts of the slaves of antiquity there was never any appeal to any ethical principle or assertion of human rights. On the contrary, they were purely and simply appeals to force by men who thought themselves sufficiently strong to rebel successfully. But while these revolts failed to abolish slavery—for there was never a successful slave revolt—Christianity succeeded, by effecting a change of spirit which gradually dissolved the old order. It transformed society by bringing about a state of things in which human values took precedence over economic values. Little by little this changed spirit came to affect the Arts. The humble worker began to gain confidence, and to think and feel on his own account. This changed feeling, combined with the communal spirit which Christianity everywhere fostered, tended to bring into existence those communal traditions of handicraft which reached their most consummate expression in Gothic Art. For Gothic Art is just as democratic in spirit as the Greek and Roman is servile. Every line of Gothic Art contradicts the popularly accepted notion that the Middle Ages was a period of gloom and repression. The riot of carving, the gaiety and vigour of the little grotesques that peer out from pillars and cornices, the pure and joyous colour of frescoes and illuminated manuscripts, the delight in work that overflowed in free and beautiful details in the common articles of daily use, tell the tale of a rich and abounding life, just as much as the unanswerable logic of Greek architecture tells of a life oppressed with the sense of fate.

It is important that these fundamental differences should be acknowledged. Gothic architecture was the visible expression, the flowering of the dogmas of Christianity, and it cannot finally be separated from them. Apart from them, it would never have come into existence. It was precisely because the men of the Middle Ages had their minds at rest about the thousand and one doubts and difficulties which perplex us, as they perplexed the Greeks,

that it was possible for them to develop that wonderful
sense of romantic beauty which enabled them to build the
cathedrals, abbeys, and churches that cover Europe.   If
the acceptance of dogmas puts boundaries to the intellect
in one direction, it does so to break down barriers in another,
for dogmas do not strangle thought, but cause it to flow
in a different direction.   Under Paganism thought flowed
inwards, giving us philosophy ; under Christianity it flows
outwards, giving us the Arts, Guilds and economics.   Gothic
Art, like Christian dogmas, rests finally upon affirmations.
It seems to say : This is the right way of treating stonework ;
this, brickwork ; this, leadwork ; and so on.   And it says
all these things with authority in terms that admit of no
ambiguity.

While Gothic Art was democratic in spirit the Mediæval
craftsman understood clearly the limits of liberty.   He
knew that liberty was only possible on the assumption that
boundaries were respected, and that there is no such thing
as liberty absolute.   Liberty is possible on certain terms.
It involves in the first place a recognition of the authority
of ultimate truth, or, in other words, of dogmas, because
authority is in the nature of things, and men who refuse
to accept the authority of dogmas will find themselves
finally compelled to acquiesce in the authority of persons.
That is why revolutions which begin by seeking to overturn
the authority of ideas invariably end by establishing the
authority of persons.   A respect for authority of ideas
is naturally accompanied by a respect for mastership, which
is a fundamentally different thing from authority of persons.
For whereas, in the latter case, the authority is necessarily
exercised arbitrarily, in the former it is not so.   The pupil
asks the master how to do a thing because he wants to know.
But the employer tells the servant what he requires doing
because the servant has no desire to know.   That is the
difference between the two relationships.   That feeling of
personal antagonism which exists between employers and
workers to-day did not exist between the masters and
journeymen of the Mediæval Guilds, because the difference
between them was not primarily a difference of economic
status, but of knowledge and skill.   Well has it been

said that " producers of good articles respect one another ; producers of bad articles despise one another." [1]

A respect for the principle of mastership permeated Mediæval society, while it informed the organization of the Guilds. " In the Middle Ages," says Professor Lethaby, " the Masons' and Carpenters' Guilds were faculties or colleges of education in those arts, and every town was, so to say, a craft university. Corporations of Masons, Carpenters, and the like, were established in the towns ; each craft aspired to have a college hall. The universities themselves had been well named by a recent historian ' Scholars' Guilds.' The Guild, which recognized all the customs of its trade, guaranteed the relations of the apprentice and master craftsman with whom he was placed ; but he was really apprenticed to the craft as a whole, and ultimately to the city whose freedom he engaged to take up. He was, in fact, a graduate of his craft college, and wore its robes. At a later stage the apprentice became a companion or bachelor of his art, or by producing a master-work, the thesis of his craft, he was admitted a master. Only then was he permitted to become an employer of labour, or was admitted as one of the governing body of his college. As a citizen, city dignities were open to him. He might become the master in building some abbey or cathedral, or, as King's mason, become a member of the royal household, the acknowledged great master of his time in mason-craft. With such a system, was it so very wonderful that the buildings of the Middle Ages, which were, indeed, wonderful, should have been produced ? " [2]

Such, then, was the foundation on which Gothic architecture was built. In its earlier phase, as we meet it in this country in the Norman architecture of the twelfth century, it is characterized by a strong handling of masses. The Norman builders had " a sense of the large proportions of things," a firm grip of things fundamental. In this early work only a bare minimum of mouldings and ornaments are used, but such as are used are strong and vigorous. The general arrangement of parts which we find in Norman work persists

---

[1] *From the Human End*, by L. P. Jacks.
[2] Lecture on *Technical Education in the Building Trades*, by W. R. Lethaby.

through all the phases of Gothic, but the details or secondary parts, the trimmings, as it were, receive more and more attention, until finally, in the sixteenth century, the last phase is reached in Tudor work, when Gothic degenerates into an uninspired formula, and the multiplication of mechanical and accessory parts entirely destroys the sense of spaciousness, which is the mark of all fine architecture. This last phase is exemplified in this country in Henry VII Chapel at Westminster Abbey and King's College Chapel, Cambridge, as in the various Hotels de Ville of Flanders. Though architecture of this kind has the admiration of Baedeker,[1] it is simply awful stuff. It is Gothic in its dotage, as anybody who knows anything about architecture is aware.

Though there is much very beautiful architecture of the fifteenth century, it is apparent that the decline of Gothic dates from the middle of the century. From that time onwards, it is, generally speaking, true to say that the most important buildings in the civic sense are the least important from an architectural point of view. Most of the best examples of later Gothic are to be found where there was not too much money to spend, for after the middle of the fifteenth century the restraining influence in design does not appear to come from the taste of the craftsmen, but from the poverty of their clients.

The most important examples of Gothic are to be found in Northern France. In the early part of the twelfth century Paris became the cultural centre of Europe, and it remained throughout the Middle Ages the centre of thought and culture. It was here that the Gothic Cathedral in its essence as a kind of energetic structure in which the various parts of pillars, vaults and buttresses balance each other was developed. In 1140 the abbey church of St. Denis, a few miles from Paris, was begun, and completed within a few years, and it established the type and set the tradition which all subsequent cathedral builders followed. First came the cathedrals of

[1] Baedeker's Guides do a great deal of harm to architecture, being entirely untrustworthy. The buildings which they ask the public to admire are those which are very old, or elaborate, or big, or because of some historic association. But they never recommend those which are simply beautiful and do not come into any of their other categories. Such buildings are ignored by them.

Paris, Chartres and Rouen, and later the celebrated culminating group of Amiens, Beauvais, Bourges and Rheims, which are generally regarded as the high-water mark of Gothic achievement.

All other Gothic architecture derives from the parent stock of France. But to me the branches are more interesting than the stem. For though there is a magnificence and daring about French Gothic, and though we are indebted to it for the germ ideas, there is too much effort about it to satisfy my taste entirely. It lacks the sobriety and reserve of the Gothic of England, Flanders, and Italy. The brick cathedrals and churches of Belgium have a wonderfully fine quality about them, though their plastered interiors are entirely devoid of interest. Only in Italy has brickwork been so successfully treated. Gothic never took root properly in Italy, and the more ambitious attempts at it, as are to be seen at Orvieto and Milan cathedrals, are dreadful failures so far as the exteriors are concerned. But the simpler forms of Italian Gothic in civil and domestic work and in some of the smaller churches are exquisite in taste. It is a thousand pities that the development of Gothic in Italy should have been arrested by the coming of the Renaissance, for there are unexplored possibilities in it which may prove to be the germ of a great revival some day in Italy, if not elsewhere.

In comparing Gothic with other styles of architecture, the most extraordinary thing is that Gothic buildings, which are badly proportioned and entirely indefensible from a strict architectural standpoint, have a way of looking quaint and interesting. Take the case of the belfry at Bruges, which Mr. Chesterton once said was like a swan with a very long neck. The tower is out of all proportion with the building, and the various stages of it are out of proportion with each other ; it was added to from time to time, and in any other style of architecture a building so badly proportioned would be a monstrosity. Yet there is a charm about this belfry which it is impossible to deny, and if we seek for the final cause of it, I think we shall find it in the vagaries of craftsmanship, in the liberty of the craftsman who was part of a great tradition. .

CHAPTER IX

THE FRANCISCANS AND THE RENAISSANCE

THE stimulus which was given to thought and discovery in the thirteenth century by the recovery of the works of Aristotle was the beginning of an awakened interest in the literature and art of Paganism which culminated in that many-sided movement which we know as the Renaissance. The movement originated in Italy and spread itself over France, England, and Germany. It is the turning-point in the history of Western Europe and is not to be understood if it is regarded as a rebellion against Christianity; for in its origin it was nothing of the kind, but a reaction against the perversion of the Christian ideal at the hands of the Franciscans. The Renaissance was at the same time a continuation of and a reaction against the forces which St. Francis set in motion, while only in a secondary sense is it to be regarded as a reaction against the scholasticism of the Dominicans.

In order to see the Renaissance in its proper perspective, it is necessary to realize the significance and influence of the Franciscans in the thirteenth century. They stood in the same relation to the Middle Ages as the Socialist Movement does to the modern world, in that the Franciscans were the central driving force which created the issues in morals and economics which occupied the thought of the Middle Ages. Moreover, as with the Socialist Movement, the problem of poverty was their primary concern, but they attacked it from a different angle and by a different method. They did not approach it from the point of view of economics, though their activities led to economic discussions, but from the point of view of human brotherhood. This different method of approach was due partly to the fact that they approached it as Christians appealing to Christians, and partly because in the Middle Ages poverty was not the problem it is to-day—something organic with the structure of society—but a thing that was essentially local and accidental. It did not owe its existence to the fact that society was organized on a basis fundamentally false as is the case to-day, but because the Mediæval organization, good as it was, was not co-extensive with society. Poverty existed on the fringes of society, not at its centres.

The problem arose as a consequence of the development of trade. The monastic orders, as we saw, were the pioneers of civilization in Western Europe. They settled down in the waste places, cleared the woods and drained the swamps, and around them there gradually grew up the hamlets and towns of Mediæval Europe. But a time came when new towns began to spring up to meet the requirements of trade, and in the new mercantile towns of Italy and Southern France the lower grades of the population were woefully neglected by the secular clergy, and in consequence had grown up wild and ignorant of every form of religious worship and secular instruction, while they lived in poverty and dirt. It was against such ignorance and neglect that the Franciscans resolved to fight, and it was in order that they might be of service to the poor that they sought identity with them in position and fortune. This was the origin of the gospel of poverty that they taught, and which by the middle of the thirteenth century their zeal and militant spirit had carried far and wide over Christendom ; for they were great preachers. But while they were a force in all the great centres of Mediæval Europe, they were exceptionally strong in their home in Italy. The huge churches built for them without piers in the interior, and which are found all over Italy, testify to the large crowds to which they were accustomed to preach. But with the success which followed them there came a perversion of their original idea. Poverty as taught by St. Francis was a means to an end. It was recommended to his followers in order that they might be of service to the poor. But after a time this original idea tended to recede into the background, and in time poverty came to be looked upon as the essence of

religion. When, therefore, the excesses of this ideal began
to make religious life impossible for all except the very poor,
it produced the inevitable reaction. An influential party
among the Franciscans sought to have the original rule
modified in order to bring it more into accord with the
dictates of reason and experience. But in this effort they
were obstinately opposed by a minority in the Order who
refused to have any part in such relaxations. The recrimina-
tions between these two branches of the Order at last became
so bitter that appeal was made to the Pope to judge between
them. He appointed a commission of cardinals and theologians to inquire into the issues involved, and quite reasonably
gave a decision in favour of the moderate party. But this
only embittered the extreme party, who now denied the
authority of the Pope to interfere with the internal discipline
of the Order, affirming that only St. Francis could undo what
St. Francis himself had bound up. From attacking the
Pope they went on to attack the wealthy clergy, maintaining
that wealth was incompatible with the teachings of Christ,
and from that they went on to attack the institution of
property as such. It was thus that the split in the Franciscans led to those discussions about the ethics of property
which occupied so much of the thought of the Mediæval
economists. This question, studied in the light of Aristotle,
led St. Thomas Aquinas to formulate those social principles,
which became accepted as the standards of Catholic orthodoxy, as at a later date led St. Antonino to affirm that
" poverty is not a good thing ; in itself it is an evil, and can
be considered to lead only accidentally to any good." [1]

Without doubt St. Antonino had the Franciscan gospel
of poverty in mind when he made this utterance. He
realized the terrible evils which would follow the divorce
of religion from everyday life if an ideal beyond the capacity
of the average normal man were insisted upon. Moreover,
in the early part of the fourteenth century the Franciscans
themselves had fallen from their high estate. It is a fact
of pyschology that an excess of idealism will be followed by
a fall from grace, and the Franciscans fell very low indeed.

[1] *St. Antonino and Mediæval Economics*, by Bede Jarrett (The Manresa
Press).

The high moral plane on which they sought to live was too much for them. The moment they relaxed from their strenuous activity they became corrupted by the degraded environment in which they found themselves, and rapidly sank to that depth of coarseness, meanness, and sinfulness which has been so well described by Chaucer. The once popular Franciscans now became objects of the same scorn and ridicule as the monks of the Benedictine and Cistercian Orders.

We saw there was a reaction against the rule of St. Francis within the Franciscan Order. There was now to come a reaction from without, and the immediate form it took was a reassertion of those very things which St. Francis forbade his followers—scholarship and the world. An insistence upon the value of these is the keynote of the Humanists whose labours inaugurated the Renaissance. The men of the Early Renaissance were not opposed to Christianity, but to what they conceived to be the perversion of its ideal at the hands of the Franciscans. Against the Franciscan conception of life they warred incessantly. Their enthusiasm for Pagan literature was inspired by the belief that its study would lead to a fuller understanding of Christianity. In it was to be found most precious material for the cultivation of the mind and for the purification of moral life. Its popularization would, moreover, tend to restore the balance between the religious and secular sides of life which the exaggerated teachings of the Franciscans had temporarily upset. They had no sympathy with the later Humanists who regarded learning as an end in itself. On the contrary, classic literature was by them only valued as a means to an end—the end being the Christian life. The position was not a new one. Classic literature, as such, had never been banned by the Church. Already in the first centuries of Christianity the Fathers of the Church had pursued and advocated the study of the literature of Greece and Rome. But they had exercised discrimination. They recognized that while many classic works had been inspired by lofty sentiments, such was not by any means always the case, and that while many books had been written in Pagan times merely to extol vice, there were many other books which, though they had no such object, might be used by

9

vicious-minded persons as apologetics for vice, and so discrimination had been made. The classic authors who were
above suspicion were taken into the bosom of the Church.
St. Augustine had based his theology upon the Platonic
philosophy. The *Æneid* of Virgil came to be looked upon
almost as a sacred book, loved and honoured as much by
Christian Fathers as by Roman scholars. Virgil had remained with the Church all through the Dark Ages and
lived to inspire the *Divina Commedia* of Dante a century
and a half before the Revival of Learning was inaugurated
by Petrarch. All through this period great value was set
upon such classic authors as the Church had sanctioned and
had survived the wreck of Roman civilization. The Benedictines preserved in their monasteries a knowledge of the
Latin classics. Virgil, Horace, Statius, Sallust, Terence,
Cicero, Quintilian, Ovid, Lucan, Martial, Cæsar, Livy and
Suetonius were known and studied by them. But though
the Latin classics and the Latin language were never wholly
lost, the fortunes of the Greek classics were very different.
After the fall of the Western Empire in the fifth century
a knowledge of classical Greek rapidly faded out of the
West, becoming practically extinct, and with it disappeared
from Western Europe any knowledge of the works of Plato,
Aristotle and other Greek authors. From about the end
of the tenth century a knowledge of the Latin classics began
to be more widely diffused. But the incipient revival of
a better literary taste was checked at the beginning of the
thirteenth century by the re-discovery of Aristotle which
was followed by such a great awakening that for the time
being he came to monopolize intellectual interests and the
Latin classics that had been studied before Aristotle came
along fell into neglect. In this light the Revival of Learning
appears in the first place as an endeavour to take up the
threads of the Latin culture of the pre-Aristotelian period
of a hundred years before, and in the next to subject them to
a more systematic study. In another later and quite secondary sense it became a movement of poets or men of letters
against philosophers.[1]   In no sense can the Revival of

---

[1] " The inveterate quarrel, which is as old as Plato, between poets, or
men of letters, and philosophers who seek wisdom by process of dialectic,

Learning in its early stages be regarded as a rebellion against
Christianity. The early Humanists were not looked upon
as dangerous and destructive innovators. Aristotle had
been made a bulwark against heresy by the efforts of Albertus
Magnus and St. Thomas Aquinas, and at the time there
seemed no reason to suppose that the study of other authors
of antiquity could not be similarly reconciled and incorporated in the Christian theology. This spirit of reconciliation
survived through the greater part of the fifteenth century,
and when, after the fall of Constantinople in 1453, a priceless
cargo of Greek manuscripts arrived in Italy together with
numerous Greek scholars, Plato was studied in this same
spirit of reconciliation. The proof that the Platonists of
the Renaissance were genuinely inspired by religious motives
is to be found in the fact that both Marsilio Ficino and Pico
della Mirandola eventually came entirely under the influence
of Savonarola. Ficino entered the Church. Pico burned
his love-poems, decided to become a friar, and was only
prevented by death.

Such was the ideal of the Early Renaissance. The
changed ideal which is the mark of the Later Renaissance
is to be accounted for by a growing consciousness on the
part of the Humanists of the ultimate irreconcilibility
between the Pagan and Christian attitudes towards life,
if not always between the Pagan and Christian philosophies.
They began to ask themselves the question whether the
Pagan world was not a bigger, broader and more humane
one than the Christian world with which they were
familiar, whether, in fact, the life of the senses which Paganism
avowed was not the life which it was intended that man should
live and whether Christianity, by placing restraints upon the
natural impulses of man, had not frustrated the ends of life.
In an earlier age under other circumstances such thoughts
would have been resisted as coming from the Devil. But
they did not appear as such to men who lived in an atmosphere of intellectual and æsthetic intoxication, in a society

must not be overlooked when we read of the judgments of the later Humanists
on a scholasticism which they despised without always understanding it.
To them, technical terms were a jargon and the subtle but exquisite distinctions of Aquinas spelt barbarism " (*Cambridge Modern History*, vol. i.
p. 633).

in which the recovery of the remains of Greek and Roman
Art was proving a new source of guidance and inspiration.

Now it is important to recognize that the ideas with which
the Humanists had now become familiar fascinated their
minds because at the time they understood neither Paganism
nor Christianity.   On the one hand they did not realize
the slough of despondency into which Pagan civilization had
fallen, while they were not familiar with Christianity as it
had been understood at an earlier age but with its perversion
at the hands of the Franciscans.   For it is well to remember
that Christianity had never denied the life of the senses.
The doctrine of the Resurrection of the Body is an eternal
witness to that fact.   For it was formulated, as we saw, as a
means of combating the Manichean heresy, which *did* deny
the sensuous life of man.   But while on the one hand Christianity thereby acknowledged " that in any final consummation the bodily life of man must find a place no
less than the spiritual," on the other it clearly apprehended
the dangers to which the sensuous life of man was exposed,
affirming that the exercise of restraint alone could guarantee
emotional continuity.   Deprived of a restraining influence,
man rapidly exhausts his emotional capacity.   The man
who is for ever seeking experience and expression, because
experience and expression are natural to the healthy normal
man, soon becomes emotionally bankrupt.   He becomes
blasé.   So it was with the later Humanists.   When the
spell which bound them to Christian beliefs had been broken
no power on earth could stop them once they were fairly
embarked on the pursuit of pleasure.   They went from excess
to excess, from debauchery to debauchery in a vain search
for new experiences, while they took especial pleasure in
the works of Petronius and the other disreputable authors
of Antiquity who sought to make vice attractive.   Whatever
else these later Humanists failed to do, they certainly succeeded
in reviving the sensuality and epicureanism of Rome.   The
Papacy, which had become associated with the revival, became
a veritable centre of corruption.   When the young Giovanni
de Medici went to Rome his father Lorenzo warned him to
beware of his conduct in that " sink of iniquity."   And
the warning was not given without good reason.   The best-

known Popes between the years 1458–1522 were all more or less unscrupulous evil-doers. Sixtus IV was an accomplice in the plot against the Medici which ended in the murder of Giuliano. Alexander VI shows an almost unparalleled record of crimes. In this society poison became a fine art, simony and theft everyday occurrences, and where the Popes led, the cardinals followed. Alexander's illegitimate son, Cæsar Borgia, chief among them, was the hero of Machiavelli. If these monsters had lived in the Middle Ages, we should never have heard the last of them. A record of their crimes would have been considered an indispensable part of every child's education. But, as it is, their story is reserved for the few, while they are treated with a certain curiosity, not to say indulgence, as patrons of culture.

What happened to religion happened to the arts. The ideas of the Renaissance were in each case their destruction. The spirit of reconciliation which was characteristic of the thought of the Early Renaissance is reflected in the arts of the period. This is especially true of the Italian architecture and the painting and sculpture of the fifteenth century, which is Gothic in spirit and general conception combined with details derived from the study of Roman work. In the work of this period the Gothic and Roman elements are always present, and the blend is exquisite. But this great moment of transition did not last for. long. The Gothic element begins to disappear, and with the arrival of Michelangelo it is entirely eliminated. The decline begins to set in, for Michelangelo introduced a manner which proved fatal to all the arts. That delight in natural objects, in flowers and birds, in quaint things and queer things, which is so peculiar to Gothic art, which probably owes its origin to the influence of St. Francis and which made the arts of the Middle Ages so democratic in their expression, is now no more. Michelangelo eliminated everything that gave to art its human interest and concentrated attention entirely upon abstract form. In the hands of a great master such a treatment of art is great, though cold and austere, but in the hands of lesser men it became ridiculous, for the manner of Michelangelo was just as much beyond the capacity of the average artist and craftsmen as the life of poverty which St. Francis recommended to his followers was normally beyond the capacity of the ordinary man.   And Michelangelo set the fashion in all the arts.   Mediaeval sculpture was rich in decorative detail, but after Michelangelo sculpture became identified with the nude.   Mediæval painting was rich in design and colour, but after Michelangelo its primary concern is with light and shade.   Paradoxically, Michelangelo introduced the very opposite principle into the treatment of architecture.   For he does not simplify, but elaborates it.   Prior to , Michelangelo architecture was simple in its treatment, while elaboration was confined to the decorative crafts, but now, having robbed painting and sculpture of their decorative qualities, he sought to obtain the contrasts he required by making architecture itself a decorative thing. This he did by multiplying the number of its mechanical parts.   Michelangelo disregarded altogether the structural basis of architectural design, and in his hands architecture became a mere theatrical exhibition of columns, pilasters, pediments, etc.   Thus he inaugurated that evil tradition in which architecture and building are divorced, against which we fight in vain to this day.

But Michelangelo was not the only cause of the decline. Architecture might have survived the introduction of his mannerisms had it not been that in the sixteenth century the works of Vitruvius were unearthed.   He had reduced Roman architecture to a system of external rules and proportions and his re-discovery was the greatest misfortune which ever befell architecture.   Though Vitruvius was a very inferior architect, absurd homage was paid to him because he happened to be the only architectural writer whose works were preserved from antiquity.   He was exalted by the architects of the time as a most certain and infallible guide as to what was and what was not a proper proportion. We know from the writings of Serlio, an architect of the period who did much to establish the reputation of Vitruvius, that the craftsmen of the time objected to the pedantic idea that only one set of proportions was allowable ; that there was one way of doing things and no other, and in a couple of pamphlets written by two German master builders

of the time, Matthew Boritzer and Lawrence Lacher [1] protests
are made against this new way of regarding architecture,
and they insist that the highest art is the result of inward
laws controlling the outward form. But such protests
availed nothing against the pedantry of the architects,
whose prestige enabled them to get their own way in spite
of the objections from the building trade. Henceforth there
is an increasing insistence everywhere upon Roman precedents
in design, and care is given to the secondary details, while
the fundamental ideas of plan and grouping are overtaken
by paralysis. Architecture, from being something vital
and organic in the nature of a growth, became a matter of
external rules and proportions, applied more or less indifferently to any type of building, quite regardless either of
internal convenience or structural necessity. When this
point of development was reached, any co-operation among
the crafts and arts which had survived from the Middle Ages
came to an end. Henceforth painting and sculpture became
entirely separated from architecture and continued an independent existence in studios and galleries, while the minor
crafts degenerated solely into matters of trade and commerce.

The growth of pedantry in architecture was assisted by
a change in the organization of the crafts which followed
the introduction of Renaissance ideas. In the Middle Ages
it was, as we saw, the custom for craftsmen to supply their
own designs, and if every craftsman were not a designer,
at any rate every designer was a craftsman. But with the
revival of Roman ideas of design there came into existence
a caste of architects and designers over and above the
craftsmen of the building trades, who supplied designs which
the craftsmen carried into execution. At first these architects
had to proceed very warily, for the craftsmen did not seem
to care very much about this new arrangement. Thus we
read that Sir Christopher Wren, when sending his small-
scale plans and directions for the library at Trinity College,
Cambridge, adds : " I suppose you have good masons ;
however, I would willingly take a further pains to give all
the mouldings in great ; we are scrupulous in small matters,
and you must pardon us, the architects are as great pedants

[1] Janssen, vol i. p. 167–8.

as critics and heralds." This letter is interesting, not only because it testifies to the existence of trained schools of masons 'and carpenters who had their own traditions of design and could be trusted to apply them, but to the growing spirit of pedantry which proved to be the death of architecture. So long as architecture had its roots firmly in the crafts such a development was impossible. But with the separation of the functions of design and execution and the rise of a school of architects who were proud of their scholarly attainments, pedantry grew apace. The craftsman, compelled to execute designs made by others, gradually lost his faculty of design, while the architect, deprived of the suggestion in design which the actual handling of material gives, naturally fell back more and more upon Roman precedent, until, finally, all power of invention in design came to an end and architecture expired at the end of the eighteenth century. Since then a succession of revivals have been attempted which have succeeded in producing a certain number of interesting buildings but not in effecting a general revival of architecture.

Fortunately during this period of decline, architects were few in number, and were only employed on the most expensive work. The great mass of building was designed, as well as executed, by builders. While the architects were engaged in producing those monstrous platitudes in the "grand manner," known as monumental architecture, these builders were engaged in the development of a style of'work which carried on the vigorous traditions of Gothic craftsmanship, while it made use of such Roman forms as could readily be assimilated. This vernacular architecture, which in this country we know by the names of Elizabethan, Jacobean, Queen Anne and Georgian, is the really genuine architecture of the Renaissance period, and it reacted to give the architects an endowment of traditional English taste which kept the academic tendencies of the Renaissance within certain bounds. But in the latter half of the eighteenth century the pedantic ideas of the architects, owing to the prestige of London, became enforced as stringent standards over the whole country, and this vernacular architecture came to an end.

While thus we see the Renaissance ended by destroying communal traditions in the arts, it destroyed also the communal traditions of culture of the Middle Ages. This culture, which had its basis in common religious ideas, was a human thing to the extent that it was capable of binding king and peasant, priest and craftsman together in a common bond of sympathy and understanding. It was, moreover, a culture which came to a man at his work. The mason who carved ornaments of some chapel or cathedral drew his inspiration from the same source of religious tradition as the ploughman who sang as he worked in the field or the minstrel who chanted a song in the evening. It was a part of the environment in which every man lived. But the later Renaissance had no sympathy with culture of this kind. It could not understand craft culture. To it culture was primarily a matter of books. It became a purely intellectual affair, whose standards were critical, and, as such, instead of operating to bind the various classes of the community together, it raised a barrier between the many and the few. There is no escape from this state of things so long as culture remains on a purely intellectual basis, for a time will never arrive when the majority in any class are vitally interested in intellectual pursuits. Mediæval culture did not expect them to be. It accepted differences among men as irrevocable, but it knew at the same time that all men had certain human interests in common, and it built up a culture to preserve them.

In the place of a communal culture, the Renaissance promoted the cult of the individual. Its history bristles with the names of brilliant men who seem almost to be ends in themselves. They have all the appearance of being great creators, but when we examine them more closely we see they are the great destroyers. For their greatness is not their own. They were men who inherited great traditions, which they thoughtlessly destroyed, much in the same way as a spendthrift squanders the fortune to which he succeeds. But while the Renaissance destroyed the great traditions, it could put nothing in their place, for its facile half-success left it ultimately impotent, and if we search for the final cause of this failure, I think we shall find it in this—that it valued means rather than ends.   It concentrated its energy upon science and criticism, but for what ends it knew not. These, it assumed, might be left to take care of themselves. And so it remained without a rudder to steer by or a goal at which to aim.   Science and criticism may be constructive, but only when used by men with well-defined ends in view. But men of this type believe in dogmas, which the men of the Renaissance did not.   Such men realize that if criticism has any validity in society it can only be on the assumption that it is in search of final and definite conclusions ; that if it seeks to destroy one set of dogmas it does so in order to create others.   But the men of the Renaissance did not understand this.   They valued criticism for the sake of criticism, not for the sake of truth but for the love of destruction.   They never understood that the final object and justification of criticism is that it destroys the need of criticism ; that the final aim and object of free thought should be the re-establishment of dogmas.

CHAPTER X

THE REFORMATION IN GERMANY

THOUGH the Reformation may be regarded at once as a development and a reaction against the Renaissance, it had yet at the same time roots of its own. Though it broke out in the sixteenth century in Germany, its intellectual foundations were laid in the fourteenth century in England by Wycliffe—"the Morning Star of the Reformation" as he is called. His ideas were carried all over Europe by wandering scholars. He was the inspirer of the Hussite Movement in Bohemia as well as of the leading men in the Reformation.

Wycliffe was no Catholic, but a religious pervert. He had no conception of the function of religion in its broadest and most catholic sense as an instrument which maintained the common life by securing the acceptance of certain beliefs and standards of thought and morals by the whole people and thus maintaining the Kingdom of God upon Earth. On the contrary, his attitude towards religion was a very narrow, self-regarding and personal one. He was concerned with the need of a man saving his own individual soul, and his teaching was a perversion of the whole idea of Christianity. If we keep steadily in our mind that the central aim of Christianity is to maintain the common life, it becomes apparent that the primary object of the priest is the maintenance of a common standard of thought and morals. A man by his words may secure respect for them, though in his individual life he may fall short of their fulfilment. But Wycliffe, viewing the corruption of the clergy of his day, laid down the dictum that only a priest who is himself without sin can preach the word of God. Though a corrupt clergy is to be deplored, it becomes evident that the remedy of Wycliffe is worse than the disease, inasmuch as it denies the humanity of the priest.   Insistence upon such a standard demands that a priest, instead of, as heretofore, being acknowledged a sinner like other men, must be a superior person.   Thus he will, knowing himself to be a sinner, become a hypocrite in the eyes of the world, or, what is far worse, he will become a prig, committing the most deadly of all sins, that of spiritual pride, and endeavour to make his own conduct the standard of truth and morals.

This constituted the central heresy of Wycliffe.   All the rest flowed from it.   Wycliffe himself was a prig of the first order ; his self-sufficiency was intolerable.   It was the elect, he taught, who constituted the community of saints— the community of God or the true Church.   According to him, the Church consisted of all true believers who had access to the Divine mercy, who approached God by their own prayers without the intervention of a priestly mediator, and who were to interpret the Scriptures according to the dictates of their consciences.   For by making the Scriptures rather than the traditions of the Church the final authority Wycliffe made personal opinion the final test of truth.   In other words, the Church consisted not of the hierarchy and the people but of all the prigs and self-elected saints whose standard of self-righteousness was henceforth to become the standard of conduct and morals.   Wycliffe was the first of the Puritans.

In the ordinary course of events, Wycliffe would have suffered death as a heretic, but like all the self-righteous Puritancial crowd he had in his composition a streak of worldly wisdom.   He took care that his new gospel would be acceptable to the hierarchy of the State if not to that of the Church, and made his position safe by securing the protection of John of Gaunt, whose personal conduct incidentally was anything but pure.   The corruption of the clergy, Wycliffe maintained, could be traced to their excessive wealth.   It was essential, therefore, to the promotion of the higher life in the community that the clergy should be reduced. Hence it was Wycliffe advised the confiscation of the Church lands by the State.   That the State itself was more corrupt than the Church, that in the hands of the lawyers who were now controlling it the State had become a shameless instrument of class oppression which was for its own ends dispossessing the peasants of their lands, did not deter Wycliffe from proposing a measure which would increase enormously the power which was so unscrupulously used. Such larger issues did not interest him. As to how the peasants were likely to fare under his new regime he never, apparently, gave a moment's thought. He was not concerned with the well-being of the people, but with the creation of a race of self-righteous plaster saints to replace the hierarchy of the Church.

Such was the fundamental heresy of Wycliffe which bore fruit a thousand-fold when the Reformation broke over Europe. Immediately, the Reformation owed its inception to the protest of Luther against the corruption of the Papacy which had come about as a consequence of the revival of Pagan thought and morals. In the year 1510, Luther visited Rome on business connected with his monastic order, and was deeply moved at the irreligion and corruption of the Papal Court. Seven years after this visit he took up a stand against the sale of Indulgences, by which at the time Leo X was seeking to raise money for the completion of St. Peter's at Rome, in the belief that the abuses attending their sale were the main source of corruption. On the 1st of November, 1517, he nailed to the doors of the Castle Church at Wittenberg his famous thesis of ninety-five propositions against the sale of Indulgences. The nailing of theses to the doors of churches was in the Middle Ages an ordinary academic procedure, and according to the usage of the times the author was not supposed to be definitely committed to the opinions he had expressed. But it was apparent that Luther did not intend the debate to be an ordinary academic one, for he had carefully chosen the day on which to nail up his thesis. For the 1st of November was All Saints' Day. It was the anniversary of the consecration of the church and was commemorated by a long series of service, while the benefits of an Indulgence were secured for all who took part in them. It was the day when the largest concourse of townsmen and strangers might be expected, and would therefore ensure a wide reading of his thesis, nor was he disappointed with the result. He had raised a question in which there happened to be widespread interest. The printers could not produce copies of this thesis fast enough to meet the demand which came from all parts of Germany.

Now why was it that Luther's act had immediately such marvellous practical results ? The answer is because it had become widely recognized that the abuse of Indulgences was a fruitful source of the corruption of the ecclesiastical organization. It is impossible here properly to discuss this question, not only because it is very involved, but because the theory on which Indulgences rest is entirely unintelligible from a purely rational or ethical standpoint. It may, however, be said that Mediæval theology did not create Indulgences ; it only followed and tried to justify the practices of the Popes and the Roman Curia. They originated in the early days of the Church. Serious sins involved separation from the fellowship of Christians, and readmission to the communion was dependent not merely upon public confession but also on the manifestation of a true repentance by the performance of certain *satisfactions,* such as the manumission of slaves, prolonged fastings, extensive almsgivings ; which were works acceptable to God and gave outward and visible proof that the penitent really desired to be received again into the fold. In course of time public confessions became private confessions to a priest, and there grew up a system of penances proportionate to the sins. In the seventh century these, under certain circumstances, became commuted for money payments, and so little by little the inward meaning receded into the background while greater importance became attached to the outward acts until, under the direction of the Renaissance Popes, Indulgences had degenerated into purely commercial transactions. They had been abused everywhere, but particularly in Germany, for Germany during the Middle Ages was the richest country in Europe and as such had become the usual resource of a Pope in financial straits. So long as the sale of Indulgences was limited and only made use of in exceptional circumstances, nobody thought of objecting. But the authority of the Holy See had been severely shaken by the Great Schism—for the spectacle of two, and at one time three, Popes claiming the allegiance of Christendom, whilst hurling anathemas at each other, was anything but an edifying one. Moreover, the Popes of the Renaissance in their pursuit of temporal power had to all intents and purposes become secular princes, using religion merely as an instrument for the furtherance of their political ambitions. These Popes greatly increased the sale of Indulgences and raised tithes and annates under the pretext of war against the Turks, though no expeditions were sent forth and the money collected was spent upon other objects. When news of the corruption of the Papacy had been noised abroad and the clergy of Germany found, as they asserted in a petition presented to the Emperor-elect, Maximilian, in 1510, that the Papacy could be restrained by no agreements or conventions seeing that it granted dispensations, suspensions, and revocations for the vilest persons while employing other devices for nullifying its promises and evading its own wholesome regulations, a time came when numberless people began to ask themselves whether the Papacy was entitled to the allegiance that it claimed and in what sense the Popes were to be considered the successors of St. Peter. All efforts at reform having failed, the only remedy lay in revolution, and Germany was ready for the signal. In 1521 the Nuncio Alexander wrote " that five years before he had mentioned to Pope Leo his dread of a German uprising, he had heard from many Germans that they were only waiting for some fool to open his mouth against Rome." [1]

The immediate popularity of Luther's protest, then, was not due to any desire for doctrinal reform but because he stood for opposition to Rome. The doctrinal changes associated with his name were largely improvised dogmas called into existence by the desire to combat Papal pretensions, for he was a man of action rather than a careful and logical thinker and only stated an abstract position when he was driven to it. The original idea of the Church had been that of salvation by faith and good works. But when Christianity triumphed and everybody was born a Christian,

[1] *Cambridge Modern History*, vol. i. p. 690.

the faith came to be taken more or less for granted and emphasis was put more and more upon good works, as being the mark of a good Christian life. It was among other things the emphasis which had been almost entirely placed upon good works that led to the abuse of Indulgences. Luther attacked this external idea of Christianity. He had told an assembly of clergy who met at Leitzkau in 1512 to discuss the reform of the Church that reformation must begin with the individual and involved a change of heart. The penitence which Christ required was something more than a momentary expression of sorrow. Hence his cardinal dogma of justification by faith. No Christian, I imagine, Catholic or Protestant, would object to what he meant by this. For though he maintained that good works were not sufficient, it is to be supposed that he meant salvation by faith and good works. But he did not say this, and the result was the Reformation produced results very different from what he had intended. Under Protestantism, stress came to be laid entirely upon questions of faith to the exclusion of good works, and morals accommodated themselves to the practice of the rich. To understand exactly why this came about we must consider the changes which Luther introduced into Church government. Like his doctrinal changes, they had their origin in political expediency.

The immediate success of Luther I said was due to the fact that he stood for opposition to Rome. Of that there can be no doubt whatsoever. But a question arises out of it that needs to be answered. If the Reformation, so far as the majority were concerned, was inspired by opposition to Rome, how was it that the movement did not take the form of a mere separation of the Church from Rome as in the first place it did in England? The answer is that the political condition of Germany made that impossible. From the date when the revival of Roman Law led the Emperors to attempt to control the Papacy, it had been the consistent policy of Rome to cripple the Empire by encouraging the congeries of sovereign princes to assert their independence against the Emperors. The result of this policy was that the power of the Emperor was only nominal. In reality it did not exist. Consequently in Germany there could be no appeal from the authority of the Pope to the authority of State, but only an appeal from the Pope to the people; that is, to the community of believers. Hence it came about that when at the Diet of Worms (1521) Luther maintained that Popes and Councils might err, in the absence of the support of the Emperor he was in the position of having either to retract or to appeal to the people. Having taken this step, certain consequences logically followed from it. In appealing to the people he not only made their authority supreme in matters of Church government, but in the interpretation of the Scriptures; a development which was made possible by the recent invention of printing. This was fatal for the ends he had in view, because it entirely destroyed the value of religion as a social force capable of binding men together, because if each individual is to interpret the Scriptures, their meaning becomes a matter of opinion, in the light of which every man is a law unto himself. For if truth is declared to be subjective, it is impossible to insist upon a moral standard which is necessarily objective. Luther was not long in finding these things out, though he would never admit to himself that he could possibly be wrong. The doubts and qualms of conscience which in later life he had with regard to the correctness of his course of action he ascribed to the suggestion of the evil spirit. Often at the beginning of his crusade Luther had expressed the confident expectation that his gospel would exercise a beneficent influence both morally and religiously. But he was terribly disappointed. It was not long before he was driven to acknowledge that things had grown seven times worse than before. " People," he said, " after hearing the Gospel steal, lie, drink, gluttonize, and indulge in all sorts of vice. Drunkenness has come upon us like a flood and swamped everything." [1] He deplored, too, the growing insubordination especially of the rising generation, but his words fell upon deaf ears. Writing of the change which followed the transfer of authority from the hands of the priests to those of the laity, Erasmus said : " The people will not listen to their own ministers when the latter do not tickle their ears ; on the contrary, these unhappy preachers must straight-

[1] Janssen, vol. iv. p. 150.

10

way be sent about their business the moment that they show any frankness, and presume to question the conduct of their hearers." In a letter to Luther in 1524 he wrote: " I see that these innovations are producing shoals of turbulent good-for-nothing people, and I dread a bloody insurrection." [1]

The trouble then, I incline to think, was very much like the trouble at the present day. Everybody wanted reform, but they had no intention of changing their own lives. They would support Luther to get rid of the incubus of Rome, but that was as far as they desired to go, for they had no really religious feeling. Germany had become corrupted by wealth, and as a matter of fact so far as Germany was concerned it was much truer to say that the people had corrupted the Church than that the Church had corrupted the people, for the Humanist Movement in Germany which owed its inception to the ecclesiastical reformer Cardinal Nicholas of Cusa never became as corruptly Pagan as in Italy, but had addressed itself to the higher emotions and had sought to train the conscience of the individual to recognize his direct responsibility to God and his fellows. On the other hand, the corruption in Germany was of secular origin and had come about as a result of the sinister influence of Roman Law reacting upon the growth and development of commerce. At the beginning of the sixteenth century Germany was the most prosperous country in Europe. It was the great universal centre of commerce, the great market for the products of nature and art. This was to be accounted for, firstly by its central geographical position, which in the days of the overland trade routes placed it in a position to trade with Italy and the Levant on the one side and with Flanders, the Scandinavian North, Poland and Russia on the other ; and secondly by the enterprising character of its merchants, who knew how to use their favourable position to the utmost advantage. In the early Middle Ages they had been averse to the business of usury and had devoted themselves exclusively to mercantile affairs. The Merchant Guilds of the German towns had organized themselves into

---

[1] Janssen, vol. iv. p. 153.

the famous Hanseatic League,[1] which had settlements in the principal ports of the countries with which they traded. The one in London known as the Steelyard[2] was surrounded by high walls after the manner of a fortress. It was required that all who lived within its walls—masters, assistants and apprentices—should be unmarried men, for they followed a life of strict discipline which was monastic in its character. It was upon this monastic basis that the broad foundations of German trade were laid in the early Middle Ages. The adventurous and dangerous calling of the merchant in those days fostered in them a simple and humble piety which expressed itself in a diligent attendance on the services of the Church and in the foundation of benevolent institutions of every kind. It was because of such things that the merchant of those early days was not looked upon askance. It was believed that the merchant who engaged in active trade and visited distant markets was rendering a service to the community, and it was considered that he was entitled to some gain for the undoubted risks he was running. But this old-time sense of responsibility was gradually undermined by the lawyers, whose teaching regarding wealth corrupted the merchants; little by little the early monastic discipline was broken down and the merchants became avaricious and corrupt. The trading corporations which had originally come into existence as a means of affording mutual protection for their members in foreign parts, for the assurance of exchange, the settling of questions of justice, taxation, and coinage, and had recognized definite responsibilities towards society, began to think of nothing else except of how to secure advantages for themselves. They became corrupt monopolies which no longer observed Guild regulations. They kept up an artificial dearness in all necessary commodities, adulterated articles ˙of food and clothing, suppressed small industries, paid low rates of wages, and forced down the prices of agricultural produce to such an extent that all through the fifteenth century there were

---

[1] The word Hansa has the same significance as Guild, and was first used in England to designate certain commercial associations (Janssen, vol. ii. p. 47).

[2] See *Pictures of Old England*, by Dr. Reinhold Pauli, chapter entitled " The Hanseatic Steelyard in London."

frequent risings of the peasants against their tyranny and oppression. All these evils were allowed to grow unhindered because the traders played into the hands of the great personages either by lending them money or borrowing it from them to speculate with.

Now why did the nobility become a party to these iniquities ? The usual Socialist answer would be, of course, that all classes exist for the purposes of exploitation, and therefore it is but natural that they should join with the merchants to exploit the peasants. This, however, is not historically true. The Feudal class, as I showed in an earlier chapter, had a dual origin, and half of it at least, probably three-quarters of it, came into existence to perform a function. Their change from protectors of communal rights to exploiters was ultimately due to the corrupting influence of Roman Law, but immediately it was due to the desire to " keep their end up " in a competition of luxury and display as against the merchants. Many of the latter had grown to be richer than kings and emperors, and vanity had prompted them to give visible evidence of their great riches in the adoption of a higher and higher standard of living. Feasting and gambling became the order of the day, while they became very extravagant in dress. Men and women were alike in this respect, though the wives and daughters of the merchants were the most extravagant. Fashions changed constantly and took the form of dressing in the costumes of other countries, of big sleeves and little sleeves and all the other foibles with which we are familiar. Many people saw the dangers in these innovations, and attempts were made to put a boundary to the growth of extravagance by the enactments of sumptuary laws. In the year 1485 the Council of Ratisbon made the following rules with regard to dress which are interesting as showing the moderate demands of reformers. " The distinguished wives and daughters of burghers shall be allowed eight dresses, six long cloaks, three dancing dresses, and one plaited mantle having three sets of sleeves, of velvet, brocade and silk : two pearl hair bands not costing more than twelve florins, a tiara of gold and pearls worth five florins, not more than three veils costing eight florins each, a clasp not having more than one ounce of gold, silk fringes to their dresses, but not gold or pearl ; a pearl necklace not costing more than five florins, a pearl stomacher worth twelve florins, two rows of pearl round the sleeve at five florins per ounce, a gold chain and pendant worth fifteen florins and a necklace of twenty florins. Except for the engagement or wedding ring, none were permitted to cost more than twenty-four florins. Three or four rosaries were allowed, but they were not to cost more than ten florins ; sashes of silk and embroidery worth three florins."[1] Few people would say that there was anything very Puritanical about such a law, though no doubt it would seem so to many women of the day who were said to wear at one time clothing worth three or four hundred florins while they had in their wardrobes adornments costing more than three or four thousand florins.

I said that many people saw the dangers of such extravagance. Wimpheling, who was one of the most widely read authors of his day, writing on the great commercial prosperity of Germany, which he pointed out she owed to the untiring industry and the energy of her citizens, artisans as well as merchants, showed the reverse of the medal adding " wealth and prosperity are attended with great dangers, as we see exemplified ; they induce extravagance in dress, in banqueting, and what is still worse, they engender a desire for still more. This desire debases the mind of man, and degenerates into contempt of God, His Church and His Commandments. These evils are to be perceived in all classes ; luxury has crept in among the clergy, particularly among those who are of noble birth ; they have no real love for souls and they try to equal the rich merchants in their mode of living." [2]

Wimpheling saw, as men in all ages have seen, that luxury leads to social catastrophe. The peril arises from the fact that it is no longer the wise but the wealthy who set the social standards, and a kind of social compulsion is brought to bear upon others to live up to it whether they can afford to do so or not. As only the very rich can afford to go the pace, a point is soon reached when the need of

[1] Janssen, vol. ii. pp. 63–4.   [2] Ibid., vol. ii. p. 62.

money is very widely felt. When in Germany that point was reached, nobody wanted to do any really productive work, but everybody wanted to go into trade where money was to be made. Mercantile houses, shops and taverns multiplied inordinately, and complaints were everywhere made that there was no money but only debts and that all districts and towns were drained by usury. Then there happened in Germany what is happening to-day. Each class attempted to save itself from bankruptcy by transferring its burdens on to the shoulder of the class beneath it, and it was then there arose in Germany a bitter enmity between the propertied and unpropertied classes. While the working class were advancing towards pauperism, the general rancour and class hatred increased in intensity as the wealthy more and more indulged in ostentation and display.

Such was the social condition of Germany on the eve of the Peasants' War which broke out in the year 1524. It is apparent that had Luther and his followers never appeared on the scenes the spirit of discontent and class hatred which was growing everywhere and which had been fermenting since the beginning of the fifteenth century would have produced tumults and seditions in the towns and provinces of Germany. But it was the special condition of things brought about by the evangelical preaching of Luther which hastened the crisis and gave to the Peasants' War its characteristics of universality and inhuman atrocity. Immediately it was a movement to restore the old communal system of land-holding which had been destroyed by the inroads of Roman Law, and was of a purely agrarian character. The demands of the peasants were moderate and bore few of the traces of the intellectual and physical violence which marked its later course. They demanded the restoration of their old *Haingerichte* and other courts, the restoration of common lands and old rights, the abolition of new exactions of rents and services, and freedom of water, forest and pasture. The revolt commenced with local risings of peasants in the south-west. But when once it had started, it gathered momentum quickly. It was joined first by one and then by another revolutionary current until it united in one stream all elements of disaffection and threatened to inundate the whole of Germany. It convulsed almost every corner of the Empire from the Alps to the Baltic. Bavaria alone was unaffected, and this is attributed to the fact that the Bavarian Government had offered strenuous resistance to religious innovations.

As the rebellion extended its area, it assimilated ideas distinct from the agrarian grievances which had prompted it. The communist spirit was rampant in the cultivated town circles, and its effect was to give a religious aspect to the revolt. " The age of Christian liberty and brotherhood had come," it was said, " and one class ought to be as rich as another." It is not improbable that the religious element came to predominate because it offered a convenient banner under which sectional interests might unite. While the merchants blamed the clergy for the troubles, the nobility blamed the rich merchants, and so it came about that in the early stages of the revolt the rich middle class gave some support to the peasants. Waldshut and Memmingen were friendly, while Zurich, Strasburg, Nuremberg and Ulm rendered active assistance. Though the bulk of the insurgents were peasants, they received others into their ranks, and along with priests, barons and ex-officials there came men of criminal tendencies, who are always ready to join any revolutionary movement because of the prospect of loot it offers. As generally happens in popular risings, these baser elements got entirely out of hand and by their excesses brought odium upon the whole movement. They brought about the reaction in which the middle class element made common cause with the nobles in suppressing the revolt. Luther, who in the early days of the rising had written a pamphlet in which he deprecates the use of violence, though admitting that the demands of the peasants were just, now became genuinely terrified at the size of the revolt and wrote a second pamphlet in which he urged the princes to kill and slay the peasants without mercy. The princes took him at his word. After lasting two years the revolt was put down with unheard-of cruelty. According to the Emperor Charles V. a hundred thousand people were killed on both sides.

From whatever point of view Luther's action is examined it remains indefensible. His first pamphlet might be defended on the grounds that it was consistent with his former attitude inasmuch as he had always taught the efficacy of the word and had repudiated appeal to the sword. But there can be no excuse whatsoever for his second one, for he must have known that the tide had begun to turn when he wrote it and that the princes needed no urging to be merciless. From being a national hero Luther sank to the level of the leader of a sect, and a sect that depended for its existence on the support of political and financial interests. Henceforth Lutheran divines leaned upon the territorial princes and repaid their support with undue servility. When the princes began to suppress the monasteries and to seize the Church lands, Luther appears to have been taken entirely by surprise. He deplored and censured the selfishness of the princes, but he was powerless to prevent it. By condemning the rising, Luther had alienated for ever the sympathy of the peasants. His action settled the future of Protestantism by identifying it entirely with vested interests. It is as supplying a version of Christianity acceptable to capitalists that the subsequent history of Lutherism interests us and is to be studied.

The appeal of Luther against the authority of the Pope had been to the traditions of the Early Church. Those traditions were communist, and it was because the early Christians despised wealth that they could approach God without the intervention of a priestly mediator and without the likelihood of abusing the privilege. But when Luther alienated the peasants, he separated his gospel from any possible communist base and identified it with a class whose traditions were not only extremely individualistic but had an inordinate love of wealth, and this made a great difference. For the merchants and shopkeepers who now supported him were not the kind of people who could be relied upon to interpret Christian ideas to any but their own advantage. They came to support Luther, not because they had any intention of living up to the ideals of the early Christians, but because they resented supervision and for long had chafed under a religion which taught that the pursuit of wealth for wealth's sake was an ignoble and degrading thing, however far its priests fell short of its ideal. So they welcomed a gospel which removed such supervision and made them answerable only to their own consciences, from which they had little to fear. Luther might have denounced merchants as usurers and lawyers as robbers, but Luther's supporters were not thin-skinned people. They saw that the principle of an elective priesthood subject to the control of the laity was a valuable one for the ends they had in view and that organized on such a basis the priesthood would soon have to do their bidding. Hence it was that the Protestant Churches speedily came to accommodate morals to the practice of the rich. The Scriptures might be studied but not such parts as denounced the wealthy. On the contrary, immorality became synonymous with sexual immorality, swearing and drunkenness—vices to which they were not particularly prone—while avarice, the one sin towards which they were powerfully drawn, the new religion was careful not to forbid. The change of attitude towards usury is not the least of the triumphs of the Reformation. The history of the change is interesting, considering that Luther's first attitude towards the problems it presented was to revert to earlier and more rigid standards than were current in his day.

The Early Church had condemned usury in all forms absolutely as immoral. But this strict view was modified somewhat by later moralists and economists, who came to realize that to forbid the taking of interest, under all circumstances, was not expedient, inasmuch as it led to serious public inconvenience. Hence the question which agitated the minds of moralists and economists in the thirteenth, fourteenth, and fifteenth centuries was to determine what was and what was not legitimate. Starting from the principle of Aristotle that money itself cannot beget money, the Mediæval moralists were puzzled as to how to justify the taking of interest. They were agreed that to seek to increase wealth in order to live on the labour of others was wrong, and to this extent the issue with them was a purely moral issue. But, on the other hand, there was the question of public convenience, as in the case of travellers who would have to carry large sums of money about with them in the absence of bills of exchange, or the question of risk involved in a loan. To all such difficult and perplexing problems the Mediæval moralists addressed themselves, not for theoretical but for practical reasons. For as commerce tended to increase, it became urgent to hammer out some principle whereby the necessities of trade could be related to some definite moral standard.

To the end the problem evaded them. In principle all were against usury, but public convenience demanded that exception be made under certain circumstances. These exceptions grew and grew in number, but no sure principle was forthcoming, and I am left to wonder whether the failure of the Mediæval moralists and economists to find an answer to the problems which usury presented may not have been due to the fact that the problem is only partly a moral one. The difficulties in which they found themselves in their attempts to justify the taking of interest in certain cases in order that public convenience might not suffer arose because the function which the usurer performed in such cases was essentially a public one, and should have been undertaken by men in some corporate capacity, and not left to the initiative of individuals. The Franciscans appear to have come to some such conclusion, for they founded the *montes pietatis* or lending houses, which advanced loans to poor people either without interest or at a very low rate, and thus prevented many from falling into the hands of usurers.

In so far as the problem was a moral one, perhaps St. Antonino [1] gave such answers as were to be given. St. Antonino was an Archbishop of Florence in the fourteenth century, and was therefore well placed for one who wished for information. He was a representative man, and to be acquainted with him is to be acquainted with the thought of his generation, for he had read widely and formed judgments on many of the vexed economic problems of his day. What is more important, his judgments were of a very practical nature, for he was constantly referred to by the bankers and merchants of Florence to give decisions on delicate points affecting the morality of trade. This fact alone is worth recording, and should be of particular interest

[1] See *St. Antonino and Mediæval Economics*, by Bede Jarrett (Manresa Press).

to Marxians who believe that no other motive but exploitation has ever existed in trade, more especially when they learn that St. Antonino anticipated Marx himself in affirming that all value depends upon labour, whether of hand or head.

Though in the early days of the Reformation the reformers were even more opposed to any compromise with usury than the Catholic theologians, the influence of the Reformation brought a breach with Mediæval doctrine in the latter half of the sixteenth century. Calvin objected to the idea of regarding money as barren when it was possible to purchase with it property from which a revenue could be obtained. Calvin's attitude may therefore justly be regarded as the turning-point. It had certainly much influence in weakening the old repugnance towards usury. But Calvin did not allow the taking of interest under any circumstances. This is evident from Calvin's own words :—

" Although I do not visit usuries (payment for the use of money) with wholesale condemnation, I cannot give them my indiscriminate approbation, nor, indeed, do I approve that any one should make a business of money-lending. Usury for money may lawfully be taken only under the following conditions, and not otherwise." Among these conditions are " That usury should not be demanded from men in need ; nor is it lawful to force any man to pay usury who is oppressed by need or calamity," and " he who receives a loan on usury should make at least as much for himself by his labour and care as he obtains who gives the loan." [1]

" What Calvin feared took place. In after centuries Calvin's great authority was invoked for the wide proposition that to take reward for the loan of money was never sinful ; and a couple of his sentences were taken from their context and quoted without regard to the conditions by which they were limited. His carefully qualified approval of the claim for usury when it was made by one business man on another was wrested into an approval of every sort of contract concerning the loan of money." [2]

What happened with regard to usury happened also in respect to the institution of property. The communist

[1] *An Introduction to English Economic History and Theory,* by W. J. Ashley, part ii. p. 459. [2] Ibid., p. 460.

theory and practice of the Church had been abandoned and the Church came to recognize the institution of private property. It was to be regarded as an evil due to the Fall, and become a necessity, because of the presence of sin in the world. Still the Church did not regard possession as absolute but as conditional, and dependent upon the fulfilment of certain duties. Such as failed in their duties might be called upon to surrender it. They had no legal or moral claim. " Private property and common use "—the formula which Aquinas borrowed from Aristotle—became the official attitude of the Church. The Roman lawyers sought to reintroduce into society the old Pagan idea of absolute property rights in the interests of the territorial princes. But the Church would have none of it, and did all in its power to resist the encroachments of the Roman Code. The Reformation changed all this by removing opposition to the inroads of Roman Law. The rights of property, from being objective and dependent upon the fulfilment of duties, became subjective and absolute. Luther, who had denounced Roman Law, came to profess the most restrictive views on property ; while Melanchthon went much further, affirming that property existed by Divine right, and that to limit it in any way would be contrary to the teachings of Jesus Christ and the Apostles.

In the face of such evidence, it is impossible to maintain the popular notion that the Reformation was a triumph of democracy. So far from this being true, the Reformation was in reality the triumph of the State, landlordism and capitalism over the Church and the people, and this tendency was present from the very start. The story which has been so sedulously promoted in order to give the Reformation a democratic flavour, that Wycliffe, its " morning star," was one of the instigators of the Peasants' Revolt, is absolutely without any foundation in fact. Considering that John of Gaunt—whom the peasants associated with the lawyers as the cause of their oppression—was Wycliffe's best friend and protector, it is foolish to connect his name with the revolt. Moreover, there is nothing in Wycliffe's writings to suggest that he favoured insurrection. Wycliffe desired to maintain the system of the State precisely as it then was, while he regarded the growing power of the Church as the menace, and it was to that he was opposed. On the contrary, it was the Friars who organized the revolt. If not officially, at any rate, unofficially ; for not a few of them actually took part in the revolt, leading some of the bands of peasants who marched to London. Anyway, suspicion fell upon them, and it may have been one of the reasons why, when the Reformation burst forth, the monasteries were suppressed.

CHAPTER XI

THE SUPPRESSION OF THE ENGLISH
MONASTERIES

THE great difference between the course of the Reformation
in England and in Germany is to be found in the fact that
whereas in Germany the Reformation was primarily a religious
and popular movement with certain political and economic
complications or consequences, in England the religious
movement was artificially promoted to bolster up the
political and economic changes initiated entirely by the
Crown. For though Wycliffe's gospel had been warmly
espoused on the Continent by Huss, Jerome and Luther,
his influence in England appears to have come to an end
with the suppression of the Lollards in the reign of
Richard II, and at the time when Henry VIII began to
suppress the monasteries there was not in existence any
popular movement demanding change. It is significant
that no serious change was made in the doctrine, worship
or ceremonials of the Church until sixteen years after
Henry VIII had repudiated Papal authority. Though Henry
at one time had given the Protestant Princes of Germany
great hopes of a religious union against both Pope and Emperor, nothing came of it. It was clearly a piece of bluff
intended to ward off a possible attack by the Emperor. For
Henry had no sympathy with Protestantism. Not only
had he opposed it and received from the Pope as a reward
for a book he had written in defence of the Catholic Faith
the title of " Defender of the Faith " (a title which English
sovereigns still use, it being popularly supposed that the
Faith referred to is. Protestantism and not Catholicism,
as is actually the case) but he had actually gone so far as
to burn as heretics men who preached Protestant doctrine.

However much room there may be for differences of opinion as to the motives which led Pope Clement VII to refuse to sanction the divorce of Henry VIII from Catherine of Arragon, there can be no doubt whatsoever that the repudiation of Papal authority by Henry which prepared the way for the Reformation in England and immediately led to the suppression of the monasteries was due to the fact that Henry entertained a passionate desire to marry Anne Boleyn and was determined that nothing should stand in his way. As to why he did so desire, there is again a difference of opinion. The most generous explanation is that Henry wanted a son, and remembering that the Wars of the Roses had resulted in the death of all possible male successors to the throne, and that while he had three sons and two daughters by Catherine only one daughter had survived, it was not an altogether unnatural desire. But such an explanation is difficult to reconcile with the facts as we know them. It might be argued that the desire for a son impelled Henry to seek a divorce if his matrimonial adventures had come to an end when he married Anne Boleyn, but the evidence in this case is strong that lust was his ruling passion, for when within a twelvemonth he had grown tired of her he said he had been induced to marry her by witchcraft, which strongly suggests he was at the mercy of his lusts. The fact that Henry's life became a succession of marriages, divorces and beheadings suggests that he was possessed of a mania which is equally difficult to reconcile with the natural desire for a son or the mere pursuit of lust. It should not be forgotten, moreover, that when he married Jane Seymour he procured a clause in the Succession Act enabling him in the event of failure of issue to dispose of the Crown by will ; it being understood at the time that this concession was made in favour of his illegitimate son the Duke of Richmond, who died shortly afterwards. If the only object of Henry's marriages was to secure the succession it may be asked why, if it was possible for him to secure this concession after he married Jane Seymour, he could not have done it while he was married to Catherine of Arragon. The grounds on which he sought to obtain a divorce from her, that he feared he had been living in sin with her because she had been formally married to his brother Prince Arthur, who had died before the marriage was consummated, will scarcely acquit a man whose subsequent life proved him to be indifferent to sin.

Whatever the truth may be as to the secret motives of Henry, there can be no doubt whatsoever as to the consequences of his actions, for the whole subsequent history of England turns on his marriage with Anne Boleyn. Having determined to marry her, and after six fruitless years being unable to persuade the Pope to take any steps towards the granting of a divorce, he resolved to overthrow the power of the Pope in England by making himself the head of the English Church. In this task he was aided and abetted by the perfidious and cold-blooded Thomas Cranmer, whom he immediately afterwards made Archbishop of Canterbury, and who speedily granted Henry the divorce he desired. By becoming a party to this disreputable business Cranmer put himself entirely into Henry's power and henceforth had to do his bidding, to perish at last amid those flames which he himself had been the chief means of kindling. All who refused to acknowledge the king's supremacy in spiritual affairs Henry mercilessly sacrificed. Sir Thomas More and John Fisher, Bishop of Rochester, with many others were executed for refusing. The executions filled the world with horror both at home and abroad. The Emperor Charles V is said to have declared that he would rather have lost the best city in his dominions than such a councillor as Sir Thomas More. Yet in spite of all Henry won through. His success is to be attributed in the first place to the fact that he found himself in an extraordinary strong position owing to the centralizing process which had been going on ever since the reign of Henry II and had concentrated in his hands more powers than any other king of England enjoyed either before or since, and in the next to the fact that Henry was a man of remarkable ability while he was entirely unscrupulous. The old nobility, who alone might have offered resistance to his policy, had been for the most part destroyed in the Wars of the Roses, while such as were left were no match for him in intelligence. They were superseded in the end by a new nobility which Henry raised out of the commercial middle class—a class of sycophants who enriched themselves by continual peculation. It was thus that covetousness and fraud came to reign in high places, and the tradition was established which identified the governing class with exploitation.

It is possible that the monasteries would not have been suppressed had not resistance to Henry been offered by the Franciscans who maintained the Pope's authority. Henry now found himself in the position of having either to abandon his policy of making himself supreme in spiritual affairs or of suppressing the whole Order, which he did not hesitate to do. It now became apparent that sweeping confiscations of monastic lands were to be made. The princes of Germany had shown him the way, and he was not slow to learn their lesson. Doubtless many of Henry's councillors and courtiers who were hoping to share in the plunder were by no means averse to such measures, for the Reformation could not have proceeded apart from the concurrence of Parliament. But this could not be said of Parliament as a whole. For the Act of 1536, which transferred the property of the smaller monasteries, three hundred and seventy-six in number, to the King and his heirs, stuck long in the Lower House and was not passed until Henry threatened to have some of their heads.

The agent to whom Henry entrusted the work of suppressing the monasteries was Thomas Cromwell. He had been an underling in the service of Cardinal Wolsey. After a roving youth spent in Italy and elsewhere he had risen by his wits, recommending himself to Henry by his sycophancy and by his treachery to his old master. He maintained his position by utter obsequiousness, and there was no kind of cruelty or tyranny of which he declined to be the agent. Yet he was a man of cultivated tastes, with a wide acquaintance of Italian literature. He had seen Machiavelli's great work in manuscript, and from it had derived the principles that guided him throughout his infamous career. He was emphatically a man of the Renaissance ; that strange combination of taste and rascality which it was so successful in producing. Henry made him a peer, and appointed him Royal Viceregent and Vicar-General. In this capacity he

11

took first place in all meetings of the clergy, sitting even before the Archbishop of Canterbury. The procedure adopted in the suppressions was first to set on foot a visitation of the monasteries. In this work Cromwell was assisted by deputies who were as villainous as himself. They prepared reports full of false accusations in order to find pretences for confiscating monastic property. They menaced those who objected with charges of high treason. Subsequent visitors appointed by Henry from among the country gentry sent in formal reports distinctly contradicting many of the facts alleged by Cromwell's agents. But such protests were of no avail. Henry was out for plunder, and as Cobbett rightly observes in this connection, "when men have power to commit and are resolved to commit acts of injustice, they are never at a loss for pretences."[1] The monastic orders were never heard in their defence. There was no charge against any particular monastery or convent ; the charges were loose and general, and levelled against all whose revenues did not exceed a certain sum. "This alone," observes Cobbett, " was sufficient to show that the charges were false ; for who will believe that the alleged wickedness extended to all whose revenues did not exceed a certain sum, and that when those revenues got above that point the wickedness stopped ? "[2]

It is clear that the reason for stopping the confiscations at the point where the revenues did not exceed a certain sum was that the public had to be brought into line before any seizure of the great monasteries could be safely attempted. The weak were first attacked, but means were soon found for attacking the remainder. Great promises were held out that the King, when in possession of these estates, would never more want taxes from the people. " Henry employed preachers and ministers who went about to preach and persuade the people that he could employ the ecclesiastical revenues in hospitals, colleges and other foundations for the public good, which would be a much better use than that they should support lazy and useless monks."[3] It is

---

[1] *A History of the Protestant Reformation*, by William Cobbett, p. 110.
[2] Ibid., p. 126.
[3] Letter written in 1540 by Marillac, the French Ambassador.

possible, of course, that Henry may have thought that he would be able to fulfil these promises; but he soon found out that he would not be able to keep the plunder for himself, and that the nobles and gentry could only be persuaded to allow him to continue his dastardly work on condition that he agreed to share the spoil with them. They so beset him that he had not a moment's peace. After four years he found himself no better off than he was before he confiscated a single convent. " When complaining to Cromwell of the rapacity of the applicants for grants he exclaimed : " By Our Lady ! the cormorants, when they have got the garbage, will devour the dish." Cromwell reminded him that there was much more yet to come. " Tut, man," said the King, " my whole realm would not staunch their maws." [1]   And thus it was that from confiscating the property of the smaller monasteries he went on to seize that of the larger ones, for there was no stopping half-way once he had begun. Where opposition was encountered, Cromwell and his ruffian visitors procured the murder of the parties under pretence of their having committed high treason. Here and there the people rose in rebellion against the devastations. But the local outbreaks came to nothing, since as nearly every one of any consequence was sharing in the plunder the people were deprived of their natural leaders.

During the Middle Ages, England had been the most prosperous and happiest country in Europe, perhaps the happiest country at any time in history. These monasteries were wealthy and full of things of gold and silver ; and society was so well ordered that these things remained untouched, though there was no standing army or police. But Cromwell and his ruffians stripped them bare of all such things. The only parallel which history affords of such a rich harvest of plunder is that of the conquest of Peru, during which Cortes and Pizarro stripped the temples bare of their gold and silver linings.

" The ruffians of Cromwell entered the convents ; they tore down the altars to get away the gold and silver, ransacked the chests and drawers of the monks and nuns, tore off the covers of the books that were ornamented with

[1] Cobbett, p. 127.

the precious metals.   These books were all in manuscript.
Single books that had taken half a long lifetime to compose
and to copy out fair ;   whole libraries, the getting of which
together had taken ages and ages and had cost immense sums
of money, were scattered abroad by these hellish ruffians
when they had robbed the covers of their rich ornaments.
The ready money in the convents, down to the last shilling,
was seized." [1]

Among the libraries so destroyed was that of St. Albans
Abbey, which was the greatest library in England.   But the
destruction of libraries at the Reformation was not confined
to those of the monasteries.   The original Guildhall Library,
founded by Whittington and Carpenter, was destroyed,
as were also the Library at St. Paul's Cathedral and the
predecessor of the Bodleian Library at Oxford.   About
the year 1440, Humphrey, Duke of Gloucester, "gave to
the University of Oxford a library containing 600 volumes,
only 120 of which were valued at more than a hundred thousand pounds.   These books are called *Novi Tractatus*, or
New Treatises, in the University register, and said to be
admirandi apparatus.   They were the most splendid and
costly copies that could be procured, finely written on
vellum, and elegantly embellished with miniatures and
illuminations.   Among the rest was a translation into French
of Ovid's *Metamorphoses*.   Only a single specimen of these
valuable volumes was suffered to remain ;   it is a beautiful
MS. in folio of Valerius Maximus, enriched with the most
elegant decorations, and written in Duke Humphrey's age,
evidently with a design of being placed in this sumptuous
collection.   All the rest of the books, which, like this, being
highly ornamented, looked like missals, and conveyed ideas
of Popish superstition, were destroyed or removed by the
pious visitors of the University in the reign of Edward
VI, whose zeal was only equalled by their avarice." [2]   Anything which was decorated apparently ranked then as
Popish superstition, which was a convenient cloak for the
pursuit of plunder.

[1] Cobbett, p. 130.
[2] *The History of English Poetry*; by Thomas Wharton, pp. 344–5, 1778
edition.

After the monasteries were plundered, sacked and gutted, they were rased to the ground, and in most cases gunpowder was employed in order to get through the job quickly. For in granting these estates, it was in most cases stipulated that they should be destroyed. The reason may be easily understood. These wonderful Gothic buildings could not be allowed to stand, for their continued existence would have been a constant reminder to the people that these estates had been plundered, while their destruction deprived them of all hope of the old order ever being restored. The loss of these splendid buildings, where formerly rich and poor received hospitality on their travels, brought a feeling of sadness to the countryside, particularly in solitary and mountainous districts—a sadness which was not diminished when the manor-houses of Elizabeth and James I were built out of their ruins. The only comfort there is in this terrible story is the knowledge that Cromwell, after he had plundered, pillaged and devastated England, was sent to the block by Henry, who had then no further use for him. But Henry, the chief instigator of these crimes, got off scot-free.

It has often been urged that the monastic orders could not have occupied the same place in the popular affections as they had done at an earlier date, or Henry would not have found it possible to suppress them. The answer is that on a straight issue they could never have been suppressed. The people would everywhere have risen in their defence. But Henry was too cunning to create such an issue. He allowed important people to share in the plunder, disarmed opposition by promises of putting their funds to a better use, and quelled rebellions by making promises that he had never any intention of fulfilling. Thus by trickery he prevented united action being taken against him. The suppression of the monasteries was for the people a loss of the first magnitude, as the following interesting picture of monastic estates at the time bears witness :—

" There was no person that came to them heavy or sad for any cause that went away comfortless ; they never revenged them of any injury, but were content to forgive it freely upon submission, and if the price of corn had begun

to start up in the market they made thereunto with wain
load of corn, and sold it under the market to poor people,
to the end to bring down the price thereof. If the highways,
bridges, or causeways were tedious to the passengers that
sought their living by their travel, their great help lacked
not towards the repairing and amending thereof—yea, often-
times they amended them on their own proper charges.

  "If any poor householder lacked seed to sow his land,
or bread, corn, or malt before harvest, and came to a monastery either of men or women, he should not have gone
away without help ; for he should have had it until harvest,
that he might easily have paid it again. Yea, if he had
made his moan for an ox, horse, or cow, he might have had
it upon his credit, and such was the good conscience of the
borrowers in those days that the thing borrowed needed
not to have been asked at the day of payment.

  " They never raised their rent, or took any income or
garsomes (fines) of their tenants, nor ever broke in or
improved any commons, although the most part and the
greatest waste grounds belonged to their possessions.

  " If any poor people had made their moan at the day
of marriage to any abbey, they should have had money
given to their great help.   And thus all sorts of people
were helped and succoured by abbeys ; yea, happy was
that person that was tenant to an abbey, for it was a rare
thing to hear that any tenant was removed by taking his
farm over his head, nor he was not afraid of any re-entry
for non-payment of rent, if necessity drove him thereonto.
And thus they fulfilled the works of charity in all the country
round about them, to the good example of all lay persons
that now have taken forth other lessons, that is, *nunc
tempus alios postulat mores.*" [1]

  When these estates passed into the hands of the landlords they speedily raised the rents and enclosed the commons.
In other cases the peasantry were simply turned out of their
holdings in order that sheep-farming might be substituted

---

[1] Cole MSS. (British Museum), XII, fol. 5, " The Fall of Religious
Houses." The author resided near Roche Abbey in Yorkshire, and had
bought some goods sold out of a church by Edward's commission. (Quoted
from Cunningham, pp. 472–3.)

for tillage. " It seems," observes Cunningham, " that the lords had the peasantry entirely in their own power, and that, since they were technically liable for incidents of the nominal servitude, into which they had returned since the failure of 1381, their lands were forfeited in law if not in equity." [1] It may be said that these changes created the problem of poverty. For though there was some poverty in the Middle Ages, the monasteries must on the whole have relieved it, for one of the charges brought against them is that they were too indiscriminate in their charity and that many beggars had become dependent on them. It is not necessary to deny the truth of such statements, but to point out that if the monasteries supported beggars they were created by the landlords who, with the help of the Roman lawyers, had dispossessed the peasants and turned them adrift because sheep-farming was more profitable than tillage. Are the monasteries to be condemned for having succoured those whom the landlords had rendered homeless ? After the suppression, the poor were deprived at one fell swoop of alms, shelter and schooling. The consequence was that great numbers, left entirely destitute of the means of existence, took to begging and thieving. Henry VIII is said to have put 72,000 thieves to death. Elizabeth complained bitterly that she could not get the laws enforced against them. " Such was the degree of beggary, of vagabondage, and of thievishness and robbery, that she resorted particularly in London and its neighbourhood to martial law." But it was all of no avail. The people had been rendered destitute, and there were only two possible policies for dealing with them if economic injustices were to be maintained—extermination or legal pauperism. Shrinking from the former, resort at last was made to the latter, and some general permanent and solid provision was made for them. In the forty-third year of her reign there was passed the measure which we know to-day as the Elizabethan Poor Law, from which our Poor Law derives.

It was not only in the realm of charity and hospitality that the monasteries were missed. It was customary for them to maintain highways and dykes, to build bridges

[1] Cunningham, p. 475.

and seawalls and other such things for the commonwealth. Many arts that had been brought to a high state of perfection in the monasteries were paralysed or migrated to the towns. Sculpture, embroidery, clock-making and bell-founding were almost entirely monastic arts. The monks had been the chroniclers and transcribers of manuscripts in the Middle Ages, and were among the first to set up printing presses. It is true that monasticism had for long been on the decline, but the monasteries had come to perform all kinds of functions which were no part of their original purpose. The consequence was that their violent suppression disorganized the social and economic life in the community in many directions. Their disappearance left a gap in the educational system of the country which the reforms of the nineteenth century have attempted in vain to fill, for the education of the people was largely in the hands of the monastic establishments ; what was not in their hands was in those of the chantry priests, who were generally the local schoolmasters. So it came about that when in the reign of Edward VI the chantries were also suppressed, all provision for education practically came to an end. The reason why so many educational endowments date from the reign of Edward VI is not to be found in the surmise that as a consequence of the Revival of Learning and the Reformation a sudden desire for enlightenment came over society, but to the fact that when the monasteries were suppressed certain people, feeling the gap which had been made in society, left money for such foundations. The destruction of the monastic system of elementary education reacted to undermine the position of the universities, which nearly disappeared ; for the monasteries not only provided probationers for them but maintained many there to complete their education. In the thirteenth century, it is said, there were 30,000[1] students at Oxford, but to such an extent did university studies decay that " in the six years from 1542 to 1548 only 191 students were admitted bachelor of arts at Cambridge and only 173 at Oxford."[2]   When the revival of the

---

[1] This number is given in Dr. Reinhold Pauli's *Pictures of Old England.* Perhaps 3,000 would be nearer the truth.

[2] *Cambridge Modern History,* vol. ii. p. 468.

universities did take place, their character was completely changed. They were no longer the democratic institutions of the Middle Ages, but finishing-schools for the rich.

Educationalists might do worse than study the Mediæval and monastic system of education, for it obviated one of the most glaring defects of the present system—the gulf between elementary and higher education. This it did by a system of local autonomy, which made every elementary school part of an institution which was primarily interested in the pursuit of learning. In consequence of this there were no elementary school teachers existing as a class apart, cut off from the main currents of intellectual life, whose individuality was strangled by the requirements of a code. On the contrary, the whole system was free and humane, while it was organic from the top to the bottom ; and this was possible because the Mediævalists were not interested in an abstraction called " education," but in certain definite things which they were anxious to teach. The problem of improvising machinery is so simple when you know what you want it to do, and so perplexing when you don't.

CHAPTER XII

THE REFORMATION IN ENGLAND

THOUGH as an explanation of the whole course of history the materialist conception is demonstrably false—since, among other things, it fails to offer any explanation why capitalism, after dominating Pagan civilization, was brought under control during the Mediæval period—it becomes more plausible from the Reformation onwards when the material factor increasingly tends to determine social development. Before the Reformation, landlordism and capitalism had, owing to the sinister influence of Roman Law, got a foothold in society ; but landlords and capitalists did not have things entirely their own way, for the Church and Crown were still sufficiently powerful to exercise a restraining influence. But after the suppression of the monasteries, the old order received a blow from which it never recovered. The monastic lands, at least a fifth of the wealth of the country, were transferred to the great landowners, and this transference tipped the scale entirely in their favour as against the peasantry.[1] Landlordism and capitalism were now triumphant, and with the change the economic equilibrium of society was upset. This in turn reacted to upset the religious and political equilibrium. The history of English politics from now onwards is to be interpreted in the light of these central facts. Henceforth, policy wavers between efforts to restore the equilibrium of society by seeking a return to the past—the direction in which social salvation was to be found and " progress " or the maintenance of vested interests—the policy that was eventually adopted.

[1] *The Servile State*, by Hilaire Belloc, p. 69. Cunningham gives the monastic lands as being only one-fifteenth ; whichever estimate is true, the consequences were the same.

With the accession of Edward VI the absolutism of Henry was relaxed. "The late king was doomed to the usual fate of despotic monarchs after their death; the very men who during his life had been the most obsequious ministers of his will, were now the first to overturn his favourite projects."[1] Though Henry had separated the English Church from Rome and had suppressed the monasteries, he had not espoused the cause of Protestantism. Whether this was from conscientious reasons, or because in his early years having written a book in defence of the Catholic Faith, that obstinacy and pride which were such very strong features in his character prevented him from appearing to retract, must be a matter of opinion. But all obstacles in the path of the spread of the Protestant Faith were removed by his death. Edward VI was a minor, and entirely in the hands of his ministers, chief among whom was the Duke of Somerset, his Protector. Somerset was a moderate man who disliked coercion and sought to govern on a basis of civil liberty and religious toleration. The first Parliament that he summoned effected a complete revolution in the spirit of the laws. The statute which at the close of Henry's reign had given the force of law to Royal proclamations was repealed. Nearly all the treasons created since 1352 were swept away, many of the felonies, the Act of Six Articles by which Henry had sought to enforce religious unity, the laws against heresy, all the prohibitions against printing the Scriptures in English, against reading, preaching, teaching or expounding the Scriptures were erased from the statute-book. The immediate consequence of it all was that the tongues of the divines were loosed and the land was filled with a Babel. Heretics and sectarians, Lutherans, Calvinists and Zwinglians flocked to England, which became one great scene of religious disputation with London as its centre, few men knowing what or what not to believe. The more trenchantly a preacher denounced the old doctrines, the greater were the crowds that gathered to hear him. The New Learning carried all before it in the large cities. This was not because the majority of the nation desired religious change, but because the Catholic population who had been

[1] Lingard's *History of England*, vol. v. p. 248.

accustomed to leave questions of theology to be settled by
the priests found themselves at a tremendous disadvantage
when discussion on religious questions had descended to
the streets. Moreover, the issues were new, and few Catholics
knew how to answer the innovators ; and indeed this is
never quite easy. We know to-day how long it often takes
to find a satisfactory answer to some heresy on social questions.
We often know a thing is wrong and yet can't find an answer
then and there. The Catholics were at this disadvantage
at the first onslaught. New interpretations of the Scriptures
came upon them like a flood, and they were no match for the
zeal and conviction of their opponents. The only answer
they had for men who affirmed the right of private judgment
was a demand for respect for the authority of the Church,
and this was for them a very weak defence in an age when
the Church had suffered so many rude shocks.

The Catholics became very embittered. They blamed
Somerset's leniency and toleration for the Babel of opinion,
and were ready to support any movement to secure his
overthrow. The plunderers, on the contrary, had no objection
to such disputation. Firstly, because it diverted attention
from them and their doings ; and secondly, because if it went
far enough it would make reunion with Rome impossible,
which was to their liking. For, they reasoned, if they were
to keep possession of their stolen property England must
be separated from Rome irrevocably. Hence the cry of
" No Popery " which figures so much in all accounts of the
Reformation. It was the watchword of the plunderers, since
popery for them meant restitution.

But while the plunderers were in accord with Somerset's
policy of religious toleration, they strongly objected to his
attitude towards the agrarian troubles that were brewing.
Though he himself was one of the greatest of the plunderers,
having managed to get into his possession over two hundred
manors, he nevertheless did not stand in with the others
in their refusal of any justice to the peasants. He was in
fact a curious mixture of the spirit of the old and the new
orders. While apparently he thought it right to get hold
of as much property as he could lay his hands on, for his
rapacity knew no bounds, on the other hand he had a firm

conviction that the ownership of property carried with it certain responsibilities, and he actually got a private Act of Parliament passed to give his tenants security of their tenure. It was his known sympathy with the cause of the peasants that brought the agrarian crisis to a head, giving rise to the Peasants' Revolt of 1549 that led to his fall.

Though the agrarian problem had been intensified by the suppression of the monasteries, it did not begin with it but dates from the thirteenth century when the Roman lawyers transformed the feudal lord, who was a functionary administering communal land, into a landlord whose possession of the land was absolute. From that time onwards land began to be bought and sold, and the peasants lost that practical security which they had enjoyed under the old Feudal System. The extension of commerce gave rise to a moneyed class which established itself on the land and gradually gained admission into governing circles. To these new landlords the feudal idea of reciprocal rights and duties was altogether foreign. They had bought the land, they regarded it primarily as an investment, and sought to apply to it the same principles that they had practised in trade, making it yield the utmost possible return for their capital. It was not long before they discovered that owing to the high price of English wool, for which there was a great market in the Netherlands, the land could be made to yield much more if employed for sheep-farming instead of tillage. It is said that by effecting this change a landlord could double his income. But sheep-farming required larger holdings and less labour. Hence it became the custom for these new landlords to exercise their manorial rights to the full by enclosing the common lands; to buy up several holdings and turn them into one. The old homesteads were left to decay, and their former tenants became either vagabonds or landless labourers.[1] Another means whereby these

---

[1] " If economic causes made a new system of farming profitable, it is not the less true that legal causes decided by whom the profits should be enjoyed. We have already pointed out that many customary tenants practised sheep-farming upon a considerable scale, and it is not easy to discover any economic reason why the cheap wool required for the development of cloth manufacturing industry should not have been supplied by the very peasants in whose cottages it was carded and spun and woven. The

new landlords sought to get greater return for their capital was to raise the rents of their tenants. This departure from custom and tradition was a thing the old feudal lords would never have thought of doing, and it was felt to be a stab in the back. The consequence of all these innovations was to pauperize a large section of the community. Great numbers became dependents of the monasteries which had come to the rescue of these homeless men ; when the monasteries were suppressed they were left entirely destitute. The new proprietors of the Church lands accepted no responsibility for them. In consequence they wandered about begging and stealing, and in other ways became a source of danger to the rest of the community.

The growth of this evil had not been allowed to pass unnoticed. Before the monasteries were suppressed Sir Thomas More had written about the evils following upon enclosures and sheep-farming. "Sheep are eating men," a phrase which he used in his *Utopia*, has become classical. In 1517 Cardinal Wolsey made vigorous efforts to stop enclosures, but without success. The cause of the peasants had also been advocated by others in high places during the reign of Henry VIII, but he was too busy getting himself divorced to trouble about the condition of the peasants; while the suppression of the monasteries, to which in the end he found himself committed if he was to be acknowledged as the head of the Church in England, not only enormously increased the evil but the resistance which he encountered from the old order led him to the creation of a new aristocracy, which differed from the old one to the extent that it did not arise to exercise a public function but to act as an instrument of oppression, and as such it identified the idea of government with oppression. It is not true, as Marxians maintain, that the history of all hitherto existing society has been the

decisive factor, this method of meeting the new situation created by the spread of pasture farming, was the fact that the tenure of the vast majority of small cultivators left them free to be squeezed out by exorbitant fines, and to be evicted when the lives for which most of them held their copies came to an end. It was their misfortune that the protection given by the courts to copyholders did not extend to more than the enforcement of existing manorial customs " (*The Agrarian Problem in the Sixteenth Century*, by R. H. Tawney, p. 407).

history of class struggles. It was not true of the Middle Ages until the revival of Roman Law began to corrupt Mediæval society, but it became entirely true after Henry VIII created his plunder-loving aristocracy. But while this generalization applies to the governing class as a whole, there have at all times been a number of highly placed men who were exceptions to this rule and sided with the people. It is of vital importance to any proper understanding of the social problem that this fact should be recognized, for the Marxian interpretation of history not only operates to unite the enemy and to bring division into the reformers' camp, but by creating a prejudice against normal forms of social organizations tends to thwart all efforts to reconstruct society on a democratic basis by diverting the energies of the people into false channels.

Somerset, as we saw, was one of these men. His known sympathy with the peasants brought the question to the front. He had denounced the misdeeds of this new aristocracy with more warmth than prudence, and a party which came to be known as the " Commonwealth's men." had come into existence. *Discourses on the Commonweal* by John Hales, its most active and earnest member, is one of the most informing documents of the age. The failure of Parliament to give satisfaction gave rise to agrarian disturbances in Hertfordshire in the spring of 1548. The Protector took advantage of the occasion to appoint a commission to enquire into enclosures. Though Hales and other reformers were members of it, the opposition of the new aristocracy was such as to reduce it to impotence. Hales had obtained from the Protector a general pardon for those who had made illegal enclosures presented by the commission. But this did not lessen the determination of their opposition. They set themselves resolutely to defeat its ends. They packed the juries with their own servants and threatened to evict any tenants who gave evidence against them. They even went so far as to have them indicted at the assizes. The consequence of such high-handed procedure was that in the spring of 1549 there was a general uprising of the peasantry. Commencing in Somersetshire, it spread to Cornwall and Devonshire, to Wiltshire, Gloucestershire, Dorsetshire, Hamp-

shire, Oxfordshire, Buckinghamshire, Surrey, Norfolk and
Suffolk. In the west changes of religion were made the
pretext of the rising. But in Norfolk no such pretext was
made. The rebels demanded satisfaction for their economic
grievances. For a time it was feared that the revolt might
develop into a general rising like the Peasants' War in Germany, and the new aristocracy was genuinely alarmed. In
general, however, the rebels acted without concert and without
leaders ; but in the counties of Devon and Cornwall, and
Norfolk and Suffolk, the risings assumed a more threatening
aspect. Armies were formed which threatened the Government and would probably have succeeded, but for the fact
that England was at the time at war with France, and the
Government was able to use Italian, Spanish and German
mercenaries which had been raised for service in France.
The rebels were defeated in the west by Lord Russell and in
the east by the Earl of Warwick. The Protector found
himself in an awkward position. His sympathy with the
insurgents had weakened his action, while his readiness to
screen and pardon offenders exasperated his colleagues.
It brought to a head the dissatisfaction with his policy.
He was charged with stirring up class hatred and with
unwillingness to take drastic action against the insurgents,
and the Catholics united with the plunderers to overthrow
him. The movement was successful, and the Earl of Warwick,
who had now become the idol of the new aristocracy, became
Protector, with the title of the Duke of Northumberland.

Reaction now set in. The masses had risen against the
classes, and the classes resolved to retaliate. " Parliament
met in a spirit of exasperation and revenge, and it went back
not only upon the radical proposals of Somerset, but also
upon the whole tenor of Tudor land legislation. Enclosures
had been forbidden again and again ; they were now expressly
declared to be legal ; and Parliament enacted that lords of
the manor might ' approve themselves of their wastes, woods,
and pastures notwithstanding the gainsaying and contradiction of their tenants.' In order that the process might
be without let or hindrance it was made treason for forty,
and felony for twelve, persons to meet for the purpose of
breaking down any enclosure or enforcing any right of way ;

to summon such an assembly or incite to such an act was also felony ; and any copyholder refusing to help in repressing it forfeited his copyhold for life. The same penalty was attached to hunting in any enclosure and to assembling with the object of abating rents or the price of corn ; but the prohibition against capitalists conspiring to raise prices was repealed, and so were the taxes which Somerset had imposed on sheep and woollen cloths." [1]

That the reaction should have assumed this form appears to have taken the Catholics entirely by surprise. They had assisted the plunderers to overthrow Somerset, not because they were unsympathetic to the cause of the peasants but because of the encouragement he had given to heretics and sectarians, and with the idea, apparently, that his overthrow would be followed by a return to the Catholic worship. What they failed entirely to understand was that Protestantism was acceptable to the new aristocracy because it made their plunder secure. They failed to perceive that capitalism was a much more deadly enemy than Protestantism of the Catholic Faith, and that finally Protestantism was nothing less than capitalism camouflaged. That they should have failed to perceive this to the extent of being willing to support the plunderers to overthrow Somerset, proves conclusively not only that they misgauged the temper of the new aristocracy but that they had themselves lost sight of the communal basis of Christianity. It is, I believe, to this fact that the defeat of the Catholic Church at the Reformation is finally to be attributed, for it led it into every imaginable political error. If the Church had kept the communal aim of Christianity clearly to the forefront of its mind, it would have reverted to the policy which it pursued in the early Middle Ages of supporting the peasants against the secular authorities. It was because the Church did this that it was feared by the secular powers, and it remained powerful so long as this aim was steadily kept in view. But when at a later date and as a consequence of the revival of Roman Law the secular powers became more powerful, the Church made the fatal mistake of seeking to combat the growing spirit of materialism, not by a reaffirmation of the communal basis of Chris-

[1] *Cambridge Modern History*, vol. ii. p. 497.

tianity, but by an ever-increasing insistence upon the
principle of authority, of obedience to the Church. And this
proved to be fatal by confusing the issues. For the real
issue was finally not whether the Church or the State was
to be uppermost, but whether the communal basis of society
was to be maintained. Yet, strange to say, though this was
the real issue at the back of all the quarrels between Church
and State, it never emerged into the light of day. The quarrel
had begun in the form of a challenge of the power of the
Pope by the Emperor, and so it remained to the end. The
real issue was lost sight of, and because it was lost sight of
the Church lost the power of popular appeal, and so finally
was reduced to attempts to maintain its position by intrigue.
Because the Church gave emphasis to the authoritarian
rather than the communal aspect of Christianity it sought
after the Reformation to prop itself up by alliance with the
temporal powers, and in order to secure such alliances found
itself obliged to support the exploiters against the peasants,
and so it came about that while the Church succeeded in
reforming itself at the counter-Reformation it still finds
it difficult to live down the suspicions associated with this
policy. So often to appearances has it sided with capitalism
that democrats fear that to submit to the authority of the
Church would be to submit to capitalism. The alliance of
the Roman Church with capitalism in Spain to-day is evidence
that this fear is not altogether unfounded. Socialists who
have no prejudice against Catholicism as such, who realize
that during the Middle Ages it was the sustainer of the
communal life, do feel that though the Church may sympathize
with the workers it must remain powerless to help them so
long as it is anxious to secure the support of the temporal
powers, for under such circumstances when vital issues are
at stake the Church becomes a house divided against itself.
" He that would save his life must lose it " is a moral principle that has a lesson for the Church as much as for the
individual.

    To return to our subject. It was not long before the
Catholics were made to suffer for their mistaken policy.
The motto of the plunderers was : Divide and conquer.
Having with the assistance of the Catholics succeeded in

defeating the peasantry, the plunderers then began to persecute the Catholics. The first Act of Uniformity, passed
early in Edward's reign, was now enforced against clerical
offenders. Its object had been to secure uniformity in
Church services by means of a compromise, which all might
be persuaded or compelled to observe. A little later a
second Act of Uniformity was passed which extended the
scope of religious persecution by imposing penalties for
recusancy upon laymen. They were required to attend
Common Prayer on Sundays and holidays. If they were
absent they were to be subject to ecclesiastical censures
and excommunication ; if they attended any but the
authorized form of worship, they were liable to six months'
imprisonment for the first offence, a year's imprisonment
for the second, and lifelong imprisonment for the third.
An incidental object of these reforms was perhaps to relieve
the financial embarrassment of the Government by the
seizure of a large quantity of Church property which became
superfluous by the extensive reduction of ritual which this
Act effected, but its main object was perhaps to prevent the
growth of faction which was such an embarrassment to
the Government. Cranmer, who during the reign of Henry
VIII condemned people to the flames for not believing in
transubstantiation, was now ready to condemn them for
believing in it.

With the accession of Mary, the policy was reversed.
An attempt was made to return to the *status quo ante*. Mary
was a devout Catholic, she sought the restoration of the
Roman religion and the suppression of the Protestant sects
to which the leading reformers and plunderers belong.
Altogether, two hundred and eighty-six persons were put
to death during her reign. Some of these may have been
martyrs to their opinions, but the majority were the scoundrels
who had plundered the monasteries and who had sought
by treachery to destroy the Queen herself. In restoring
the Catholic Faith and in acting against these scoundrels
there can be little doubt that Mary's actions were popular.
Only three years before her accession, the peasants had
risen against the new aristocracy and religious innovations
in many parts of the kingdom, and the insurrection, as we

saw, had only been put down with the help of foreign mercenaries. Was it not natural, therefore, that a Queen who sought to restore the old worship and acted against a gang of ruffians should be popular ?

It had been Mary's intention to take the stolen property away from the plunderers and to restore it to the Church. But this was no easy matter, for there was scarcely a man of any note who had not in some degree partaken of the spoils. Moreover, the lapse of time had created a vested interest in the new order. Though the spoils of the Church had been originally divided between a few, they had now by sales and bequests become divided and subdivided among thousands, while a new economic life had come to organize itself around the new order. Cardinal Pole, the Pope's envoy, came at last to the conclusion that to demand the restitution of the stolen property under conditions which involved the compulsory surrender of the whole or a part of its possessions by almost every family of opulence in the kingdom was impracticable. So the Papacy decided to leave the plunderers in the undisturbed possession of their property, and to confine their demands to a restoration of the Catholic Faith and worship. On these terms, the Houses of Parliament agreed to recognize the Papal supremacy and allowed Pole to pronounce the reconciliation of England and the Church of Rome.

Though Mary assented to this compromise because no alternative, except civil war, was open to her, she was resolved to keep none of the plunder herself. She gave up the tenth and first-fruits ; that is to say, the tenth part of the annual worth of each Church benefice and the first year's income of each, which hitherto had gone to the Papacy, the Church and monastic lands, in fact, everything which Henry had confiscated and which were in her possession. Her intention was to apply the revenues as nearly as possible to their former purposes, and she did, in fact, make a start with the restoration of institutions which her predecessors had suppressed, in the face of great opposition. She did it against the remonstrances of her Council and of Parliament, which feared that her generous example would awaken in the people a hatred of themselves and the desire for vengeance. Not to be undone, the plunderers entered into a conspiracy against her. Before she had been on the throne many months a rebellion was raised. The rebels were defeated and the leaders executed, as was the case in a second rebellion which followed shortly afterwards. Mary's experience seems indeed to prove that it would have been better for her to have risked civil war against the plunderers at the very start than to have allowed them to keep their spoil whilst giving hers up ; since from the enmity which she incurred by surrendering the property her father had confiscated, arose those troubles which harassed her during the remainder of her short reign, and which were to some extent responsible for her early death.

Had Mary lived, it is possible that, having defeated two rebellions and disposed of the leading conspirators, her example might have been followed to some extent by the nobility and gentry. But she reigned only five years, and Elizabeth, who succeeded, undid her good work and took back the plunder. The reasons which led Elizabeth to reverse Mary's policy are probably to be found in a regard for her own personal safety. For she had no religious convictions like her sister, and her choice in favour of Protestantism was more a matter of policy than of principle. In the first two years of her reign she ran simultaneously two policies —a Catholic and a Protestant one—until she could be sure which way the wind was blowing. The arguments for and against maintaining the Catholic worship were for her, apart from personal considerations of safety, almost equally divided. On the one side of her were the clergy in possession, who stood for the Roman supremacy and were determined not to yield, and the peasantry who favoured the Catholic worship. On the other was the new aristocracy of plunderers, who clearly understood that their position would not be safe until Protestantism triumphed, and the population of the towns which was mainly in favour of religious change. If, therefore, she chose to continue Mary's policy, she might have to face conspiracies and be worn out by them like her sister. On the other hand if she espoused Protestantism she was probably committed to a policy of religious persecution so far as the major part of the nation was concerned.

Her choice was a difficult one for a person without religious convictions, and in the circumstances it is not surprising that she sought to make her own position secure by the adoption of Protestantism. But there was a difficulty in the way. Scotland was Catholic. Mary Queen of Scots, when married to the Dauphin of France, was styled at her court the Queen of England and used the arms of England. So long, therefore, as Scotland remained Catholic England, if Protestant, could not be free from attack. Elizabeth therefore decided to second John Knox in his efforts to win Scotland for the cause of Protestantism, and to supply him with money and arms. In 1555 he returned from Geneva, to conduct an evangelical campaign. He was a great organizer as well as preacher, and as he went through Scotland new Churches sprang into existence everywhere. His campaign was followed speedily by an insurrection, for the strife between Catholicism and Calvinism was also a strife for the delivery of Scotland from a foreign army. The Scottish Protestants besieged a small French force in Leith, and a small English force was sent to support the insurgents. The campaign was soon over. The French force surrendered, very few Scots openly siding with the Queen and her French force. Scotland now became Protestant, and danger was no longer to be apprehended from an attack by land.

The issue was now clear. Elizabeth no longer hesitated, but threw herself into the work of consolidating her position by forcing Protestantism on England. If the Scottish revolt had miscarried it would have been different. In the event of failure she had intended to marry one of the Austrian cousins of Philip of Spain and to pursue a Catholic policy. The English people were now irrevocably committed to Protestantism, landlordism and capitalism, if they were to retain their national independence. It was only by supporting Elizabeth through thick and thin that they could keep themselves free from foreign complications.

Elizabeth, then, had finally decided that England should become a Protestant country. To attain this end she stuck at nothing. In spite of all that had happened, the English people were still mainly Catholic in their sympathies, and rivers of blood had to flow before they could be changed.

" The Protestant religion," says Cobbett, " was established by gibbets, racks, and ripping knives." A series of Acts of Parliament were passed which by degrees put down the Catholic worship and reintroduced the Protestant form as it existed under Edward VI. Catholics were compelled to attend Protestant worship under enormous penalties, and when this failed an Act was passed compelling all persons to take the oath of supremacy, acknowledging her instead of the Pope supreme in spiritual matters on pain of death. Thus were thousands of people condemned to death for no other crime than adhering to the religion of their fathers, the religion, in fact, in which Elizabeth herself had professed to believe until she became queen and had turned against it, not from conscientious motives, but from considerations of convenience. " Elizabeth," says Cobbett, " put, in one way or another, more persons to death in one year, for not becoming apostates to the religion which she had sworn to be hers, and to be the only true one, than Mary put to death in the whole of her reign. . . . Yet the former is called or has been called ' good Queen Bess,' and the latter ' bloody Queen Mary.' " [1]

Elizabeth's successor, James I, continued her policy of persecuting the Catholics. Before he came to the throne he had promised to mitigate the penal laws which made their lives a burden, but he actually made them more severe than ever, while there came with him from Scotland a horde of rapacious minions who preyed upon the Catholic population, filling their pockets by extracting from them the maximum in fines which the statutes allowed. The consequence of this was the Gunpowder Plot which was organized by a group of Catholics " to blow the Scotch beggars back to their native mountains," as Guy Fawkes replied when asked why he had collected so many barrels of gunpowder.

Mention has been made of the fact that the Duke of Somerset encouraged the sectarians who flocked to England from the Continent to preach their doctrines in order to make the breach with Rome final and irrevocable. These sectarians were men of the same mentality as the heretics of the Middle Ages, that is, men who were temperamentally incapable

[1] Cobbett's *History of the Protestant Reformation*, p. 244.

of seeing truth as a whole, but would fasten themselves upon
one aspect of it which they insisted upon in a spirit of narrow
fanaticism to the neglect and denial of all other aspects of
truth.   At all times men of this type are a danger to society,
and in the Middle Ages they were kept well in hand.   But
after the Reformation, when the Bible was translated, and
copies of it multiplied by the thousand by the printing press,
recently invented, these men got their chance.   They challenged the Catholic tradition upon which the Roman Church
had based its authority with the authority of the Bible,
upon which without note or comment they took their stand.
As every one now began to interpret it in his own way, it
led to the growth of innumerable sects who poisoned the
minds of nearly the whole community.   " Hence all sorts
of monstrous crimes.   At Dover a woman cut off the head
of her child, alleging that, like Abraham, she had had a
particular command from God.   A woman was executed
at York for crucifying her mother ;   she had, at the same
time, sacrificed a calf and a cock.   These are only a few
amongst the horrors of that ' thorough godly Reformation.'
We read of killings in the Bible ;   and if every man is to be
his own interpreter of that book, who is to say that he acts
contrary to his own interpretation ? " [1]   This is what making
truth subjective comes to in the sphere of religion.   Only
the affirmation that truth is objective can make the common
sense of men prevail.

Out of the medley of conflicting beliefs and opinions there
gradually emerged the Puritan Movement, which became
such a formidable power in the reign of Charles I.   Its
members were not bound together by a community of beliefs
but by a community of disbeliefs.   They were united in
their hatred of all ritual and ceremonies, and in a longing for
liberty of conscience for all who subscribed to the " No
Popery " cry, but not for such as thought otherwise.   This
new religious development is in one sense perhaps to be
ascribed to the separation of religion from the practical
affairs of life which made it a personal rather than a social
consideration.   The Catholic and Mediæval idea had been
that of salvation by faith and good works, but with the rise

[1] Corbett's *History of the the Protestant Reformation*, p. 303.

of Protestantism there came the idea of salvation by faith alone. This idea, which found a ready support among the commercial class who desired to be at liberty to determine their own standards of morality in respect to their trade-relationships, changed entirely the meaning of the idea of salvation by faith. From being considered as a means to an end—the end being good works—faith came to be regarded as the end in itself. And with this change, religious faith lost its social significance. Instead of implying the acceptance of certain moral, objective and revealed truths which experience had proved to be necessary for the proper ordering of society, it came to imply the acceptance of certain peculiar views as to the personal nature of God. Religion became a matter of keeping on the right side of God, whom the Puritans interpreted as a narrow-minded, jealously disposed person, much inferior to the average human being. Hence the endless religious discussions to decide the best method of propitiating the Deity, which naturally came about when religion lost its original aim of seeking the establishment of the Kingdom of God upon Earth and concerned itself with the less dignified aim of saving the individual soul from eternal damnation.

Charles I, who came to the throne on the death of his father in 1625, came into violent collision with this new power. He was one of the most moral and religious men who ever wore a crown ; but his autocratic methods made him the last person in the world to deal with the Puritans. Many were the grounds of quarrel between him and his Parliament and people, but the great ground was that of religion. So far as the people were concerned, the quarrel was genuine. They were Protestants and Puritans by conviction, and they looked with suspicion upon Charles, who had married a Catholic wife and was therefore suspected of designs to restore the Catholic worship. His action in repealing the Sunday Observance Laws was taken as evidence of such intention. But with the Parliament the trouble was different. The landlords of whom it was composed had grievances of their own. Under the two preceding reigns they had been accustomed to have things very much their own way, and they resented Charles's attempts to curb their power. Realizing the troubles which arise from absenteeism, he requested the landowners to live on their estates instead of spending their time in London. He appointed a Commission—" to inquire touching Depopulations and conversions of Lands to Pasture "—an evil which was destroying rural life and pressed hard upon the poorer inhabitants. Charles was determined to put a stop to this scandal and imposed heavy fines upon delinquents. Sir Anthony Roper was fined no less than £30,000 for committing Depopulations. Further, Charles so arranged matters that the weight of taxation fell entirely upon the trading and wealthy class, and for this he was not forgiven. Parliament resolved to checkmate him. Government was impossible without supplies, and they refused to vote him any. Charles answered them by seeking to impose taxation without their consent. Here was a clear issue about which they could fight with some prospect of securing popular support. They raised the cry of arbitrary government. That this arbitrary power was exercised in the interests of the people against the landlords did not prevent the cry from catching on, for when people put their faith in means rather than ends they can be easily misled. The landlords artfully connected their own political grievances, the exact nature of which they concealed from the people, with the Puritan demand for religious liberty, whatever that may have meant. " If it were not for their reiterated cry about religion," said Hampden, " they would never be sure of keeping the people on their side." [1] It was by such means that Parliament secured the support of London, which was the centre of Puritanism and which played such a decisive part in the Civil War. The end was as we all know. Charles was defeated, and eventually executed. The landlords triumphed, and Parliament rewarded the people for their support by transferring to their shoulders the burden of taxation which was taken off land and profits on trade and put upon food. It was thus that the foundations of English " liberty " were laid upon a firm and democratic basis, and taxation broadened.

[1] *Commentaries on the Life and Reign of Charles I*, by Isaac Disraeli, pp. 330-1, vol i., quoted in Ludovici's *Defence of Aristocracy*.

Since the defeat of Charles, no monarch or statesman has seriously attempted to put a boundary to the depredations of landlordism and capitalism. In his *Defence of Aristocracy* [1] Mr. Ludovici has exalted Charles as a national hero who led a forlorn hope against the stronghold of capitalism and landlordism under which England still groans. Though he glosses over the weaker side of Charles's character, he certainly makes a very strong case out for him which leaves little doubt in one's mind that Charles did try to govern England in the interests of the people rather than in that of the landlords and capitalists ; and, moreover, that it was because he made this valiant attempt that he eventually came to grief. So much we are willing to grant. But Mr. Ludovici goes further, and seeks to make of his example a case for the revival of aristocracy, forgetting, apparently, that the evil influences against which Charles fought in vain were largely the creation of another aristocrat, Henry VIII, and that while it can be shown that individual aristocrats have placed the public interest before their own, it is not true of any aristocracy considered as a class since the revival of Roman Law.

With the reasons which have led Mr. Ludovici and others to advocate a revival of aristocracy I have every sympathy. Like him, I realize the practical difficulty of initiating measures for the public good, apart from a recognition of the principle of authority. From one point of view the problem confronting modern society is that of the re-establishment of authority. But I contend that this difficulty is not to be met by any attempted revival of aristocracy, because the authority of which we stand in need is not primarily the authority of persons, but of *ideas* or *things* as Mr. de Maeztu terms them. The authority of the aristocrat presupposes the existence of certain common standards of thought and action throughout the community ; and if these are non-existent, as is the case to-day, it is vain to seek a remedy in the authority of persons. The thing to do is to seek the re-creation of the intellectual unity of a common culture by bringing ideas and values into a true relationship with each other. In proportion as this end can be attained

[1] *A Defence of Aristocracy*, by Anthony M. Ludovici (Constable & Co.).

authority will reappear in society, for ideas tend to become authoritative once they are accepted. When this is secured, the difficulties which make Mr. Ludovici yearn for a revival of aristocracy will have disappeared. Democracy and authority will no longer present themselves as mutually exclusive principles, but as complementary ones.

CHAPTER XIII

THE FRENCH REVOLUTION

" It is no idle Hibernianism," says Mr. Chesterton, " to
say that towards the end of the eighteenth century the
most important event in English history happened in France.
It would seem still more perverse, yet it would be still more
precise, to say that the most important event in English
history was the event that never happened at all—the
English Revolution on the lines of the French Revolution." [1]
That such a revolution did not materialize in England
was not due to any lack of ardour on the part of those who
would have brought it about, but to the fact that the English
governing classes and the rising manufacturing class, landlords, churchmen, judges, and manufacturers, stood firmly
together in order to save themselves from the fate which
had overtaken the privileged classes in France. By such
means they postponed the crisis which threatened England
towards the end of the eighteenth century, until the development of railway building came to their rescue by effecting
a general revival of trade, and, within certain limits, a redistribution of the wealth of the community.

The fact that the experiment in Revolution, to which
all Western European countries were moving towards the
end of the eighteenth century, was tried in France is
to be attributed to the writings of Rousseau. " But
for Rousseau," said Napoleon, " there would have been
no Revolution," a conclusion which it is difficult to avoid,
for it was Rousseau who formulated the ideas which exercised
such a profound influence on the course of the Revolution.
Apart from Rousseau, great social, political, and economic
changes would have taken place ; for the contrasts between

[1] *The Victorian Age in Literature*, by G. K. Chesterton.

wealth and poverty had become so great, famine so prevalent, and the monarchical system of government so unworkable that something had to be done. But there is strong evidence to support the idea that if Rousseau and the intellectuals associated with him had not inflamed the imagination of the French people with impossible dreams, the change would not have taken the direction it did. It would have moved towards a revival of Mediæval institutions, for though it so happened that such Mediæval institutions as had survived to their day had been corrupted by Roman Law, the Mediæval tradition among the peasants was still strong, as evidenced by the fact that in the years following the American War, when systematic and widespread agitations broke out in many parts of France, notably in the East, against the dearness of food, the peasants, acting on their own initiative, sought a solution of the problem by a revival of the central economic idea of the Middle Ages—the idea of the Just Price. The rebel bands would compel those who had brought corn to market to sell it at a Just Price, or else they seized the corn and divided it among themselves at a Just Price.[1] This fact alone is of the greatest significance ; its importance cannot be exaggerated, for it indicates clearly the direction in which a solution would have been sought had not the influence of Rousseau and the intellectuals of his generation operated to confuse the issue by the popularization of ideas which were antipathetic to the political and economic philosophy of the Middle Ages.

The social, political and economic crisis which precipitated the Revolution was accompanied by a paralysis of the body politic. The Revolution came because the machinery of government would work no longer. This state of things had been brought into existence by Louis XIV, whose policy it had been to concentrate all power in the Crown. Early in his reign he had sought to exclude the nobility from the chief posts in the Government. This led to the revolt of the aristocracy known as the Fronde, which he succeeded in quelling ; after which he summoned the nobles to his court, where he undermined what independence they still retained by corrupting them with favours and pleasures. He overcame the

[1] Cf. *The Great French Revolution*, by P. A. Kropotkin, p. 40.

resistance of Parliament to his encroachments by haughtily imposing upon it a silence and submission of sixty years' duration. Having by such means succeeded in destroying the independence of all who might offer resistance to his authority, he directed his immense power internally against the Protestants and externally in pursuing an aggressive policy against Germany and the Netherlands. For a time success seemed to follow him everywhere. Internal dissatisfaction with his policy was drowned in songs of victory. But at length the tide turned, the men of genius died, the victories ceased, industry emigrated with the Protestants who fled from the country, and money became scarcer and scarcer. Indeed, before his death Louis began to find, as other despots have found, that the successes of despotism exhaust its resources and mortgage its future.

The death of Louis was the signal of reaction; there was a sudden transition from intolerance to incredulity, from the spirit of servility to that of discussion and assertion. From then onwards, all through the eighteenth century, the disintegration of society increased daily while the Government fell into the hands of royal mistresses. Opposition increased. The Third Estate, which possessed scarcely a third of the land and was burdened with feudal rents to the lords of the manor, tithes to the clergy and taxes to the king, without enjoying any corresponding political rights and privileges, became more and more opposed to the nobility who were exempt from taxation and to the wealthy clergy who swallowed the rich revenues of the bishoprics and abbeys. Though they were divided among themselves, they were united in their desire to remove such inequality of burdens, while they bitterly resented the contempt with which they were treated by the upper classes. As time wore on they became more and more united and increased in strength, wealth and intelligence, until, finally, they successfully revolted. Meanwhile, the finances got into a more and more difficult condition, bringing about, finally, the state of things that in the reign of Louis XVI led to the summoning of the States-General which in turn led immediately to revolution.

Such was the problem which was developing when Rousseau made his appearance. There was little or no understanding of the nature of the problem with which France was then perplexed; but there was strong and justifiable resentment at certain obvious and concrete evils. It was apparent that the concentration of absolute power in the hands of the monarchy was an evil of the first magnitude, while it was apparent that the survival of feudal rights—of privileges without corresponding responsibilities—was not merely an anachronism that needed to be abolished, but that it imposed a crushing burden upon the poor, who were called upon to support the system. Had Rousseau been familiar with the historical growth of this problem he would have known that the concentration of power in the hands of the monarchy and the corruption of Feudalism were alike due to the influence of Roman Law, and that the solution of the problem demanded, among other things, its supersession by the Mediæval Law which it had replaced. But not only was Rousseau unaware of the extent to which the evils of society were to be traced back to the revival of Roman Law but, like most, if not all, of his contemporaries, he had a great admiration for it. He was a child of the Renaissance, and as such was an admirer of the institutions of Greece and Rome, of which, like the scholars who idealized them, he was altogether uncritical. He was apparently unaware that the civilizations of both Greece and Rome had been undermined by the unregulated use of currency, and that the problem of its regulation which had eluded the statesmen of Greece had found a solution in the Guilds of the Middle Ages, which had been rendered economically possible by the triumph of Christianity. On the contrary, not understanding that Paganism had proved itself to be morally weak, he ascribed its decline to the spread of Christian doctrines, which he considered had undermined the antique virtues. He was ignorant of the fact that Christianity had triumphed because it was a moral tonic capable of bracing up the fibre of decadent civilizations. He had been prejudiced against Christianity in the days of his youth because, brought up in Geneva, he had only known the Calvinist version of it; and being interested in the things of this world, while Calvinism was only interested in the things of the next, he jumped to the conclusion that if ever society was to be regenerated it would be necessary to abolish Christianity in favour of a revival of Paganism.

It is in this light that the *Social Contract*, which lit the flames of the Revolution, should be studied. Rousseau's ideas on civil religion do not appear until the last chapter, but they provide the key to his whole position. In order to understand Rousseau, it is necessary to read him backwards. The immediate problem with which he was concerned and which made him favour a Pagan form of worship was his desire to see an identity between Church and State, which he recognized did not exist in Christian societies! That such a union might not be desirable, that its disadvantages might outweigh the advantages, never for a moment occurred to him. So obsessed was he with the idea of unity that he never saw that religion and politics, when real, never were and never can be the same thing. Hence it was that in his search for unity he fused the categories of religious and political thought. It would be more strictly true to say that he confused them, for clear thinking demands that they should remain in their separate categories. While religion concerns itself with the ideal, politics must concern itself with the real if it is to give practical results. Hitherto this difference of function had been clearly recognized. In the normal society as it existed in the Middle Ages it was clearly recognized that while it was the function of the Church to make good men, it was the function of government to build them into the social structure. Moreover, it was recognized that the success of the legislator was ultimately dependent upon the success of the priest. The maintenance of the Just Price presupposes the existence of just men, and no one in the Middle Ages ever entertained the contrary idea that the arrival of an ideal social system could precede the arrival of ideal men. But when, after the Renaissance, scepticism in regard to religion invaded the intellectual world and capitalism triumphed and privileges were abused, men of religious temperament, instead of entering the Church as they would have done in the Middle Ages, remained outside and turned to political speculation. The consequence of this was that they infused the sphere of politics with the idealism which is proper to religion, but which can have no place in

13

politics because politics must concern itself with men as
they are and not with men as they might be. In this mood
Rousseau, realizing that certain evils which he saw around
him were attributable to bad government, and wishing to
see them remedied, turned from speculating on ways and
means of remedying these abuses to speculation on the form
which an ideal State should take. But instead of setting to
work in the way Mediævalists would have done—to consider,
firstly, how to produce good men, and then to determine
what form of government would be best suited for giving
the best results from the material so produced—good, bad,
and indifferent—Rousseau began by first thinking out how
the ideal State should be constituted, and then turned to
consider how men might be disciplined in order that his
ideal State could be maintained in its integrity. This
inversion of the natural order of thought runs all through
the *Social Contract*, and it was this that led to the tyrannies
and violence of the Revolution. For while religion seeks
to discipline man by an appeal to his heart and conscience,
the State is powerless to maintain a discipline except through
the exercise of force. The Jacobins, when they sought to
regenerate France by sending delegates with guillotines
into the provinces, were in their crude way attempting to
give practical application to a principle which Rousseau
had enunciated.

It was because Rousseau made morality wholly dependent
upon law, as at a later date Marx made it wholly dependent
upon economic conditions, that he was so anxious to devise
a State which would be mechanically perfect in its workings.
If morality is to be dependent upon law it is a matter of
vital importance that the State should be so constructed that
the evil desires in man will balance and neutralize each
other in an equilibrium of good. But, of course, it cannot be
done. The search for perpetual motion is not a more hopeless
quest, for man cannot by laws be made to go straight in
spite of himself. The utmost laws are capable of doing is
to secure outward observance of the moral standards of those
in power. They may, like Mediæval Law, aim at enabling
good men to live among bad; or, like Roman Law, at enabling
rich men to live among poor ; but to create living standards

of morality they are powerless, for if the law attempts to get ahead of public opinion it will not be observed, while the attempt of a Government to secure observance under such conditions would be to institute a tyranny that would be its undoing.

The particular form of government which Rousseau thought would automatically promote the public welfare was one based upon the sovereignty of the people. He says :

" One essential and inevitable defect which will render a monarchical government inferior to a republican one is that in the latter the public voice hardly ever raises to the highest posts any but enlightened and capable men, who fill them honourably ; whereas those who succeed in monarchies are most frequently only petty mischief-makers, petty knaves, petty intriguers, whose petty talents, which enable them to obtain high posts in courts, only serve to show the public their ineptitude as soon as they have attained them. The people are much less mistaken about their choice than the prince is ; and a man of real merit is almost as rare in a royal ministry as a fool at the head of a republican government. Therefore, when by some fortunate chance one of these born rulers takes the helm of affairs in a monarchy almost wrecked by such a fine set of ministers, it is quite astonishing what resources he finds, and his accession to power forms an epoch in a country."

From the foregoing passage as from others which might be quoted, it is evident that Rousseau did not believe in Equality as it is understood by democrats to-day. He would have answered the democrat who asserts that the people have a right to exercise power regardless of the use which they make of it, by saying that democrats in that case take their stand on precisely the same ground as the authoritarian who believes in the divine right of kings. Both have one thing in common : they make power subjective and absolute instead of objective and conditional upon the fulfilment of duties. This was not Rousseau's idea. Strictly speaking, Rousseau did not believe in Equality at all, but in natural inequalities. He wanted to get rid of the inequalities based upon wealth and influence in order to clear the way for what may be termed the free movement in society of natural

inequalities. He believed in government by the wise.
" It is," he says, " the best and most natural order of things
that the wise should govern the multitude, when we are sure
they will govern it for its advantage and not for their own."
The wise were to be the executive officers of the State, but
he wanted the people to be sovereign in order that they
might keep a check on them. In this sense only did Rousseau
believe in Equality. He did not regard it as an end in itself,
but as a means to an end, the end being government by
the best and wisest. There is something very simple and
unsophisticated about all this. The whole trouble of the
world from one point of view is precisely that the best and
wisest do not automatically come to the top under democracy
any more than they do under any other form of government.
It is the clever rather than the wise who do, and, unfortunately,
the wise are rarely clever, nor are the clever usually wise.
When the wise do come to the top the millennium will have
arrived.

Rousseau himself realized this difficulty when he considered the problem of the legislator. He was of the opinion
that neither the sovereign people nor the executive were
wise enough to frame good laws. The successful accomplish-
ment of such a task required a superman. Of the legislator
or lawgiver he says :—

" Wise men who want to speak to the vulgar in their
own language instead of in a popular way will not be understood. Now, there are a thousand kinds of ideas which it
is impossible to translate into the language of the people.
Views very general and objects very remote are alike beyond
its reach ; and each individual approving of no other plan
of government than that which promotes his own interests,
does not readily perceive the benefits which he is to derive
from the continual deprivations which good laws impose.
In order that a newly formed nation might approve sound
maxims of politics and observe the fundamental rules of
State policy, it would be necessary that the effect should
become the cause ; that the social spirit, which should
be the work of the institution, should preside over the institution itself, and that men should be, prior to the laws, what
they ought to become by means of them. Since, then,

the legislator cannot employ either force or reasoning, he must needs have recourse to an authority of a different order, which can compel without violence and persuade without convincing.

" It is this which in all ages has constrained the founders of nations to resort to the intervention of Heaven, and to give the gods the credit for their own wisdom, in order that the nations, subjected to the laws of the State as to those of nature, and recognizing the same power in the formation of man and in that of the State, might obey willingly and bear submissively the yoke of the public welfare. The legislator puts into the mouths of the immortals that sublime reason which soars beyond the reach of common men, in order that he may win over by divine authority those whom human prudence could not move. But it does not belong to every man to make the gods his oracles, nor to be believed when he proclaims himself their interpreter. The great soul of the legislator is the real miracle which must give proof of his mission. . . . The choice of the moment for the establishment of a government is one of the surest marks for distinguishing the work of the legislator from that of the tyrant."

Apart from the exceptional problem which the law-giver presents, Rousseau quite rightly realized that in general there are certain external circumstances which favour the rise to power of the wise as there are certain others which tend to obstruct them. He saw that the wise stood the best chance of success in the world, where men were well known to each other, and where a certain measure of economic equality obtained. Hence his advocacy of small States and of small property. But he was not a leveller. He says, " with regard to Equality we should not understand that the degrees of power and wealth should be absolutely the same ; but that, as to power, it should fall short of all violence, and never be exercised except by virtue of station and of the laws ; while as to wealth, no citizen should be rich enough to be able to buy another, and none poor enough to be forced to sell himself. . . . It is precisely because the force of circumstances is ever tending to destroy Equality that the force of legislation should always tend to maintain it." Rousseau's attitude towards property was not that of the Collectivist.

It will make the position clearer to say that the ideal of Rousseau was that of the City States of Greece, which existed independently of each other while they were federated for the purpose of defence. He saw that this meant putting the clock back ; but this did not deter him./ He realized, as all men do whose reasoning faculties have not been atrophied by the idea of Progress, that any fundamental change in the social system involves in some degree a return to a former social condition. All Socialist ideas imply reversion, but the fact that Socialists are afraid to admit it has led them into the maze of intellectual confusion in which they find themselves. / But Rousseau lived in an age when men were not afraid of words, and so boldly advocated a return to the conditions of primitive society. In an earlier work he had demanded the renunciation of cultivated life which he asserted led to " a distinction of the talents and a disparage-ment of the virtues," in favour of a return to nature which was to be made the starting-point for a nobler form of exist-ence. His description of the life of primitive society was so vivid and full of detail, while it gave such a feeling of reality to the existence of a golden age in the past, that Voltaire said " it made one desire to walk on all fours." Though Rousseau's description was a work of pure fiction—for of primitive man he knew nothing—it came to be believed in as gospel truth, because it served its purpose of contrasting a simple, unsophisticated mode of existence with the arti-ficiality and corruption of France, and gave emphasis to his denunciations of property, privileges and tyranny. In the *Social Contract* his enthusiasm for primitive man appears to have abated somewhat. Perhaps, after all, there was something to be said for civilization. It was not to be regarded merely as a disease. If many natural advantages are lost, equal or greater ones are secured. Law and morality replace appetite and instincts ; moreover, there are certain advantages in co-operation. Hence, though it is necessary to return to the past, he considers that it will not be necessary to return to any state of society prior to the civilization of early Greece.

It was because Rousseau was mistaken as to the historical nature of the problem which confronted society that he was led to regard the Greek States as models. Remembering that these States were entirely undermined by unregulated currency, Rousseau, to have been consistent, should have demanded the abolition of currency. That he did not is to be explained by the circumstance that he was apparently as ignorant of the fact that unregulated currency had destroyed the civilization of Greece and Rome as of the further fact that the solution of this problem was found by the Mediæval Guilds. Had he known these facts, the course of history might have been different. Instead of seeking a solution that was primarily political he would have sought one that was primarily economic. He would have supported the peasants in their demand for the re-establishment of the Just Price, and would have considered ways and means of restoring the Guilds to maintain it. He would, moreover, have seen that within the Guilds the people were sovereign in the Middle Ages, while their sovereignty was not based upon slavery, as was the case with the sovereign peoples of Greece. On this issue Rousseau was not honest with himself. Though he condemns slavery, he glosses over the fact that the States which he exalted as models were based upon slavery. " Slavery," he says, " is one of the unfortunate inconveniences of civilized society."

The technical cause of the confusion in which Rousseau found himself is to be found in the revived interest in Roman Law which had established the tradition of thinking about economic problems entirely in terms of property. In my chapter on Greece and Rome I drew attention to the mutual dependence of Roman Law and an unregulated currency, pointing out that Roman Law came into being not for the purpose of securing justice, but to postpone the dissolution of a society which had been rendered politically unstable through the growth of capitalism—itself the consequence of unregulated currency. Despairing of the effort to secure justice, the Roman jurists addressed themselves to the more immediately urgent task of maintaining order by following the line of least resistance. Not understanding how to regulate currency even if it had been practicable in Rome, they sought to give protection and security to private property as the easiest way of avoiding continual strife among neighbours. The consequence of this was that when after the Reformation thinkers went to Roman Law for guidance in their speculations as to how to render government stable, the tradition became established of thinking about social and political questions primarily in terms of property instead of in currency. The result of this has been that down to this day social theory is presented statically rather than dynamically. Rousseau's social theory was no exception to this rule. It did not deal with the sequential steps which would have to be taken towards the realization of his ideal society, but presented a new society already full grown. This limitation of Rousseau's theory became increasingly apparent as the Revolution developed. Not only did his constructive ideas bear no particular relationship to the problems which had to be met, but they were a positive obstruction in the path of their solution, by filling the minds of the revolutionaries with *a priori* ideas which obscured the real issues. The Revolution rapidly became a collision between theorists fired with a new ideal and the political, social and economic conditions of which they had no comprehension. Not comprehending them, they sought in vain to direct the course of events until, exasperated by failure, they came to commit crimes of which they had no presentiment at the beginning.

Rousseau misled the revolutionaries by focusing attention upon the wrong aspect of the economic problem. He talked about property and ignored currency. I make bold to say that the centre of gravity of the economic problem is not in property, but in currency, for currency is the vital thing, the thing of movement. It is the active principle in economic development, while property is the passive. It is true that profits which are made by the manipulation of currency, sooner or later assume the form of property. All the same, the root mischief is not to be found in property but in unregulated currency. To solve the problem of currency by the institution of a Just Price under a system of Guilds for the regulation of exchanges, and the adjustment of the balance between demand and supply, is to bring

order into the economic problem at its active centre. Having
solved the problem at its centre, it will be a comparatively
easy matter to deal with property which lies at the circumference. Property-owners would be able to offer no more
effective resistance to change than hitherto landlordism
has been able to offer to the growth of capitalism. By
such means the reconstruction of society would proceed upon
orderly lines. All that it would be necessary to do would
be for the democratic movement to exert a steady and
constant pressure over a decade or so, and society would be
transformed without so much as a riot, much less a revolution.
But to begin with property is to get things out of their natural
order, for it is to proceed from the circumference to the
centre, which is contrary to the law of growth. It is to
precipitate economic confusion by dragging society up by its
roots ; and this defeats the ends of revolution by strengthen-
ing the hands of the profiteer, for the profiteer thrives on
economic confusion. Of what use is it to seek to effect
a redistribution of wealth before the profiteer has been got
under control ? So long as men are at liberty to manipulate
exchange, they will manage to get the wealth of the community
into their hands. This is no idle theory. All through the
French Revolution, as, indeed, according to reports, in the
Russian Revolution of to-day, speculation was rife, paper
money depreciated, while a class of *nouveaux riches* came
into existence and the Assemblies were powerless against
them. Marat might call for " the accursed brood of capitalists, stock-jobbers and monopolists to be destroyed." But
it was easier said than done. For these men exercised a
function which was absolutely indispensable to the life of
the community. They organized distribution, and it was
because the leaders of the Revolution entirely failed to see
the primacy of distribution that they let the profiteers in.
Under the pressure of circumstances the Jacobins decreed
a maximum price for provisions. But its effect was only to
cause continual dearth. Though the Jacobins could terrorize
the Convention, they could not control the revolutionary
profiteers. For the control of currency and exchange,
which would have been a comparatively simple proposition at the start, was altogether impracticable when the

country was in the throes of revolution. If instead of beginning with the destruction of Feudalism, the revolutionaries had begun with the regulation of currency and exchange, the chaos of the Revolution would have been avoided, and Feudalism would have fallen later as dead leaves fall from a tree. The solution of the social problem, as of every other problem in this universe, resolves itself finally into one of order. Take issues in their natural order and everything will straighten itself out beautifully, all the minor details or secondary parts will fall into their proper places. But approach these same issues in a wrong order and confusion results. No subsequent adjustments can remedy the initial error. This principle is universally true. It is as true of writing a book, of designing a building, as of conducting a revolution. The secret of success in each case will be found finally to rest upon the perception of the order in which the various issues should be taken.

It was because Rousseau had built the elaborate superstructure of his reasoning upon a foundation of false history that he was driven to postulate the existence of something at the centre of society which he termed the General Will, and upon which he relied to usher in the new social order. Exactly what he meant by this General Will is most difficult to determine, for while on the one hand he exalts it into a fetish capable of performing every imaginable kind of political miracle, on the other he proceeds to qualify his original proposition in so many ways as almost to rob it of any definite meaning. " So long," he says, " as a number of men in combination are considered as a single body they have but one will, which relates to the common preservation and the general well-being. In such a case all the forces of nature are vigorous and simple, and its principles are clear and luminous ; it has no confused and conflicting interests ; the common good is everywhere plainly manifest, and only good sense is required to perceive it. Peace, union and equality are foes to political subtleties. Upright and simple-minded men are hard to deceive because of their simplicity ; allurements and refined pretexts do not impose upon them ; they are not even cunning enough to be dupes. . . . A State thus governed needs very few laws ; and in so far as it becomes necessary to promulgate new ones the necessity is universally recognized. The first man to propose them only gives expression to what all have previously felt, and neither factions nor eloquence will be needed to pass into law what every one has already resolved to do, so soon as he is sure that the rest will act as he does." The General Will, he goes on to say, is indestructible. It is always constant, unalterable, and pure ; but when private interests begin to make themselves felt, it is subordinated to other wills which get the better of it. After telling us all these fine things he has some misgivings, and proceeds : " the General Will is always right, but the judgment which guides it is not always enlightened," and that " there is no general will with reference to a particular object." After making these qualifications there does not appear to be very much of the General Will left, and we begin to wonder what was at the bottom of his mind. The only explanation I can offer of these apparent contradictions is that the General Will is something which relates to the subliminal consciousness of mankind, but is not a part of his normal consciousness. Mr. de Maeztu says there is no such thing as a General Will, since " men cannot unite immediately among one another ; they unite in things, in common values, in the pursuit of common ends," [1] and Mr. de Maeztu, I think, is right.

What Rousseau feared came about. All the careful detailed reservations he made to protect possible misapplications of the principles he enunciated were disregarded by his followers. All the ideas which he regarded as means to ends came to be exalted as ends in themselves, and to be believed in with all the fervour of strong religious conviction. Nature, the Rights of Man, Liberty, Equality, the Social Contract, hatred of tyrants and popular sovereignty were for the Jacobins the articles of a faith which was above and beyond discussion. They did not believe these things in the more or less philosophic spirit in which Rousseau believed them, but in the way that only men of simple and violent temperaments can believe things. Their firm conviction made them the driving force of the Revolution, for it gave them great strength of will, which enabled them

[1] *Authority, Liberty, and Function*, by Ramiro de Maeztu.

completely to dominate the more intelligent but weaker-willed members of the Assemblies, while it created a kind of revolutionary religion in France which inspired the armies of the Revolution.

In the Constituent Assembly the Jacobins were a small group, and at no time were they very numerous, though during the Convention they dominated France. The Revolution had not yet got its stride. This first Assembly consisted of land-lords, magistrates, physicians, and lawyers. It was what in these days would be called a business Government; that is, a Government of men who wanted to see things changed politically, but not economically, who believed in liberty, but not in equality. ́ They enjoyed the illusion which business men generally enjoy, that what is in their personal interests is necessarily in the interests of the community./ This limitation, though it gives annoyance to others, may not, under normal conditions, have serious consequences, but in a time of crisis it is a fatal defect for a class who seek to wield power, for it raises a barrier between them and popular feeling. So it was that the Constituent Assembly forfeited the confidence of the people by two of their actions. They thought they could decree the abolition of feudal rights while asking the peasants to pay for their surrender, and that they could limit the franchise to property-owners while men were preaching daily Liberty, Equality and Fraternity. Their attempt to distinguish between property-owners whom they termed *active citizens*, and other members of the community whom they termed *passive citizens*, was unfortunate for them. For this distinction was open to an interpretation the exact contrary of that which they had intended. Journalists protested that those who stormed the Bastille and cleared the lands regarded themselves as the *active citizens*, and objected to being treated as the mere raw material of a revolution for the benefit of others. But such protests were in vain. The members of the Constituent Assembly were entirely out of touch with popular feeling. And they remained out of touch until the people of Paris, armed with pikes, invaded the Assembly Hall to break up their deliberations—a habit which, once formed, continued almost daily throughout the Revolution. The Convention,

while under the influence of the Girondins, corrected the
blunder of the Constituent Assembly by removing the distinction between the *active* and *passive citizens*, but in other
respects it was equally out of touch with popular sentiment.
As a result, power in the Assembly passed entirely into the
hands of the Jacobins, who, whatever their shortcomings,
at least enjoyed the confidence of the people of Paris.

The rise to power of the Jacobins—known in the Convention as the Mountain as distinguished from the Plain, which
designated all its other members—is to be attributed to
many causes, but the principal one was the imperative
necessity of firm government. The Girondins, who had
hitherto led the Assembly, were Liberals in temperament,
and like Liberals all the world over they had little sense of
reality. They were hostile to a strong executive in the name
of Liberty, hostile to Paris in the name of Federalism, and
hostile to the economic aspirations of the people in the name
of Order. The result was as might be expected : they were
conquered by the force of circumstances. A time came at
length when the growth of economic anarchy and civil
war at home, combined with the need of defending the
Republic against other European Powers, demanded strong
and vigorous measures, and these the Girondins were unable
to supply. Power passed into the hands of the Jacobins,
because they alone were capable of determined action.

The situation had been of the Jacobins' own creating.
Earlier on they had been the means of bringing about the
execution of the King, which proved to be the turning-point
of the Revolution, for not only did it bring about civil war,
but armed Europe against France. In order to save the
Republic from its enemies without, and from disruption within,
the Jacobins resorted to the most ruthless measures. They
massacred people wholesale. In the Vendée alone it is
estimated that over half a million suffered at their hands.
Old men, women, and children were all massacred, and villages
and crops were burned. Yet in spite of all their savagery,
despite the delegates sent with guillotines into the provinces
and the Draconian laws which they enforced, they had to
struggle perpetually against riots, insurrections and conspiracies. But the reaction upon themselves is the interest-

ing sequel. They would brook no opposition, and in order
to carry through such ruthless measures they had to be
equally ruthless with their critics. It was in order to rid
themselves of them that they instituted the Terror, which,
after a run of ten months, came to an end with the execution of Robespierre and the lead'ng Jacobins. Not that
Robespierre was by any means the worst offender. On the
contrary, his influence had not unfrequently been exerted
in favour of moderation. At a time when to be considered
an " Indulgent " was an accusation pointing to the scaffold,
he successfully opposed the arrest of seventy-three members
of the Convention, saved Catherine Théot and her companions, and defended his rival Danton when his arrest was
first suggested ; while he repeatedly refused to sign warrants
for intended arrests, and had earned the lasting enmity of
Fouché, Carrier, Collôt, Tallien, Billaud-Varennes and others
by his denunciation of their atrocities, and had been the
means of effecting their return from the provinces. It
was the action of these men that immediately led to his
downfall. So intent was Robespierre on carrying the
system of virtue to its logical conclusion that a time came
when they felt their lives were no longer safe, and so they
combined with the Moderates to effect his overthrow.
Robespierre gave them the opportunity. Naturally suspicious, he complained of conspiracies, and his over-confidence
led him to attempt to get the Assembly to vote a measure
which would permit deputies to be sent to the Revolutionary
Tribunal without authorization of the Assembly. Certain
members, feeling that Robespierre was aiming at them,
and who had therefore nothing to lose, met this proposal
with a vigorous opposition. Such determined action
broke the spell that Robespierre had cast over the Assembly.
Members who had been afraid were afraid no longer, and the
next day the attack was vigorously renewed. Robespierre
tried to defend himself, but was met with cries of " Down
with the tyrant ! " From that moment Robespierre was lost.
Thanks to mental contagion, the cry instantly became general,
and his voice was drowned in the uproar. Without losing
a moment the Assembly decreed his accusation and outlawed
him. He appealed to the Commune of Paris, but the Conven-

tion was triumphant against his supporters. After the lapse of a few days Robespierre and his band of Jacobins to the number of a hundred and four were guillotined. As his name had become popularly associated with the Terror, his execution was interpreted by the people as having put an end to it. The Committee of Public Safety, recognizing this, acted as if all along such had been their intention, and the Terror came to an end.

But there were deeper reasons than personal enmities to account for the fall of Robespierre. The Revolution had entered its decadent phase. When the property of the nobles and clergy had been confiscated, instead of being returned to the people to be held communally, it was sold by the Assemblies to private individuals when they were in need of money. These large estates were on sale for several years on terms extremely favourable to purchasers, and had not only been bought by such peasants as could get hold of money, army contractors and food profiteers, but by members of the Convention itself ; while, moreover, thousands of Jacobins had secured posts under the Government for themselves. It was thus that the Revolution had created new vested interests and the corruption had not only penetrated the Convention but the Jacobin Party itself. Honest Republicans found themselves helpless against it. Robespierre was oblivious to these changes. He remained as upright and fanatical as ever, never wavering in his revolutionary faith, for ever reminding the people of the principles of Republicanism, and threatening those keenest after the spoils with the guillotine. So a coalition came into existence which regarded the overthrow of Robespierre as the first point to be gained. They had supported him so long as they feared a return of the *ancien régime*, but when the Allies had been defeated they had no further use for him. " What," said they, " is the good of a revolutionary government now that the war is over ? " The ends of the Revolution, so far as the great mass of its supporters were concerned, having been attained, they desired it to be brought to an end and to be confirmed in the possession of their riches. It was because Robespierre failed to realize the change that had taken place that he eventually came to grief. The only true Republicans now left were the young men, and they were to be found in the armies spreading the revolutionary ideas over Europe.

The fall of Robespierre prepared the way for the counter-revolution that took place a little over a twelvemonth after his death. It took the form of a rebellion of the *nouveaux riche*. During the course of the Revolution production steadily declined, and the wholesale issue of paper money had depreciated the currency to such an extent that the general want was terrible. A time came when Republican idealism vanished before the general demand for food and security, and this played into the hands of the rich, who asserted that on the maintenance of property depended the cultivation of the fields, all production, every means of work and the whole social order. The absence of it, they contended, had resulted in a general want of confidence on the part of producers, merchants and traders, and was responsible for the economic confusion and depression. Indeed, from the point of view of the Republicans there was no answer. They had rejected the idea of the communal ownership of land in favour of private ownership. They had sold the confiscated estates, and it was now up to the Government to guarantee the new owners in the possession of their lands. The counter-revolution was successful, confidence was restored and trade revived. It was thus that power passed out of the hands of the nobility into the hands of the bourgeoisie. The Revolution had miscarried.

As the Revolution proceeded, power became concentrated in fewer and fewer hands. The Committee of Public Safety, which had dominated the Convention, consisted of eight members. Under the Directory which followed, the executive power was vested in the hands of five men. This was provided for in its constitution, the framing of which was the last act of the Convention. In so far as the change was accompanied by a change of policy it was in the direction of not seeking to reorganize France but to leave it to organize itself, yet though the Directory left France to make its own economic readjustment, it was quite as ruthless as the Convention in its efforts to preserve the Republic, for it had to struggle against a succession of conspiracies against its power. Recognizing that a revival of Catholicism was taking place, the Directors imagined that the priests were conspiring against them and deported in one year nearly fifteen hundred of them under conditions which gave them little chance of survival, to say nothing of large numbers who were summarily executed, for though the Terror was abandoned, their methods were no less sanguinary. But in spite of their efforts things went for them steadily from bad to worse. Finance, administration, everything, in fact, was crumbling, until at length a point was reached when the Directors, feeling that things could not go on much longer, themselves sought a dictator who was at the same time capable of restoring order and protecting them. This is the explanation of the *coup d'état* which placed Napoleon in power. It was arranged by the Directors themselves as the only escape from an impossible situation.

It is a mistake to suppose that Napoleon overthrew the Revolution. On the contrary, he ratified and consolidated it. As early as 1795, at the end of the Convention, the idea had been canvassed of restoring the monarchy, but Louis XVIII having been tactless enough to declare that he would restore the *ancien régime* in its entirety, return all property to its original owners and punish the men of the Revolution, put himself out of court for the position. Indeed, the Royalists must have been impossible people. Even Le Bon says : " The Royalists gave proof during the whole of the Revolution of an incapacity and narrowness of mind which justified most of the measures taken against them." The Monarchy being impossible, it was necessary to find a general. Only one existed whose name carried weight —Bonaparte. The campaign of Italy had made him famous. He had been repeatedly pressed by the most influential and enlightened generals to place himself at the head of the Republic, but he refused to act upon their advice. He saw very clearly the difficulties which would beset him if he acted prematurely. He saw that the task of rebuilding France was impossible unless he were in a position to exercise absolute power in order that measures might be carried through with the greatest possible speed, which, of course, was impossible if every measure had to be preceded by a long discussion in the Assemblies. He saw, moreover, that he must be

14

beyond the reach of parties, and so he preferred to wait until the Directorate itself should seek his assistance. Conscious of the fact that his ideas upon the art of governing differed fundamentally from theirs, he refused to have anything to do with the government of France until they were willing to allow him to govern in his own way, and he had sufficient insight to see that a time was bound to come when conditions would have reached such a pass that they would be willing to grant him his terms.

Napoleon reserved to himself the right of initiating all laws, and he restricted the duties of the Assemblies to confirming or rejecting them. Yet while he insisted upon having the last word in the framing of all new laws, he always conferred with the two other Consuls with whom he was associated before proceeding even with the most trivial measures. He chose his agents of government indifferently from the Royalists, Girondins, or Jacobins, having regard only to their capacities. But although in his Council he sought the assistance of eminent jurists, he appears to have been always up against them, for he is reported to have said that any measure which is promoted for the public good is sure to meet with the opposition of lawyers. This fact is not surprising when we remember that lawyers are trained in the tenets of Roman Law, which is individualistic in intention, while measures for the public good are necessarily communal in aim.

I said that Napoleon ratified and consolidated the Revolution. His authority speedily put an end to the Parisian insurrections and attempts at monarchical resistance and restored moral unity where there had only been division and hatred. He provided work for the unemployed in building, the construction of military roads, and in minor ways, such as giving large orders for furniture for the Tuilleries. He was wise enough to see that no restoration of the *ancien régime* was possible, and so made no such foolish attempt, for he saw that order could only be restored on the assumption that those in possession of the land were confirmed in their ownership. With the law passed by the Convention enacting that all estates should be divided up at death equally among the children of the owner he did not interfere, nor with many other useful measures which had been enacted during the Revolution, such as the establishment of the metric system and the creation of important colleges. Indeed, all through the Revolution, much useful work of this kind was done by technical committees, in which the majority of the members of the Assemblies took refuge in order to escape from the political conflicts which threatened their lives.

The only statesman in history whose work may be compared with Napoleon is Augustus, since he undertook the task of reorganizing the Roman Empire after the Civil Wars as Napoleon did France after the Revolution. They both had recourse to similar methods of government. Both sought a solution in the organization of a highly centralized bureaucracy. Though we have no love for bureaucracy, we yet must recognize that when the traditions of a country have been destroyed there is no other way of delivering it from anarchy, and the popularity of the Napoleonic regime is a sure witness that though it was despotic it could not have been so intolerable as that which the people had endured during the Revolution.

The French Revolution does not appear to me to be a thing to be defended or denounced, but to be studied, for it is a rich field for the study of economics and psychology. We should aim at understanding it in order that we may profit by its mistakes. The convulsions of the Revolution were due to the fact that it attempted an impossible task. The revolutionists thought society could be reconstructed anew on a purely theoretical foundation, not understanding that the basis of every social order is to be found in certain traditions, and that it is only possible to reshape them within definite limits, for society can only exist by imposing certain restraints, laws, manners and customs to constitute a check upon the natural instincts of barbarism which never entirely disappear. The revolutionary gospel of nature, by removing these restraints, without which no society can exist, transformed a political society into a barbarian horde, for, misled by Rousseau, they did not understand that the aim of civilization was to escape from nature and not to return to it. Hence it was that while the Revolution had its moral sanction in the demand for the redress of certain definite social grievances, the feeling of unrest was exploited by idealists and theorists in an attempt to realize an unrealizable thing. Among other things, the events of the Revolution gave the lie to what might be called the spontaneous creation theory of democracy—the idea that the will of the people is omnipotent and final—for democracy cannot spontaneously create itself. Democracy will arrive when it knows how to choose the right ideas and *not a day before*, for there is a law of gravitation in human affairs which is as constant as the law of gravitation in the physical universe, and which all who aspire to govern society must obey. It was because the revolutionists did not understand this that the Revolution ended by establishing not the sovereign people, but a bureaucratic despotism.

It is remarkable how slow mankind is to learn by experience. A crisis has overtaken the modern world which has many parallels with the crisis which overtook France before the Revolution, and yet with the experience of the French Revolution to guide us, there is little or no attempt to learn the lessons which it has to teach. On the one hand we have a governing class, crying " Peace, peace," when there is no peace, as jealous of maintaining their privileges as the French nobility, and as unwilling as them to meet the need of additional taxation and equally blind to the inevitable consequences of their short-sightedness. On the other hand, just as in France there was a movement of peasants groping its way back to Mediævalism demanding the Just Price, so we have a popular movement on a similar quest demanding a fixed price and the control of profiteers. Just as this movement back to Mediævalism was frustrated by the French intellectuals who exploited the popular unrest in the interests of impossible ideals, so we have the Socialist Movement doing just the same thing. For in all the big fundamental things there is little to choose between the Socialists to-day and the French Revolutionaries. Both have got their ideas upside down. Rousseau made morality dependent upon Law, while Marx made it dependent upon economic condition. In theory this is a difference ;

in practice it is not, for both make morality dependent upon the maintenance of administrative machinery. Both concentrate upon property and ignore currency. Both search for a fool-proof State. And so it is in respect of the whole range of Socialist ideas. They differ from Rousseau only in being one degree further removed from reality ; for Rousseau did realize that the basis of society must rest upon agriculture, but Socialists to-day appear to have forgotten it. The difference of their ideas regarding property is a matter of minor importance, since the more they differ the more they are alike. They are alike in their belief that evil resides finally in institutions and not in men, and in their faith absolute in the natural perfection of mankind.

CHAPTER XIV

CAPITALISM AND THE GUILDS

WITH the French Revolution and the wars that followed it there fell what remained in Western Europe of the old Mediæval Order. Henceforth political thought no longer troubles itself with the issue of Church and State but with Capitalism which becomes the dominating power in the world. It will be necessary therefore for us, before proceeding further with the political problem, to retrace our steps to watch the rise of capitalist industry.

Capitalism, as we saw, had its origin in the growth of foreign trade, which offered merchants abundant opportunities for making profits by the manipulation of currency, unchecked by Guild regulations. But capitalist exploitation began on the land, when the merchants began to invest the wealth they had accumulated in land, and proceeded to convert tillage into pasturage. That such a development was possible was due, as we saw, to Roman Law, which corrupted the old Feudal order by instituting private ownership in land. Apart from Roman Law, the Feudal system would have been transformed, for the spread of currency into rural areas had gradually undermined its old stability by substituting money payments for payments in kind. But the fact that the transformation proceeded from Feudalism to landlordism and capitalism instead of from Feudalism to agricultural Guilds, which would have regulated currency by a system of fixed prices such as obtained in the towns, was due entirely to Roman Law, which, by instituting private property in land, paved the way to capitalist exploitation. Roman Law, then, created capitalism, and capitalism, we shall see, destroyed the Guilds.

From having commercialized agriculture, capitalists

turned their attention to the capture of industry. In the towns, capitalist exploitation was impossible, for the detailed regulations of the Guilds covered every condition of production. But outside of the towns in the rural areas no such regulations existed. The capitalist there was at liberty to do as he pleased. He could manufacture what he liked, use inferior material, pay low wages and sell at whatever price he liked, and there was no one to stop him. The capitalists who had taken to sheep-farming were not long in turning such circumstances to their advantage. They employed many of those whom they evicted from their holdings in the manufacture of cloth and articles made from it. It was thus there came into existence that " domestic system " of industry which was destined to be the destruction of the Guilds. As early as the fourteenth century the Guilds began to feel the competition of this domestic industry. The Guildsmen complained that the goods so produced were made of inferior material; that one master would employ many journeymen, have too many apprentices, and pay them a lower wage than was allowed by the Guilds, while some trades, as, for instance, the cappers and fullers, began to suffer from the competition of wares produced by machinery driven by water-mills. This led to so much improverishment among the craftsmen of the towns that fulling-mills were forbidden by statute in 1483.

Not only were the Guilds at a disadvantage in meeting such competition owing to the high standard of quality which they existed to uphold, but they were further handicapped by the fact that the towns came in for taxation which manufacturers outside of the towns were able to escape. " The pressure of the Apprenticeship Act of Henry IV, the heavy assessment which they paid for the wars with France, and for Henry VII's unnecessary exactions, and lastly, the regulations made by the Guilds with regard to apprentices and journeymen, were all telling against the old corporate towns ; they were at a disadvantage as compared with neighbouring villages, and there was in consequence a considerable displacement of industry from old centres to new ones, or to suburbs." [1] During the fifteenth century

[1] *Growth of English Industry and Commerce*, by W. Cunningham, pp. 460-1.

a general decay of English towns set in. Migration was no longer from the country to the towns, but from the towns back to the country, and with this change there came the decay of the Guilds which had grown up within the corporate towns.

There can be little doubt that the newer regulations of the Guilds which were regarded as tyrannical, and which we hear of in the fifteenth century, were brought about by the desire of those already in the Guilds to protect themselves against the competition of the rising capitalist industry. At an earlier date, it had been possible for every journeyman in the Guild to look forward to a day when he would be able to set up in business on his own account as a master. But now, when the monopoly of the Guilds was clearly breaking down before the rise of capitalist industry, and the masters were beginning to feel the pressure of competition, they began to frame regulations not with an eye to the interests of the craft as a whole, which was beyond their power, but solely to protect their own individual interests. Such undoubtedly was the origin of the grievance of the journeymen, for which they obtained redress in 1536, whereby, on becoming apprentices, they were made to swear upon oath not to set up in business in the towns without the consent and licence of the masters, wardens and fellowship of their Guild, upon pain of forfeiting their freedom or like penalty. One of the results of this restriction was to aggravate the tendency of journeymen to withdraw from the towns and set up shop in the villages where they were outside of Guild jurisdiction. To do this was often their only chance of getting employment, for the competition of the rural industries inclined the masters more and more to overstock their shops with an undue proportion of apprentices.

The growth of such abuses demonstrated clearly that the craft Guilds were breaking down before the rise of capitalist industry ; and it became evident that if industry was to continue to be subject to regulation, the Guild system would need to be reorganized upon national lines, or, in other words, that Guild regulation should be made co-extensive with industry and the various local Guilds linked up or federated into national ones. Some such general notion appears to have inspired the attempts at Guild reorganization by Henry VII and Henry VIII, who tried to get the Guilds placed entirely under the control of public authorities by enacting that in the future all Guild ordinances should be approved by the justices. This was the one reform which complainants had demanded in 1376 and 1473, as well as from the Tudors. Subject to such control, the Guilds were encouraged. But the measures they took were altogether inadequate to cope with the economic situation which was developing. Instead of seeking to establish a national system of Guilds, they merely extended certain local privileges, giving certain Guilds the right to search in rural areas within a certain radius of the towns. Justices of the peace were to appoint searchers for the shires.

We can easily imagine why such measures were ineffective. Capitalism had already got a firm foothold, and it could not be brought under control except by the most determined action on the part of the authorities, and justices of the peace would not be the kind of people to act in such a way. If regulations are going to be enforced, those empowered to enforce them must be made to suffer if they neglect in their duty, as is the case with democratically constituted Guilds. Such Guilds might have been established in the rural areas at the time of the Great Revolt. But the opportunity which then presented itself was lost. The peasants threw away their opportunity when they demanded the liberty to buy and sell instead of the protection of Guilds, and now the problem was not such a simple one. The development of foreign trade made the fixing and regulating of prices an extremely difficult one, and nothing short of a great popular movement demanding such reforms would have sufficed to render such measures practicable. But no such movement existed. The peasants, who had been driven off the land to make room for sheep, resented the monopolies of the Guilds. They had no idea of the value of their services in regulating currency, and welcomed action which removed their monopoly.

The Guilds received their death-blow when they found themselves no longer able to fix the prices of commodities, for everything turns upon this. If prices can be fixed, then it is a comparatively easy matter to enforce a standard of quality and maintain the internal discipline of the Guilds, but if prices cannot be fixed, then a standard of quality cannot be enforced, and the Guilds' jurisdiction over their members tends to become restricted within increasingly narrow limits.   The Guilds found themselves unable to determine prices during the sixteenth century.   In 1503 they lost their autonomy in this respect, when it was enacted that any change in the price of wares had to be "approved by the Chancellor, Treasurer of England and Chief Justices of either Bench, or three of them; or before both the Justices of Assizes in their circuit."[1]   But what finally broke the monopoly of the Guilds was the growing desire of the public to have prices fixed by *the haggling of the market*.[2]   No doubt they had acquired this taste through buying the products of the capitalist industry, which was subject to no regulation; and they came to demand the same terms from the Guild masters, who, presumably, suffering from competition, were unable to offer effective resistance.   But there was a deeper cause for the change.   The moral sanction of the Just Price had been undermined by the lawyers, who maintained the right of every man to make the best bargain he could—a right which was recognized in the Justinian Code.   St. Thomas Aquinas, in challenging the lawyers, defended the principle of the Just Price on purely moral grounds.   He failed altogether to perceive its economic significance, contending that "human law can only prohibit what would break up society.   Other wrong acts it treats as quasi-lawful in the sense that while not approving them, it does not punish them"—a strange conclusion to come to, considering how ruthlessly profiteering all through the Middle Ages was suppressed, and that failure to suppress it has in these days nearly broken society up.   It is thus we see the economic significance of the Guilds was not understood, and they had no official defenders.[3]   From this time onwards the Guilds lose their public functions.   In the seventeenth century, journeymen were excluded from

---

[1] Ashley, vol. i. part ii. p. 159.
[2] Ibid., vol i. part ii. p. 160.
[3] See Ashley, vol. i. part i. pp. 135–6.

their membership, and they continue as societies of employers. Two or three, even a dozen occupations, become united in one company (for they cease to be called Guilds), which bears the name of the occupation followed by the more influential citizens. Such companies continue to exist to this day in old towns in the provinces, as well as in London, and have given rise to the various Chambers of Commerce of our day. The property in the possession of these companies to-day is the property that remained in the possession of the Guilds after the confiscations made under the Chantries Bill (1547), in the reign of Edward VI. This Bill did not attack the Guilds as economic organizations, as is commonly supposed, nor did it seek to confiscate the whole of the property of the Guilds, but only such part of their revenues as had already been devoted to certain specified religious purposes. A great part of their wealth had been spent in providing masses for the souls of the deceased brethren, and it was the lands whose revenues were spent on such purposes that were confiscated. The revenues of the craft companies devoted to social and charitable purposes remained with the Guilds. All the same " the disendowment of religion in the misteries evidently accelerated the transformation of the system; for it removed one strong bond of union among the members, and limited their common efforts to the range of their material interests." [1]

The Elizabethan Statute of Apprentices, passed in 1563, may perhaps be regarded as an honest attempt to save something from the wreck. The Mediæval policy of regulating prices having broken down, it sought to protect the position of the skilled worker from deteriorating under competition.

" According to it no one could lawfully exercise, either as master or as journeyman, any art, mystery, or manual occupation, except he had been brought up therein seven years, at least, as an apprentice. Every householder dwelling in a city, town-corporate or market town, might take apprentices for seven years at least. But only those youths might be taken as apprentices whose parents possessed a certain fortune; and none could be bound but those who

[1] Ashley, vol. i. part ii. p. 158.

were under twenty-one years of age. Whoever had three apprentices must keep one journeyman ; and for every other apprentice above three, one other journeyman. As to journeymen, it was enacted that, in most trades, no person should retain a servant under one whole year, and no servant was to depart or be put away but upon a quarter's warning. The hours of work were fixed by the Act to about twelve in summer, and from day-dawn till night in winter. Wages were to be assessed yearly by the justices of the peace or the town magistrates, at every general session first to be holden after Easter. The same authorities were to settle all disputes between masters and apprentices, and protect the latter.[1]

Though this was, I believe, an honest attempt to protect the skilled workers, its mischief lay in the power given to the justices of the peace to determine wages, for in effect it handed the workers over to the mercy of their employers. Thorold Rogers condemns it severely on this account, affirming that it brought down wages to a bare subsistence. All the same, the Act does not appear to have been unpopular among the workers, for in the eighteenth century, when the assessment of wages had fallen into disuse, and wages had begun to be settled by competition, the workers in the skilled trades repeatedly petitioned Parliament to compel the justices to carry out the regulations as to apprentices, which they recognized would tend, by limiting the number practising a particular craft, to keep up the standard of wages. " When year after year, notwithstanding all the petitions of the workmen, the Acts regulating woollen manufacture were suspended, a factory was burnt down ; and in September, 1805, the London Fire Insurance Companies received letters of caution from workmen, wherein they declared that as Parliament refused to protect their rights they would do it themselves." It was determined action of this kind that brought the whole question to a head and led to the repeal of the statute in the woollen trade in 1806, and for all trades in 1814. And this, in spite of the fact that in petitions presented to Parliament 300,000 were for the maintenance of the statute and only 2,000 for its repeal.[2]

[1] Brentano : *History and Development of Gilds*, p. 103.   [2] Ibid., p. 128.

The repeal of this statute declared the state of industrial disorganization and disorder as the only lawful state. This state became only too soon the prevailing one in all trades. Parliamentary reports on the condition of the ribbon trade and the silk manufacture at Coventry, Nuneaton, and Macclesfield describe as the immediate consequence of the repeal, such a growth of the system of sweaters and half-pay apprentices, that the journeymen were driven to famine, and the female workers to prostitution. " Whilst the statute of the 5th Elizabeth was in force," says the report, " the distressing circumstances now complained of never occurred." The whole of the masters and weavers therefore petitioned in 1818 for the extension of the Spitalfields Acts to the silk trade in the said places. Reports of the year 1817 and 1818 give an absolutely identical account of the condition of the watchmakers at Coventry. Further, as the justices of the peace no longer assessed wages after having heard masters and men, the workmen now endeavoured to introduce regulation of wages by statement-lists of prices, agreed upon by masters and men. But they were violated upon every occasion by the employers. The words which Pitt spoke on the subject of the Arbitration Act were now completely fulfilled. " The time will come," he said, "when manufactures will have been so long established, and the operatives not having any other business to flee to, that it will be in the power of any one man in a town to reduce the wages, and all the other manufacturers must follow. If ever it does arrive at this pitch, Parliament, if it be not then sitting, ought to be called together, and if it cannot redress your grievances its power is at an end. Tell me not that Parliament cannot—it is omnipotent to protect." The workmen were quite of the opinion of Pitt, and numberless were the petitions which, after 1814, they addressed to Parliament for the legal regulation of their trades. But as Parliament thought it could not redress their grievances, they tried self-help. After the repeal of the Act of Elizabeth, combinations and unions therefore arose in all trades. But whilst, on the one hand, the workmen were refused legal protection, self-help, in consequence of the 39th and 40th George III, c. 106, was considered a crime. In 1818, bail to the amount of £200 and two sureties for £100 each were required for the appearance of a common workman at the next session to answer a charge of combining. The greatest mischief was, however, that the Combination Laws, by confounding right and wrong, led men to regard with less aversion things really vicious. The people, in their despair, did not shrink from the greatest deeds of violence and the most infamous crimes in self-defence."[1]

The consequence of these acts of violence was that in 1825 the Combination Laws were repealed. A London Radical, Francis Place, having by dexterously stage-managing the evidence given before a Royal Commission, succeeded in persuading the Government that Trade Unions owed their existence entirely to the irritation caused by the Combination Laws and that they would disappear with their repeal. Workmen were not granted full liberty of association, but a half-liberty. They were allowed to combine to determine rates of wages and hours of labour, but they were not allowed to limit the number of apprentices or to prevent piecework. Six months' hard labour was to be imposed on any one who should resort to violence, threats, molestation or obstruction in order to secure a rise of wages. The judges interpreted this clause as extending to workmen on strike who reproached other workmen for continuing to labour, thus making picketing illegal. They also decided that Trade Unions had no legal position, could not hold title to property nor maintain actions in the courts in defence of their rights. These grievances, along with a law which discriminated between the penalties meted out to employer and employee in the event of either breaking a contract, were removed by the Trade Union Act of 1871, which gave the Unions legal recognition. But it was not out of any largeness of heart of the employers, or any political insight of the governing class, that such status was given, but because an outbreak of working-class violence in Sheffield had led them to suppose that the existing law, by denying legal status to the Unions, tended rather to provoke than to repress violent action. It was thus at last the principles of Roman Law were successfully challenged, and the lie given to the Roman theory

[1] Brentano: *History and Development of Gilds*, pp. 129-131.

that only by sapping every tie between man and man could stability be given to the State.

In these days we recognize in the Trade Union Movement the first step towards a restoration of the Guilds. Already the Unions, with their elaborate organizations, exercise many of the functions which were formerly performed by the Guilds—such as the regulation of wages and hours of labour, in addition to the more social duty of giving timely help to the sick and unfortunate. Like the Guilds, the Unions have grown from small beginnings until they now control whole trades. Like the Guilds also, they are not political creations, but voluntary organizations which have arisen spontaneously to protect the weaker members of society against the oppression of the more powerful. They differ from them as industrial organizations only to the extent that, not being in possession of industry and of corresponding privileges, they are unable to accept responsibility for the quality of work done, and to regulate the prices. But these differences are the differences inherent in a stage of transition, and will disappear as the Unions trespass on the domains of the capitalist.

CHAPTER XV

POLITICAL AND ECONOMIC THOUGHT AFTER THE REFORMATION

By the end of the sixteenth century capitalism had triumphed. Not only had it succeeded in capturing agriculture and entirely undermining the position of the Guilds, but it had come to exercise a preponderating influence in the counsels of the State. The way for its advance in England had been opened by Henry VIII, who found himself compelled to create a new aristocracy out of the capitalists in order to destroy the power of the Church. It was not long after the political arrival of this new aristocracy that there came a new valuation of political and economic philosophy.

During the Middle Ages the theory obtained that national prosperity and well-being had its foundation in agriculture rather than commerce. Work and not wealth or property was the bestower of all worth and dignity. Mediæval economists deprecated any politico-economic movement that encouraged the people to give up the pursuit of agriculture for trade and commerce. Thus we read :—

" Among manual industries none stood higher in the estimation of the Canon Law than agriculture. It was looked upon as the mother and producer of all social organization and all culture, as the fosterer of all other industries, and consequently as the basis of national well-being. The Canon Law exacted special consideration for agriculture, and partly for this reason, that it tended in a higher degree than any other branch of labour to teach those who practised it godly fear and uprightness. ' The farmer,' so it is written in *A Christian Admonition*, ' must in all things be protected and encouraged, for all depends on his labour, from the Emperor to the humblest of mankind, and his handiwork

is in particular honourable and well-pleasing to God.' Therefore both the spiritual and the secular law protect him."

" Next to agriculture came handiwork. ' This is praise-
worthy in the sight of God, especially in so far as it represents
necessary and useful things.' And when the articles are
made with care and art, then both God and men take pleasure in them ; and it is good and true work when artistic
men, by the skill and cunning of their hands, in beautiful
building and sculpture, spread the glory of God and make
men gentle in their spirits, so that they find delight in beautiful things, and look reverently on all art and handicraft
as a gift of God for use, enjoyment, and edification of mankind."

" Trade and commerce were held in lower esteem. ' An
honourable merchant,' says Trithemius, ' who does not
only think of large profits, and who is guided in all his dealings
by the laws of God and man, and who gladly gives to the
needy of his wealth and earnings, deserves the same esteem
as any other worker. But it is no easy matter to be always
honourable in mercantile dealings, and with the increase
of gain not to become avaricious. Without commerce no
community, of course, can exist, but immoderate commerce
is rather hurtful than beneficial, because it fosters greed of
gain and gold, and enervates and emasculates the nation
through love of pleasure and luxury.' "

" The Canonical writers did not think it was conducive
to the well-being of the people that the merchants ' like
spiders should everywhere collect together and draw everything into their webs.' With the ever-increasing growth
and predominance of the mercantile spirit before their eyes,
they were sufficiently justified in their condemnation of the
tyranny and iniquity of trade which, as St. Thomas Aquinas
had already said, made all civic life corrupt, and by the
casting aside of good faith and honesty opened the door
wide to fraudulence ; while each one thought only of his
personal profit without regard to the public good." [1]

This attitude towards social questions came to an end at
the Reformation, when, with the destruction of the Church,

---

[1] *History of the German People at the Close of the Middle Ages*, by Johannes
Janssen, vol. ii. pp. 97–8.

power passed entirely into the hands of the capitalists who came to dominate the State. The political philosophy which gradually came into existence under their auspices looks at things from a very different angle. It makes no attempt to interpret society in the light of the principle of function, to conceive of society as a whole the parts of which are organically related to each other. There is little or no attempt on the part of Government to protect the interest of the labourer ; to take measures to see that the fruits of his labour are secured. for him. On the contrary, regard is paid only to the interests of the merchant, while the labourer is left to shift for himself as best he can, with only such doubtful protection as the Statute of Apprentices gave to the town workers. Though the claims of agriculture were not altogether neglected, yet the tendency in the long run was for statesmen and theorists to exalt manufacturers above agriculture and exchange above production. This came about because it was through foreign trade that the money was made which was the main source of revenue to the State and because there was a general tendency in the thought of the governing and merchant classes to identify money with wealth. The governing class of capitalists with their henchmen the lawyers consisted no longer of men capable of taking large and comprehensive views of society, but of men whose minds were entirely preoccupied with its material aspects. They concentrated all their attention upon finding ways and means to increase the wealth of the nation but for reasons perhaps best known to themselves they chose to ignore the problem as to how it was to be distributed.

External circumstances favoured the growth of this point of view in the governing class. The suppression of the monasteries had been followed by a period of great economic depression, when the people felt the pressure of poverty. There was great dislocation of industry everywhere and a debased coinage had not improved matters. The low-water mark was reached during the reign of Edward VI. Under Elizabeth things were lifted out of the mire and the country rescued from economic stagnation and depression by the encouragement given to manufacturers and foreign trade. The popularity of Elizabeth—for in spite of her

religious persecutions she was popular—was due to the
fact that the support she gave to the policy of William
Cecil, Lord Burghley, had the effect towards the close of her
reign of restoring the national prosperity. Immediately
the policy of Burghley was prompted by the likelihood of
a war with Spain. England had become Protestant, and
as she had hitherto been dependent for war material both
as regards gunpowder and the metals necessary for the
making of ordnance upon supplies that came from ports
controlled by the Roman Catholic Powers, it was urgent if
she was to retain her independence for her to have a supply
of her own. Every means therefore was taken to foster the
manufacture of munitions of war at home, and to such an
extent was the effort successful that when at last the storm
burst and the Spanish Armada sailed for England, it was
found that the leeway had been entirely made up and that
English guns were as good if not better than those of Spain.

But the new policy did not end here. Agriculture was
encouraged for military as well as for economic reasons.
Measures were taken to make tillage as profitable as pasturage
by removing the embargo upon the export of grain, while
enclosures were stopped. The fishing trades were supported
not merely for the wealth they produced but as a school
of seamanship to train men for the mercantile and naval
marine. These things did much to mitigate the evil of
unemployment which had become so chronic under previous
reigns, but further measures were taken to deal with it
definitely and to diffuse a general prosperity by the establishment of a great number of new industries that made goods
in England which hitherto had only been obtainable from
abroad. Industries for the manufacture of hardware,
sailcloth, glass-paper, starch, soap and other commodities
of common consumption were successfully established.
Mines also were opened. The assistance of German engineers
was called in for this. A new method of pumping which
they had invented made mining a more practicable and
commercial proposition.

The circumstances of the age were particularly favourable
to these new developments. The religious wars in the
Netherlands and elsewhere led to the emigration of great

numbers of skilled workmen, who found a haven of refuge
in England and brought a technical knowledge of new
industries with them.   Moreover, there was the change of
trade routes so favourable to English industry.   During the
Middle Ages these routes had been overland, and it was this
circumstance that brought such prosperity to the Hanseatic
towns of Germany whose central European position was
then so enviable.   But with the invention of the mariner's
compass, the discovery of America and the sea route to
India, overland trade routes gave place to sea routes, and
this took prosperity away from the Hanseatic and other
inland towns and countries and transferred it to seaports
and countries with a good seaboard.   This transformation,
which occupied the space of about fifty years, was very
profitable to English merchants and manufacturers, who
now began to secure a larger share of the commerce of
the world, and helped enormously to restore the national
prosperity.

It would have been a fortunate thing for England if the
political speculation which accompanied these changes had
kept its mental balance and reconciled in their true proportions the old with the new.   But unfortunately such was
not the case.   Prosperity had been restored not by efforts
to re-establish justice in the internal ordering of society
but by seizing the opportunities which a period of economic
transition afforded for the making of money.   And so faith
in the old order tended to decline while confidence in the
new increased.   Capitalism had been able to restore prosperity,
and so the opinions of capitalists came to weigh more and
more in the counsels of the State.,   Success in the new order
depended upon adaptability, and so the opinion grew that a
country lived not by its wisdom or its justice but by its
wits.   The State, which during the Middle Ages had concerned
itself exclusively with the functions of military protection
and the administration of the law, and since the reign of
Henry VIII had made itself responsible for the religious
life of the people, now began to concern itself with the promotion of industry and commerce.   According to the new
dispensation, wealth, or to be more strictly correct, bullion,
was the great alchemy.   Success in the race for wealth was

the precursor of all other desirable things. Hence it was the first concern of the State to see to it that there was always a large store of the precious metal on hand. To achieve this end, considered of such vital importance, every expedient was considered legitimate. The Government might prohibit the import or export of certain commodities. This industry was to be encouraged to export by subsidizing it with bounties, that was to be discouraged by the imposition of duties. Charters were granted giving private monopolies to certain companies. The test of success was to show a balance of trade in favour of the nation and an increase in the gold reserve. This system of the control of production and exchange by the State is known as Mercantilism. It is, as its name implies the interpretation, of national policy in the terms of the counting-house. Its defect was that it placed the State at the mercy of vested interests and was a source of political corruption, while it became a fruitful source of wars. In the Middle Ages wars had been territorial and dynastic. Now they became economic and were fought over tariffs, concessions and privileges. It was the inevitable consequence of the defeat of the Guilds, which, changing the ideal of industry from a qualitative to a quantitative one, necessarily brought those who pursued it in collision with economic interests beyond the seas. The wars with the Dutch were deliberately provoked by the Navigation Act, which prohibited the importation in foreign vessels of any but the products of the countries to which they belonged. It was intended to strike a fatal blow at the carrying trade of the Dutch from which they drew their wealth and to secure our supremacy on the seas ; and it was successful. The Mercantilists clearly grasped the fundamental economic fact, that under competitive conditions of industry the commercial advantage of one country is often only to be obtained at the expense of another, and that " Trade follows the flag," as Conservatives believe to this day. Mercantilism is not dead, it is the living faith of the commercial classes to-day in all countries of the world. Free Traders in these days are unwilling to face the unpleasant fact that the terms of the economic struggle are laid down by law and maintained by force, though Adam Smith did say, " As defence is of

much more importance than opulence, the Act of Navigation
is, perhaps, the wisest of all the regulations of England."
People who believe in commercialism ought to believe in
militarism. If one of these is to be deprecated, then the
other is. To believe in commercialism and regret militarism
is to live in a world of unrealities, as Free Traders in these
days are finding out.

Mercantilism was not a social theory but a commercial
policy evolved by men who were satisfied to assume that a
policy which suited their own immediate interests must be
good for society. It began its career during the reign of
James I, when Gerard Malynes, a specialist in currency,
whose advice on mercantile affairs was often sought by the
Privy Council, set forth his views in a series of pamphlets
in which he urged the Government to forbid the export of
bullion. The idea was a Mediæval one, and is altogether
unintelligible apart from the Mediæval system of thought,
which, refusing to divorce economies from moral considerations, placed the maintenance of the social order before the
interests of capital and trade. Viewing the social and economic
evils which accompanied the growth of foreign trade, it was
but natural that the Mediævalists, like Aristotle, should regard
its increase with alarm and suspicion and seek to put obstruc-
tions in the path of its advance, and that the support of the
State should be secured for obstructionist tactics by the
convenient theory that armies and fleets could only be maintained in distant countries if there is money to pay for them,
and that such money would not be forthcoming when wanted
if bullion were exported from the country. But Malynes,
writing at a later date, urged his case upon other grounds—
that as exchange implied value for value, the operation of
the exchanges defrauded the revenue.

Taking his stand upon such purely technical grounds, the
first Mercantilists found no difficulty in refuting him. If
the increase of foreign trade was a good and desirable thing
quite apart from how the increased wealth was distributed—
and in official quarters this assumption was taken for granted
—then the Mercantilists were easily able to show that
restrictions on the export of bullion impeded the growth of
foreign trade. " They represented, first, that the exporta-

tion of gold and silver, in order to purchase foreign goods, did not always diminish the quantity of those metals in the kingdom. That, on the contrary, it might frequently increase that quantity ; because if the consumption of foreign goods was not thereby increased in the country, those goods might be re-exported to foreign countries, and, being there sold for a large profit, might bring back much more treasure than was originally sent out to purchase them." [1] Thomas Mun, who is sometimes described as the founder of Mercantilism and whose treatise *England's Treasure in Foreign Trade* which, often reprinted during the seventeenth and eighteenth centuries, retained almost canonical authority until it was displaced by *The Wealth of Nations*, declared that " Money begets trade and trade increases money." He compared the operations of foreign trade to the seed-time and harvest of agriculture. " If we only behold," he says, " the actions of the husbandman in the seed-time, when he casteth away much good corn unto the ground, we shall account him rather a madman than a husbandman. But when we consider his labours in the harvest, which is the end of his endeavours, we shall find the worth and plentiful increase of his actions."

The sub-title of the treatise declares that " the balance of our foreign trade is the rule of Treasury," and the object is declared to be to exhibit the means by which a kingdom may be enriched. " The ordinary means to increase our wealth and treasure is by foreign trade, wherein we must ever observe this rule—to sell more to strangers yearly than we consume of theirs in value. For that part of our stock which is not returned to us in wares must necessarily be brought home in treasure." Every effort must therefore be devoted to increase our exports and to decrease our consumption of foreign commodities. Waste land should be used to grow hemp, flax and other articles which are now imported. We might also diminish our imports if we would lessen our demand for foreign wares in diet and raiment. The vagaries and excesses of fashion might be corrected by adopting sumptuary laws prevailing in other countries. " If in our raiment we will be prodigal, let this be done by our own manufactures, where the success of the rich may be the

[1] *Wealth of Nations*, by Adam Smith, book iv. chap. i.

employment of the poor, whose labours, notwithstanding, would be more profitable if they were done to the use of strangers." We may charge a high price for articles which our neighbours need and which no other country can supply ; but those of which we do not possess the monopoly must be sold as cheap as possible. Foreign materials worked up in England for export should be duty free. Our exports should be carried in our own ships, and our fisheries should be developed. Writing as a Director of the East India Company, Mun pronounced our trade with the East Indies the most profitable of our commercial activities, not only because we obtain its products cheaply for ourselves, but because we sell the surplus at a high price to our neighbours. This " may well stir up our utmost endeavours to maintain and enlarge this great and noble business, so much importing the public wealth, strength and happiness." [1]

Such was the faith of Mercantilism as it was most widely accepted. Apart from what he has to say about sumptuary laws, which has a fifteenth-century ring about it, it is the same faith as that of the average commercial man to-day. Subsequent writers sought to widen out the Mercantile theory. They deprecated the exaggerated importance given to foreign trade and emphasized the importance of home markets and agriculture. Rejecting the notion that the national wealth depended on cash, they maintained that goods paid for goods and that nature and labour were the ultimate source of wealth. To this extent their thought showed a reversion towards the Mediæval point of view. But on the other hand they were modernist, being the fore-runners of the Free Traders. They attacked the elaborate system of prohibitions, duties, bounties and monopolies as an impediment rather than an encouragement to trade. Dudley North anticipated Adam Smith when he declared, " The world as to trade is but as one nation, and nations are but as persons. No trade is unprofitable to the public ; for if any prove so, men leave it off ; and wherever the trader thrives the public thrives also." Charles Davanent, another of the school, maintained that loss by balance in one trade may cause profit in another. " Trade," he says, " is in its

---

[1] *Political Thought from Bacon to Halifax*, by G. P. Gooch, pp. 232–4.

own nature free, finds its own channel, and best directeth its own course." But he forgets that the same arguments may be turned against him. For while it is true that trade when untrammelled will find its own channel, it does not follow that the channel it finds is a socially desirable one ; for while loss in one trade may cause profit in another, one man is called to bear the loss while another gets the profits, resulting in an unequal distribution of wealth that is anything but socially advantageous.

The next development of Mercantilism is associated with the name of Adam Smith. I call it the next development because though it is true the Manchester School reversed the economic maxims of the Mercantilists, yet finally they only differed from them to the extent of carrying their ideas to their logical conclusion. The Mercantile theory of Mun was a theory of the business of making money by foreign trade. As such it provided a theory or policy for a group of interests which it assumed was in the public interest, but it took no particular pains to explain how and why. The Free Traders who followed him attempted to give the theory a wider application, demanding the abolition of privileges in trade. But they went little further than making this demand. To secure acceptance for such proposals something more was needed. Free Trade would remain unacceptable as an administrative proposal so long as political and economic thought was dominated largely by Mediæval preconceptions, and it became necessary, therefore, to secure acceptation for the Free Trade policy to undermine what remained of Mediæval political and economic thought. This was the work of Adam Smith. To the Mediæval idea of privileges for all he opposed the idea of the abolition of all privileges and unfettered individual competition which he associated with the gospel of Free Trade. To the Mediæval idea of the Just Price he opposed the idea that prices were best settled by competition. "To buy in the cheapest market and to sell in the dearest" was a policy calculated to secure the greatest good of the greatest number. But such economic principles were incompatible with the Mediæval and Christian ideal of human unselfishness. Then, concluded Adam Smith, such principles had no relevance in economics. Not unselfishness but enlightened self-interest was the ideal to be aimed at.

In his *Theory of Moral Sentiments* Adam Smith postulates the doctrine of sympathy as the real bond between human beings in their ethical relations. But in the *Wealth of Nations* he makes it clear that human sympathy has no place in economic relationships. " It is not from the benevolence of the butcher, the brewer, or the baker," he tells us, " that we expect our dinner, but from their regard to their own self-interest. We address ourselves, not to their humanity, but to their self-love, and never talk to them of our necessities, but of their advantage." This perverted attitude of mind permeates the whole of Adam Smith's writings. According to him the public well-being was secured, not by the assertion of communal interests, by the subordination of individual interests to those of the community, but by the deliberate removal of all economic restraints in order that each individual might be at liberty to pursue his own selfish ends without let or hindrance. *Laissez-faire, laissez passer* was the key to unlock all economic problems, the sole panacea for all human ills, the only hope of social regeneration. Give free play to enlightened self-interest and natural liberty, and prosperity would soon shine in all its splendour on every department of the national life, for the effect of urging each individual to pursue his interests under a system of unfettered individual competition would be to so stimulate trade and cheapen production that there would soon be plenty for all and to spare.

That Adam Smith should have been hailed as a prophet can only be explained on the hypothesis that the moral tone of society had already reached its nadir ere he wrote. Ruskin's allusion to him as " the half-bred and half-witted Scotchman who taught the deliberate blasphemy : Thou shalt hate the Lord thy God, damn His laws and covet thy neighbour's goods," was well deserved, and is not the less true because he was sufficiently cunning to wrap up his devilish advice in language of plausible sophistry instead of presenting it in the raw. The apology of all who act as Adam Smith would have them do is that they take the world as they find it, but they conceal the fact that they are content to leave it worse than they found it. Of no one is this truer than of Adam Smith. He was the pioneer of that economic fatalism which during its fifty years of power paralysed society. In the hands of his followers all his half-hearted qualifications were torn away and political economy became the rigid soulless doctrine of every man for himself and the devil take the hindermost, and all sympathy for the exploited was strangled by the Ricardian "iron law of wages." That Ruskin entirely annihilated the brazen doctrine in the first three pages of *Unto this Last*, published in 1862, by exposing the fallacy underlying the method of reasoning of the Manchester economists, any one with an ounce of logic in his composition is well aware. Yet in spite of this it showed no signs of weakening until its most distinguished adherent, John Stuart Mill, disowned the superstition seven years afterwards, in 1869.

Apologists of Adam Smith urge in his defence that the governing class took only so much from his teaching as suited them and ignored the rest, and he is therefore not to be blamed for the misinterpretation or misapplication of his principles. While this plea may be urged in defence of other men, it cannot be urged in the case of Adam Smith. Most pioneers of thought have to complain that their followers have been true to the letter of their advice while their spirit has been neglected, but the governing class were true to the spirit of Adam Smith's gospel if not to the letter. If Adam Smith really thought that he could on the one hand urge individuals to pursue their own selfish interests and at the same time forgo in the public interest any privileges they might possess, he is to be regarded as a fool of the first order, half-witted as Ruskin called him, entirely destitute of any understanding of the human psychology, for the heartless competition to which he condemned those without privileges made those who possessed privileges cling to them more tenaciously than ever.

But the evil of Adam Smith's gospel does not end with the fact that it confirmed the governing class in the pursuit of their own selfish interests ; it operated to force the working class to pursue the same policy in self-defence. Hence the theory of Adam Smith leads logically to that of Marx.

The doctrine of individualism leads inevitably to that of the Class War, which is the natural and inevitable rebellion of the masses against a governing class that has become, in the words of Sir Thomas More, " a certain conspiracy of rich men procuring their own commodities under the name and title of the Common Wealth."

CHAPTER XVI

THE INDUSTRIAL REVOLUTION

In the latter half of the eighteenth century there was inaugurated a series of changes in methods of production which gradually changed England from being a country mainly rural and agricultural into one largely urban and industrial. The period of transition is known as the Industrial Revolution, and is roughly dated from about 1770 to 1840, though of course these dates are entirely arbitrary inasmuch as industry had been moving in this direction for at least the two preceding centuries, while the development and expansion of the forces then set in motion have continued ever since. But it was during those years that the really dramatic changes were made. In 1769 Watts made the steam engine of Newcomen into a really practical and commercial thing by the introduction of a separate condenser, and this invention was the central agency for transforming industry from a basis of handicraft to machine production. Meanwhile the textile industry was becoming rapidly mechanized. In 1730 Kay invented the flying shuttle; in 1770 Hargreaves the spinning jenny. Arkwright, Compton and Cartwright followed with their inventions which made possible the application of steam power to textile production. The ball was now fairly set rolling; inventions in one trade promoted inventions in another. The inventions of the cotton industry were adapted to the woollen and linen trades, to hosiery, silk and lace-making. First one trade and then another succumbed to the new inventions until in our day this tendency has reached its climax in the growth of automatic machinery to which the war gave such an impetus.

For some time before the Industrial Revolution burst

upon the world industry had been becoming more mechanical. The introduction into the workshops of the system of the division of labour in the seventeenth century by splitting up the handicrafts into simple detailed operations paved the way for change. For as machinery in its infancy was only capable of performing separate and simplified operations, it is evident that so long as all the operations necessary to production in any of the handicrafts were the work of a skilled handicraftsman machinery could make very little headway. But when the individual labourer was confined in his operations to a single simple mechanical task, the road was paved for the introduction of machinery by simplifying the problem of the inventor.

This change from a qualitative to a quantitative basis for industry was not introduced without a considerable amount of opposition, which came both from above and from below. The craftsmen hated it, and it is safe to say the change would never have been made but for the defeat of the Guilds, since so long as the workers retained any control over the conditions of their employment they would resist changes in production which destroyed pleasure in work and involved their personal degradation. The instinct of the craftsman is always against factory production. There is no *Mediæval prejudice* about this, for in this respect craftsmen have not changed since the Middle Ages. The hand-loom weavers refused to go into the factories in Lancashire, though the wages were higher, because they hated the discipline of the factories and felt it a moral surrender to accept voluntarily such conditions of servitude. "Although to the authors of the books on the advantages of machinery, invention seemed to have lightened the drudgery of men and women, it had introduced a wearing tension ; the nervous strain of watching machinery and working with machinery aged men and women faster than the heaviest physical exertions." [1] Every craftsman instinctively knows this, and it is this that lies at the bottom of their hatred of machinery. The class to-day, as at the time of the Industrial Revolution, which is most certain

[1] *The Town Labourer*, 1760–1832, by J. L. Hammond and Barbara Hammond, p. 21.

of the benefits of machinery is the class the farthest removed from it, who profit by the conveniences it brings them and who are not called upon to support its burden. As the class which was required to attend machinery viewed the matter otherwise, it is apparent that its introduction pre-supposes the existence of a slave class in society that can be exploited. Indeed, it was from such a class that the first factory operatives came. "There were three main disturbances of the regular life of the time to account for the great stream of population into Lancashire and the adjacent counties. There was, first, the agrarian revolution in England, dispossessing a large number of small agricul-turists and breaking down the life and economy of the old village. There was, secondly, the congestion of Ireland and the acute distress caused by the exactions of an absentee landlord-class. There was, in the third place, the long war ; the disbanding of a huge army let loose a flood of men whose ties with their own homes were broken. The building of canals and bridges helped to make labour more mobile, and these enterprises drew people to the districts where labour was wanted for the factories." [1]

Until the middle of the seventeenth century the efforts of the workers to resist mechanical innovations found support in high quarters. It is well known that the Tudors were consistently opposed to the introduction of machinery which was injurious to handicraftsmen or would lower the standard of quality in the articles produced. For a long period they appear to have regarded machinery with the same hostility as did the Luddites in the early years of the nineteenth century. Inventive genius was then termed "subtle imagination," and any substitute for the manufacture by hands and feet was regarded as the ruin of the industry concerned. For this reason the fulling mill in 1482, the gig mill in 1552, and the tucking mill in 1555 were discountenanced. The advisers of Edward VI and Elizabeth, though they encouraged foreign trade, were equally opposed to mechanical innovations. James I and Charles I assumed the same attitude. They stood by the

[1] *The Town Labourer*, 1760–1832, by J. L. Hammond and Barbara Hammond, p. 13.

handicraftsmen and insisted that manufacturers should not dismiss their workmen owing to fluctuations of trade which had been artificially created by themselves in their pursuit of a quantitative ideal in production. Next to keeping men in employment, the chief object which the first of the Stuarts set before themselves was the maintenance of a high standard of quality in the goods produced, and for this purpose they sought to arrest that steady deterioration of quality in wares which had followed the defeat of the Guilds, by providing supervision for existing industries.

For a long time the opposition was successful in checking the mechanical tendency in industry. But it was broken down finally by the combined influence of two forces— the growth of foreign trade and the Puritan Movement. The discovery of America had provided England with an apparently inexhaustible market for its commodities. This removed the economic objection to change by providing an outlet for the surplus products which accompanied efforts to place production on a quantitative basis. As the fear of unemployment was diminished the opposition was deprived of its strongest argument—the only one perhaps that would carry any weight with the middle-class Puritans, who were now becoming such a power in the land, and who joined with the landlords to overthrow Charles at the Civil War. With the defeat of Charles the old order came to an end. Nothing now stood in the way of business and enterprise, sweating and mechanical industry. The mind of the Puritan was hard and mechanical, devoid alike of any love of beauty or human sympathy. The Puritans were in the main recruited from the trading classes of the community, and denounced the restrictions which Charles imposed on machinery as an interference with personal liberty. Any thought of putting a boundary to mechanical development was to them insufferable tyranny, and there can be little doubt that the attitude of the Stuarts towards machinery and their attempts to stem the tide of capitalist industry was a chief contributory cause of the Civil War. Their interferences naturally gave rise to discontent among men whose ruling passion was that of avarice and whose natures were so corrupted as to exalt this besetting sin of theirs to the level of a virtue, celebrated at a later day by Samuel Smiles. This perversion of the nature of the Puritan is to be attributed to the fact that he denied himself all the normal pleasures of life. He was cruel to himself, and so he found no difficulty in being cruel to others, especially when it was of assistance to him in the making of money.

It was because the Industrial Revolution was dominated by the Puritan spirit that it was so relentless in its cruelty. When we read of the terrible conditions of factory life in Lancashire during this period, of workers locked in factories, of the heartless exploitation of women and young children, of the ceaseless day and night work, of children working by relays and sleeping in filthy beds that were never allowed to cool, of weary hands and feet following rapidly the quick movements of the never-tiring machines, we realize that it was dominated by men who had become dehumanized, and that the personal independence of the workers must have entirely disappeared, for no class of human beings would consent to submit to such conditions who retained a scrap of independence. It was not until 1832 that the factory working day was reduced to twelve hours and to ten hours in 1847. It was not without good reason that at Ashton in 1831 it was declared " that the negroes were slaves in name but the factory employees were slaves in reality." [1]

What happened in England appears to have happened wherever industrialism has been introduced. The Prussian Government deliberately dispossessed the Polish peasantry of their lands in order to ensure a cheap supply of labour for their factories. America still exploits the cheap labour of Eastern Europeans, while until quite recently child labour was exploited in the cotton mills of the Southern States almost as mercilessly as it was in England before the passing of the Factory Acts. The Swadeshi Movement is closely associated with the introduction of Industrialism into India, and under its auspices the same evils are being created. Just what the factory system is beginning to

[1] *The Town Labourer,* 1760–1832, by J. L. Hammond and Barbara Hammond, p. 18.

16

mean for India is to be inferred from a recent report of
the Indian Factory Commission : " In daylight mills the
average working time for the whole year is twelve hours
and five minutes ; in mills fitted with electric light thirteen
to thirteen and a half hours." But the Commissioners say
" in some provinces the law is ignored to an extent not
hitherto imagined. The law referring to the half-hour's
recess is generally disregarded in rice mills, grinding factories
and flour mills throughout India." In Bombay the factory
operatives inhabit slums of the most wretched character,
crowded and insanitary. Indeed, India appears to be light-
heartedly plunging into the sufferings which are the
inevitable accompaniment of factory production.[1]

Nowadays the Industrial system encompasses us on
all sides, and the question may be asked, Has the system
come to stay or are the difficulties in which it finds itself
to-day the beginning of the end ? If the answer to this
question depended upon votes I doubt not there would
be an overwhelming majority in favour of its retention,
for the mass of people to-day are so much a part of the
system as to be incapable of understanding how the needs
of society could be met apart from our huge machinery.
They fail altogether to realize that in the fifteenth century
the wages of the town artisan worked out at six or seven
times the cost of his board, and the agricultural labourer
earned two-thirds of this amount. Though nearly everybody is dissatisfied with the present order of society, very
few people suspect that there is any connection between
the evils they deplore and industrial methods of production.
Others, realizing that the social problem preceded the
Industrial Revolution, are disposed to dismiss the industrial
problem as a false issue. Neither our own nor future generations, they contend, can escape the influence of modern
technology.

Now quite apart from the issue as to whether modern
technology is entitled to the respect with which it is customary to regard it, it is manifest that it has been reared
on a base of social and economic injustice and that it is

[1] See *Essays in National Idealism*, by Ananda K. Coomaraswamy,
pp. 157–8 (P. Natesan & Co., Madras; Probsthain & Co., London).

maintained to-day by a highly complex system of finance. It follows, therefore, that any change which threatens this basis must react on the technology. If the highly complex system of finance were to break down, as it already shows signs of doing, modern technology would be involved in the catastrophe. A very few years of social confusion and the fabric of technology would be in pieces. For whereas a simple or primitive technology can speedily recover from violent upheavals, a highly complex and artificial one cannot, because its maintenance is dependent upon a high degree of co-operation. The imminence of an economic breakdown which is becoming generally admitted, raises, therefore, the question, Could the modern technology be rebuilt after the breakdown ?

Now, it is my contention that the economic and psychological conditions necessary to reconstruct it will be absent. Once there is a breakdown the spell that blinds the modern world will be broken and all the anarchistic tendencies of the modern man will be liberated. Every popular demand to-day is for something which is incompatible with the industrial order. That this incompatibility is not recognized is due to the fact that few people trouble to carry ideas to their logical conclusions and imagine they can eat their cake and have it at the same time. The realization of these demands will, so far as the Industrial system is concerned, be like putting new wine into old bottles, and it will burst the bottles. The Industrial system demands for its maintenance the servitude of the workers, while the workers demand liberty. The life and soul of the system is the race for profits ; the workers demand production shall be for use and not for profit. Its finance and technology involve a highly centralized control ; the workers demand a distributive initiative. This demand for something which is incompatible with the industrial ideal is not only confined to the consciously organized political workers ; it is made by individuals in their private capacity in every rank of society. Industrialism, built upon the division of labour, denies men pleasure in their work. The consequence is that men seek happiness in other ways, in the pursuit of pleasure in their leisure, in the excitement of gambling. Both of these things tend to undermine the old hard Puritanical morale which built up and maintained the system. The gambling spirit in trade has, through profiteering, dislocated the economic system, and led men to trust to chance rather than hard work for success in life. The craving for pleasure has become such that only the external pressure of circumstances can keep men at work. The reaction against speeding up has come. Nobody nowadays wants to do any work. The old incentives are gone. Interest has gone out of work, and there is no prospect of the workmen setting up in business on his own account, which up to a generation ago preserved a certain morale in industry. Experience in large organizations has taught men that success and promotion do not come to the conscientious or capable worker, but to the toady and bluffer. All this is demoralizing, and provides no basis for the future reconstruction of industry on a mechanical basis. Now that the workers are organized, the demand of the rank and file is not to control industry. They have too strong a sense of human values to desire that but to get through the day with the least possible effort. The reason for this is that what the workers in their hearts really desire is control of their own lives in the same way that the hand-loom weavers had control; and it is because mass production everywhere stands between them and such control that subconsciously they everywhere seek the destruction of the industrial system.[1]

In these circumstances, if industry is to be rebuilt after the economic breakdown, it will have to be rebuilt upon a different foundation, and its central aim must be to give back to men pleasure in their work. A rebuilt Industrialism cannot do this, because its central principle is that of the division of labour. It is all very well for would-be industrial reformers to talk about stimulating the creative impulse of industry, but the system of the division of labour precludes this possibility. I confess to a complete inability to understand reformers who talk

---

[1] " Capitalism cannot be controlled. But it can be destroyed and replaced by a workers' Industrial Republic " (*The State : its Origin and Function*, by Wm. Paul, p. 195).

about "stimulating the impulses of youth for creative existence" and don't challenge the system of the division of labour. I doubt very much whether they mean anything. Nay, I do not doubt it ; I am sure of it. We know that the system of the division of labour was the great factor in the destruction of the creative impulse, and we may be sure that the impulse will not reappear until the system is destroyed. It came into existence for the purposes of exploitation, and it will go with it. If men are ever to regain control over their environment, the system of the division of labour will need to be broken, since so long as it remains the mass of workers will be at the mercy of the power that directs the system.

But, it will be asked, is machinery to disappear ? It will need to in so far as its effect has been to enslave man. Generally speaking, this would mean that small machines would be permitted, while large ones would be forbidden on the principle that a large machine tends to enslave man, because he must sacrifice himself mentally and morally to keep it in commission, whereas a small one has not this effect, because it can be turned on and off at will. Exceptions would have to be made to this rule, as in the case of pumping and lifting machinery where no question of keeping it in commission necessarily enters. The difficulty of deciding where a machine was and was not harmful would not be difficult to determine once the general principle were admitted that machinery needs to be subordinated to man.

CHAPTER XVII

PARLIAMENTARIANISM AND THE NINETEENTH CENTURY

BY the end of the eighteenth century the regime established by the Reformation in England began to show signs of breaking down. The pursuit of wealth which had been the vitalizing principle of the period was bringing in its train all manner of economic and political complications. It had resulted in the concentration of wealth in the hands of the few. Class divisions and class hatred were increasing. Money made in trade was employed in land speculation. Rents were raised and wages reduced. After the Napoleonic wars there came economic stagnation and widespread unemployment. Government had fallen into the hands of an oligarchy who wielded all political power. Spiritually, society was dead. Religion had reached its lowest ebb. Architecture had become a lifeless formula. The crafts, from being media of æsthetic expression, had degenerated into affairs of trade and commerce. Some slight tradition of art lingered in painting, which henceforth monopolized the name of art. Political science as a theory of the social organism had entirely disappeared, and its place had been taken by a new political economy which revived the laws of the jungle. Nothing now remained of the old mediæval order but its human tradition which survived among the poor. Mankind was left

> Wandering between two worlds, one dead,
> The other powerless to be born.

The nineteenth century is the story of the wandering.

Though the world was dead, it was not without hope. The old order was gone. Most people thought it had gone for ever, for out of its ashes new hopes had arisen. The French Revolution and the Industrial Revolution combined to give the age a vision. It was not the vision of a new social order, but of idealized anarchy, for the impulse of the century was destructive rather than constructive. Social order is impossible apart from privileges involving reciprocal rights and duties. But privileges in the post-Reformation period had come into disrepute, partly because they were monopolized by the few instead of being shared by the many, as was the case in the Middle Ages, but mainly because they were so grossly abused by those who claimed rights but repudiated responsibilities. Hence it was that as privileges were associated with tyranny, liberty, in the minds of Radicals, became associated with the abolition of privileges, with the negation of social order, with anarchy. The French Revolution had given men the hope that the governing class might be overthrown. But its influence was ephemeral and had evaporated by the middle of the century. It is less to the influence of the French Revolution than to that of the Industrial Revolution that we must look for an interpretation of the nineteenth century, for it was the central driving force which completely disrupted what remained of the old social order, reducing it to atomic units which lacked the principle of cohesion except for the purposes of economic and military defence. That so little resistance was offered to the socially disintegrating influence of machinery was due to the fact that the automaton came to exercise an influence over the minds of men akin to that of magic. It hypnotized them into the belief that there was some virtue in change for the sake of change, that what was new was in some mysterious way superior to the old and that in some way unknown to themselves the machine would, if given free play, solve all social problems. For so many generations had the descendants of the men who stole the Church lands drilled into the minds of the people the idea that the Middle Ages was a period of black tyranny, ignorance, superstition and poverty, that a prejudice had been created which was fatal to all clear thinking on social questions and credence was given to the idea, enunciated by Adam Smith, that poverty was due to lack

of productive power instead of to gross social and economic
injustice, as was actually the case.   It was thus that during
the nineteenth century faith in the benevolence of machinery
became the faith of the people. ; Its sufficiency was exalted
into a dogma above and beyond discussion.   A man might
question God but not the machine—to do so was heresy
in the nineteenth century. ; Hence the key to the century
is not to be found in ideas, for the great men of the century
left no permanent impression on their age, but in this
hypnotic belief in progress which carried all before it.   As
the machine created problem after problem, barrier after
barrier was swept away, and as each one was swept away
civilization found itself somewhere where it never expected
to be.

The change in the material and economic base of society
was accompanied by the growth of an intellectual fluidity
" which is really not so much a definite conviction or
emotion as a rotting or a deliquescence, a melting and
confounding of the outlines of beliefs and desires, a going
to slush of all values, a thawing and liquefaction of all that
was hard and permanent in the world. . . ∕ The whole of
modernism is an attempt to obliterate distinctions—to
discover similarity and unity everywhere.   All men are
equal, men are the same as women, good is the same as
evil, freewill does not exist, catastrophe has no place in
the universe, and everything is gradually evolved." [1]   The
first step in this movement towards the obliteration of
varieties was taken by Adam Smith in the *Wealth of
Nations* ; the last was taken by Mr. Bernard Shaw in
the *Quintessence of Ibsenism.*   It was Mr. Shaw's strange
ambition to emancipate mankind by emptying life of its
remaining contents, but the more Mr. Shaw seeks to change
things the more he reveals himself a child of the established
material fact, who is content to take the material achievement for granted as a thing of permanence and stability.
He had lived all his life in a world of illusions, vainly
imagining he was at work laying the foundations of a new
social order, whereas in reality he was doing nothing more
or less than assisting to remove the last barrier that stood

[1] Letter to the *New Age*, by E. Cowley, November 13, 1913.

between industrial civilization and its final catastrophe. For catastrophe became inevitable from the day it became the fashion for men to deny its possibility; for when the fear of catastrophe was removed no power remained capable of restraining the forces of social destruction. These crazy heretical philosophers were followed in the nineteenth century because they were the only people who could set things in motion. After the Napoleonic wars economic stagnation had overtaken England as a consequence of the concentration of wealth in the hands of a few. In the normal course of affairs this undue concentration would have led to a revolution in England as it did in France, but this was averted by following the advice of these false prophets who taught the governing class the art of postponing the crisis by extending the area of exploitation. This was the secret of the success of the Free Trade policy; of the economic relief which uncontrolled machinery brought. By producing large quantities of goods cheaply, which enabled our manufacturers to exploit distant markets, by the development of railway building which offered new opportunities for investment and caused a great shifting of the centres of population from villages to small towns and from small towns to big ones, activity was stimulated in every direction. This temporarily decentralized wealth and brought about a distributed initiative. The prosperity thus artificially created led people to suppose that the principles of the new political economy were eternally true instead of being a mere theoretical justification of measures of economic expediency, useful at a particular juncture but with no finality about them. The supposed central truth of the new economics having been established in this way, sophists found no difficulty in persuading the world that all other ideas and traditions which clashed with the demands of " progress " were of themselves dated. Such ideas, they affirmed, might be true at one stage of social evolution but not at another. All truth, they maintained, was relative; absolute truth did not exist.

Meanwhile people who had preserved their mental balance found themselves at a disadvantage. To them the fallacies of the new gospel were manifest. They found it easy to expose them, but impossible to base any practical activity upon the truth as they understood it. The reason for this was to be found in the fact that since the decline of religion and art the links between them and the popular mind had been broken. They were no longer understood. Hence it came about that throughout the nineteenth century efforts were made by means of experiments and historical research to find lost roads and to recover lost truths. Efforts were made to revive religion, art and social science. This is the secret of the great intellectual and scholastic activity of the nineteenth century. Its aim was to enable men to regain that grip on reality which they had lost. To talk about the nineteenth century as being an age of enlightenment is nonsense. It was perhaps the darkest period in history, when the great traditions were dead; when great men groped for the light and ordinary men were saved from despair by the hypnotism of the machine.

But the world heeded such workers little. The problems of the immediate present pressed so heavily upon the majority that they were in no mood to listen to any gospel that could not promise immediate results. They were impatient with men who took longer views. Hence it was all through the nineteenth century the blind led the blind. Politics concerned themselves with appearances; realities lived underground. Two men only who were prominent in political life were possessed of a strong sense of reality —Cobbett and Disraeli. The former made a desperate effort to pump realities into politics from below; the latter having failed to pump realities into them from above, came to accept the situation and exploit it.

Cobbett towers above all his contemporaries as a man in touch with realities. He associated himself with all the Radicals of his age in their demand for the reform of Parliament. Though he differed with them fundamentally as to the nature of the problems of society, he saw as clearly as they did the need of Parliamentary reform. The ideal of government as it existed in the Middle Ages was to give protection to the workers. It was for this purpose that charters were given to the Guilds and the Feudal Lord held his position. But since the revival of Roman Law, government had become increasingly associated with exploitation, and after the Reformation it existed for little else. The plutocrats who controlled it not only refused to give the people economic protection, but forbade them to organize to protect themselves. In these circumstances the necessary first step towards reform was to change the Government, but as Parliament was elected upon a franchise which was limited and corrupt, and the people were deprived of any place in the social scheme, this involved electoral reform, upon which, after the Napoleonic wars came to an end, the Radicals concentrated their attention.

Though for the attainment of electoral reform Cobbett co-operated with the Radicals, he took a different view to them on almost everything, and looking at the situation from the point of view of to-day it is possible to say that Cobbett was in the main right. He exhibited a wider grip of the social problem than perhaps any one in the nineteenth century, not to forget Ruskin. Though he recognized that the governing class was corrupt, he nevertheless recognized that the Tory stood for many things that were true. He did not fall into that most hopeless of modern errors of assuming that because men did not live up to their professions therefore their professed faith was at fault, or that because a creed contained a certain admixture of error it might not contain a large element of truth. In the main Cobbett was content to take the old political philosophies and traditions for granted, and directed his attacks at the governing class for misusing them. His fine traditional and historic sense was here his salvation. Cobbett's *History of the Reformation* may not be a work of scholarship, but it is a work of genius. In it he shows an insight into the Reformation and its political and economic consequence which throws a flood of light on history and the economic problem. It is superior to the economic histories of more recent times to the extent that it recognizes the existence of other things than economics.

While Cobbett rose superior to the current historical prejudices he saw more clearly than any other man the trend of his age. Industrialism and Adam Smith he hated, and indeed it was the combination of the two that made Industrialism such a scourge. But in his protests against factory life he appears to have stood alone among prominent reformers. The Radicals who came after him accepted Industrialism as an established fact, and Radicalism lost its hold on the rural population. There can but be one reason for this—that the peasantry felt that the Radicals in accepting Industrialism and Adam Smith had deserted their cause and that, bad as the Tories were, the Liberals stood for something far worse. They felt instinctively that the Radicals' gospel of salvation was calculated to make things worse for them by rendering the circumstances of their life even more unstable ; and they were right.

Not only did Radicalism by the support it gave to the Manchester School lose the peasantry, but it divided the forces of reform in the towns. It separated Middle-Class from Working-Class reformers. The Reform Bill of 1832 incorporated the new industrial towns and abolished the rotten boroughs, but it did not secure payment of members. Disappointment with the Reform Bill led to the Chartist agitation, which was a combination of the old Radical political party and the new Socialist and Trade Union Movements. It revived the Radical programme of 1816. The agitation, after being carried on for eleven years, reached a climax when the Revolution of 1848 in France aroused them to their last great effort. But it all came to nothing. After 1848 the Trade Unionists retired from political agitation and directed their attention exclusively to the work of building up their own internal organizations—a policy which they continued until in our day the Socialist agitation brought them once more into the political field. But in the meantime they succeeded in so consolidating their strength that with their re-emergence they have become a force to be reckoned with both in the political and industrial world. There is no reason to doubt, therefore, that their decision in 1848 to retire from political agitation was the one that wisdom dictated.

But there was another cause for the decline of working-class political agitation after 1848—the development of ailway building. It was this perhaps more than anything

else that broke the power of the Chartist agitation by providing an abundance of employment, which, except for
short periods of trade depression, lasted until the end of
the century, and which reconciled the workers to the fact
of Industrialism, if not whole-heartedly, at least to the
extent of persuading them that resistance to it was hopeless. It is well to remember that the workers at any time
have never really believed in it. In its early days they
definitely disbelieved in it and did all in their power to
resist its encroachments, going so far in the days of the
Luddite riots as to break up machinery. If they came
finally to acquiesce if not to believe in Industrialism, it
is because the old order had so completely disappeared
that they had no longer anything with which to compare
it. But still they are restless under it and must increasingly
become so until it is finally destroyed; for a force so
mechanical runs contrary to every healthy normal human
instinct, and no peace or social and political stability is
possible so long as it remains.

The immediate political effect of the acquiescence of
the working class in industrialism was their acceptance
of the political leadership of the new capitalists into whose
hands political power had passed. They were wealthy,
and were able successfully to dispute political power with
the landed plutocracy (whom it is customary to call the old
aristocracy), of whose rule the people had had such a bitter
experience. The new capitalists had restored prosperity.
Perhaps after all there was something to be said for them.
There are two sides to every question; the working class
might not be the entire receptacles of political wisdom.
In some such way as this, I imagine, a working man would
reason. Though he could not see eye to eye with the
capitalists, he nevertheless was up against the fact that
trade boomed and the condition of the working class was
improving. In such circumstances perhaps the best policy
was to support the capitalists in their general policy, while
by means of better working-class organization to secure
for the workers a greater share of the wealth produced.
It was a perfectly intelligible position, and it is not surprising that it gained the day.

But there was another reason for the support they gave —the success of the Free Trade policy as exemplified by the repeal of the Corn Laws. England had become to some extent dependent on the supply of foreign corn. During the Napoleonic wars this supply was so hampered that wheat rose to famine prices, and with this rise there came an increase in rents and the price of land. But after peace was made prices began to fall, and the landlords demanded duties on corn to keep up the price of wheat. The manufacturers, on the other hand, wanted cheap food for their workpeople in order to be able to pay them low wages. As a compromise, the Corn Laws of 1814 and 1828 were enacted. They provided a sliding scale of duties which rose as prices fell, and fell as prices rose. But the compromise did not for long remain satisfactory to the manufacturers. While the Chartists were agitating for political reform an Anti-Corn-Law League was started to procure the abolition of import duties on grain. The agitation which they carried on all over the country secured the support of the workers, who were persuaded that the repeal of the Corn Laws would increase the value of their wages. As a consequence of the agitation, the failure of the potato crop in Ireland and a bad harvest in England, Sir Robert Peel in 1846 carried a measure for the gradual abolition of the corn duties. The repeal of the duties did not immediately affect the price of corn, but it enormously increased the supply. The price of corn fell later, when the English consumer got the benefit of the decreasing prices which followed the exploitation of virgin lands in America and the colonies. The repeal of the Corn Laws was followed by the abolition of duties on hundreds of articles and the reduction of duties on others ; direct taxation in the form of income tax being resorted to in order to replace the loss of revenue.

Free Trade during the nineteenth century became such a fundamental principle of English financial policy, and it coincided so entirely with the period of industrial expansion and prosperity, that it has come to be believed in by numberless people as something sacrosanct—the magic formula of Free being sufficient to invest it for such people with a halo of sanctity which renders them entirely oblivious to its practical consequences. But are there any real grounds for such a faith ? As a measure of temporary economic expediency, the repeal of the Corn Laws may be justified, though as far as I can see there are no grounds for supposing that the prosperity of the years which followed the repeal was caused by it. It coincided with the period of railway building, and there are far stronger reasons for supposing that money began to circulate freely because of the employment that railway building gave than because of the Free Trade policy. It would have been well for England if the repeal of the Corn Laws had only been justified as a measure of expediency, but unfortunately, as it was exalted into a principle that was sacrosanct, it was followed at a later date by most serious consequences. Firstly, it allowed the importation of sweated goods to bring down the wages of labour in certain trades ; then it operated to destroy agriculture and depopulated rural areas by. bringing the English wheat into competition with the wheat grown on the virgin lands of America and the colonies ; while, lastly, it has built up a vested interest inimical to the interests of the country. It is well that we should not lose sight of the fact that Free Trade confers privileges just as much as Protection ; the difference being that whereas manufacturers and farmers profit by Protection, merchants and shippers profit by Free Trade. Both give rise to political corruption, but whereas in one case it is open corruption, in the other it is concealed.

That both Free Trade and Protection should give such unsatisfactory results is due to the fact that the issue between them is a false issue that arises in the absence of Guilds to control production and prices. No stable economic system would begin with economic expediency, whether in the interests of manufacturers or merchants, but with the protection of the standard of life of the worker. In the absence of Guilds it is better for a community to suffer from the corruption incidental to Protection than from the corruption incidental to Free Trade, for its social and economic effects are less harmful, not only because the corruption which accompanies Protection is more open, and can therefore be more easily attacked, but because it must remain impossible for a community to attain economic stability that allows the workers in any industry to be placed at the mercy of the fluctuations of prices in distant markets and to be undercut by the importation of sweated goods from other countries as happened under Free Trade. The only remedy finally is to be found in a restoration of the Guilds, in connection with which Protection would take its place as the natural corollary of a system of fixed prices controlling the currency.

But there are further evils. Free Trade having placed power in the hands of merchants and financiers, establishes the trader's point of view in politics. With it has come the pernicious habit of viewing social and industrial activities primarily from the point of view of the profit accruing from them rather than from that of the well-being of the community as a whole, and this, as we have had experience during the war, may on occasion bring disaster. In peace-times this point of view was operative in the work of social disintegration. It has led to the decrease of the production of necessary and desirable things and diverted labour to the production of useless and undesirable things, or, in other words, it has exalted secondary above primary production. Only a Government controlled by trading interests could be blind to the folly of allowing things to drift in this way, or if not blind, at any rate powerless to devise means of changing the current. The Nemesis that is overtaking us is the natural and inevitable consequence of allowing the direction of the politics and industry of the country to be determined solely by considerations of the markets. Societies that are stable act otherwise. The Mediævalists, like Aristotle, recognized the danger inherent in allowing the trading class to exercise an undue preponderance of influence in national policy.

The reason why in the nineteenth century the trading interest was able to carry all before it was ultimately due to the complete disappearance of religion and art and the communal ideal of society, though immediately it was due to intellectual confusion, stupidity, and the hypnotic influence of machinery which prevented men from giving

serious consideration to any line of reasoning that came
into collision with its uncontrolled use. This was the
reason why Ruskin was thrown aside. He laid the basis
of a tradition of thought that might have borne fruit in
these days if men could only have held fast to that which
was good when appearances were against them. But faith
in reality was weak in the nineteenth century ; men trusted
entirely in appearances, and so it came about that when
the conclusions of the Manchester School were cast aside
they still clung to its utilitarian philosophy and habit of
mind. Disraeli in the days of his youth made an effort
to bring the age back to realities. *Sybil* was a valiant
attempt to persuade the governing class to face the facts
of the situation. He saw the trouble arising from intellectual confusion, class stupidity, the absurdity and unreality of the Party System, and from the stiff-necked
attitude of capital towards labour. *Sybil* having missed
fire, he became disheartened, and by the time he came to
write *Lothair* he had abandoned his generous dreams and
taken to ironical badinage. *Popanilla* is a magnificent
burlesque on the utilitarian philosophy. It demonstrates
clearly that he was alive to the contradictions and absurd-
ities in which the Radicals were involved. But while he
saw clearly what was wrong, he had no clear vision as to
what was right. This was perhaps the secret of his political
career, and has led to much misunderstanding and misrepresentation. He came to fight on the Conservative
side, not because he believed in the Conservatives, but
because he disbelieved in the Radicals; not because his
sympathies were undemocratic, but because he disbelieved
in the democratic leaders, whom he had sufficient insight
to see did not represent the people. In his efforts to defeat
a party of unconscious humbugs he became a conscious
humbug himself, for he came cynically to accept plutocracy
though inwardly despising it, while Gladstone idealized
its achievements because he never understood their inwardness. Still, in spite of their difference, Disraeli and
Gladstone really co-operated for the same end, to retain
power for the plutocracy, and under their combined
leadership politics drifted farther and farther away

17

from realities. The smugness and complacency of the later Victorian age was only shaken by the emergence of the Irish problem into the forefront of political issues. Yet all the while great changes were being prepared underground. But Parliament was cognizant of none of them. It floated about on the surface of things, skilfully evading every real issue until at length, in 1906, it was awakened from its dreams of false security by the arrival of the Labour Party at the House of Commons, when the governing class first became seriously aware of the democratic upheaval that was taking place. The popular disappointment with the performances of the Labour Party led to a reaction against Parliamentarianism which coincided with the great strikes of 1911, from which time the Industrial Movement may be dated.

CHAPTER XVIII

ON LIMITED LIABILITY COMPANIES

In the middle of the nineteenth century a series of Acts of Parliament were passed conferring upon joint-stock companies the privilege of limited liability. As the conduct of industry has been completely revolutionized and the structure of society transformed through the promotion of limited companies which followed the passing of these Acts, they are to be reckoned among the most important events of the century, and it is necessary for an understanding of the problems of to-day that their significance be understood. Their reaction upon the social and industrial life of the community has been to place society at the mercy of an impersonal and intangible tyranny which by paralysing all healthy and normal activities reacts to introduce a kind of fatalism into economic, social and political developments by placing every one at the mercy of an elusive financial machine. It is to be observed that this new economic development which carried the principle of exploitation to its logical conclusion by divorcing possession from the control of industry was, like all previous economic developments, preceded by acts of legislation.

Something approximating to limited liability existed in the reign of Elizabeth. When in the year 1600 she acceded to the request of the East India merchants for a Charter of Incorporation, when they had urged that the trade with the Indies was too remote to be capable of proper management without a "joint and united stock," she created *ipso facto* a limited liability company. For as the Common Law then only recognized individuals and corporations as legal entities, the effect of the grant of a charter to a trading company was to grant a species of limited liability such as exists in the case of a company limited by shares that are fully paid up, under the Acts now in force ; though as the trade of the East India Company was so profitable, no question of the liability for debts ever arose. Hitherto merchants engaged in foreign trade had been organized under " regulated " companies like the Russia, the Turkey, and the Eastland Companies. They were really Merchant Guilds whose members enjoyed a monopoly of their specific trade in a given district, but were originally in no sense financially associated or liable for one another's engagements. The Charter of the East India Company in acknowledging joint-stock introduced a new principle of trade organization which was not by any means popular with merchants generally. The merchants of the " regulated " companies sneered at the incorporated joint-stock East India Company because the latter were unable to " breed-up " merchants, seeing that " any one who is a master of money may purchase a share of their trade and joint-stock."

On account of its unpopularity the joint-stock principle made little headway. As late as the end of the seventeenth century there were only three joint-stock companies in existence—the East India, the Royal African, and the Hudson Bay Companies. In the early eighteenth century private joint-stock companies began to be formed whose legal position was uncertain, for monopolies for foreign trade had been abolished in the latter part of the reign of James I. One of these, the South Sea Company, which was organized to exploit the unknown wealth of South America, managed by bribes to ministers and by promising to reduce the national debt to secure in 1720 a Charter of Incorporation. It was in vain that Walpole warned the Ministry and the country against this dream of wealth. Both went mad. A wave of reckless financial speculation overwhelmed the country. Bubble company was followed by bubble company until the inevitable crash came, bringing a general ruin in its train. It was followed by the Bubble Act, which forbade the formation of companies without the sanction of Crown or Parliament as " a mischievous delusion calculated to ensnare the unwary public." The Act appears to have remained largely a dead letter, probably because after the South Sea Bubble, in which many companies came to grief in addition to the one bearing its name, political and mercantile opinion was so averse to the formation of joint-stock companies that few attempts at company promotion were made, and so things remained until the early part of the nineteenth century, when the Industrial Revolution, by opening out new fields of industry with which it was impossible for individual capitalists to cope, gradually introduced a change in public opinion. In 1825 an Act was passed repealing the Bubble Act, and encouragement was given to the formation of companies. By this statute the Crown was empowered to grant Charters of Incorporation, and at the same time to declare that the persons incorporated should be individually liable for the debts of the body corporated. Public opinion in those days did not think it desirable that the members of joint-stock companies should be allowed to limit their liability to a specified amount. In 1834 an Act was passed giving such companies the privilege of bringing and defending actions and other legal proceedings in the name of an officer of a company.

Hitherto, in order for a joint-stock company to be incorporated, it was necessary for it to obtain a charter from the Crown or a special Act of Parliament, but in 1844 a new departure was made enabling companies, with certain exceptions, to obtain a Certificate of Incorporation from the Registrar without having recourse to Crown or Parliament, but still with unlimited liability. In 1855 the principle of limited liability triumphed when power was given to companies to obtain a Certificate of Incorporation with limited liability. The change of opinion which made this possible was due to the ruin which unlimited liability had brought upon innocent men. At the period of the collapse of the railway boom in 1845 many such men liable for calls had to fly the country and to live abroad for many years upon what remnants of their property they could manage to save from the wreck. But it was not until a bank failure in Glasgow, when the holder of a small share was made liable for a thousand times its amount, that public

opinion was roused. The Act of 1855 which first acknowledged the principle of limited liability was repealed and
replaced by one in 1856, which served in many respects
as a model for the Act of 1862 which forms the basis of
the existing code of Joint-Stock Company Law.

Before the passing of these Acts, joint-stock companies
were few and far between, but once the principle of limited
liability was admitted in law they rapidly grew in numbers.
They have invaded every branch of industry with the
exception of agriculture, though as these pages are being
written I read of the coming of a movement for applying
limited liability company methods to agriculture and an
announcement that a company is to be formed to exploit
an estate of 19,000 acres in Lincolnshire, the purchase
money for which amounts to over £2,000,000. The great
boom when private concerns were turned into limited
companies and new companies promoted came in the
nineties, when, in the eight years from 1892 to 1899, 30,061
new companies were registered in the United Kingdom
and 10,578 were wound up. In April, 1899, there were
27,969 registered joint-stock companies in the United
Kingdom with a share capital, having an aggregate paid-up
capital of £1,512,098,098. In April, 1914, the latest return
before the war broke upon us, the number of companies
had increased to 64,692 with a capital of £2,531,947,661.
The latest return, that of 1916, gives the number of companies registered as 66,094 with a capital of £2,719,989,129.[1]
These figures are all the more striking when it is remembered
that they do not include most of our great railway, gas,
water, canal and other similar companies which have
private Acts of Parliament of their own.

To such an extent have limited liability companies
got a grip of modern business that it is impossible to
separate the two. But that they are not an unmixed
blessing, from whatever point of view examined, no one
will be found to deny. There is no doubt whatsoever that
they have been the main factor in the creation of that flood
of commercial dishonesty and legalized fraud which in these

[1] These figures are taken from the Board of Trade (Inspector-General's)
Reports.

days carries all before it. Companies have been formed simply in order to put money into the pockets of promoters, to get rid of declining businesses so that the existing owners may withdraw their capital to invest in something else while leaving the shareholders with nothing but the debts to pay. In other cases companies have been formed in order to create a dummy behind which some sinister figure might move. Such abuses are admitted. But to the business man of to-day these disadvantages are more than counterbalanced by the advantages they are supposed to bring, in that they have rendered possible an enormous number of undertakings which from the amount of capital required could not have been carried out by an individual capitalist or group of capitalists. This has been said so often that people are inclined to accept the statement without further examination. Yet it very much needs examination, for the real question is not whether it has rendered possible undertakings which otherwise could not have been promoted, but whether it was in the public interest that such undertakings should be entered upon at all ; for remember, such enterprises as those of railways, water, gas, etc., rest on private Acts of Parliament and are not to be confused with the general issue of limited liability.

Now it will clear the issue if we begin with the opinion of Adam Smith, who in the *Wealth of Nations* probably expressed the current view on the subject of joint-stock companies when he said that the only trades a joint-stock company not having a monopoly can carry on successfully are those in which all the operations are capable of being reduced to routine or of such a uniformity of method as admits of little or no variation. Only four trades, in his opinion, answer the test of suitability which he thus laid down, namely, those of banking, of fire and marine insurance, of making and maintaining canals, and of water supply. Railways, tramways, gas and electric supply he would doubtless have added as belonging to the same category if such things had existed in his time. Manufacturing by a joint-stock company, he considers, would not only be unsuccessful as a business, but would be injurious to the public welfare

Now the question comes, Was Adam Smith right ? Has modern experience controverted him or are appearances only against him ? I do not hesitate to say that he was absolutely right when he said that manufacturing by joint-stock companies would be injurious to the public interest, but experience has proved him to be wrong when he said they would be unsuccessful. If success for them depended upon efficiency as producers, they would certainly fail. But success for limited liability companies does not depend upon any such efficiency but upon an ability to corner the market in some way. The usual ways are either to use their great capital for keeping others out by advertising ; by manipulating prices in such a way that a market is secured for certain things at very enhanced prices while underselling small men in others, thus preventing any one from competing with them who is not on a similar scale of business ; or by securing a tied market by judiciously distributing shares among those who can be of service to the company in recommending business. Each of these methods is corrupting. I will not enlarge on the evils attendant upon advertising and manipulated prices,[1] since both of these illegitimate methods of trade were pursued by private firms before limited companies held the field, but will dwell upon the third of these methods, because it is the one thing, apart from its ease in getting hold of capital, that gives the limited company an illegitimate advantage over the private firm, while it is the most corrupting of its corrupting influences.

By distributing shares among those who can be of service to it, the limited company corrupts the public by obtaining business in an illicit way while at the same time it closes the market to new men. Henceforward the competent man who would set up in business is unable to do so because the market is rigged against him. It is no longer possible for a man, however competent he may be, to come to any position in industry apart from the favour of those already established, except he be possessed of large capital or great influence, as the case might be, such as

---

[1] The evil of manipulated prices is examined in my *Old Worlds for New*, chap. xiv.

would enable him to weather the storm and difficulties of getting established. These circumstances immediately produced a change in the psychology of industry. Hitherto, success had come to the man of grit and competence. Such qualities were the ones that made for success under the system of competition. But men soon found that so far from such qualities being an asset to them under a system of limited liability companies, they were a positive hindrance ; for success came not to men of an independent spirit, but to men whose temperament was characterized by flexibility and subservience, or, in other words, the qualities of mastership which told to advantage in the open market when combined, it should be added, with some commercial instinct were no longer in demand under a system of large organizations and limited companies ; the demand being entirely for men of secondary talents, not for men of initiative, but for men of routine. Hence talent was discouraged and mediocrity preferred. This tendency has gathered strength ever since limited companies came to dominate the situation. It has been well defined as " the principle of inverted selection." Its application guaranteed company directors a temporary tranquillity, but has so completely undermined the morale of industry as to leave them entirely without reliable counsellors when industry is required to adjust itself to a new situation, as the present crisis bears witness.

The reason for these changed circumstances is easy to understand. They came about because the joint-stock principle in placing the final authority in shareholders places it in the hands of amateurs. Amateurs, however, are never allowed to see things as they really are, but only what it is convenient for others to let them see. Hence there is a tendency for reality and appearances to drift ever farther apart. A man has not to work long inside of a large organization before he discovers that doing good work and securing promotion are two entirely separate and distinct propositions, and that so far from good work (except of the routine kind) helping him, it may actually stand in his way by bringing him into collision with others who have a vested interest in things remaining as they are, and who therefore will do everything to defeat the ends of the innovator. Promotion, on the contrary, goes with being a "good fellow"; with toadying to men in position; with maintaining an appearance of doing things but not with actually doing them, since that is much more likely to lead to trouble; with managing things in such a way as to secure the credit for things that are successful for oneself and to shuffle off responsibility for failure on to the shoulders of others. This is not difficult in large organizations, for it is generally impossible for any except those inside to know exactly for what work any particular individual is responsible. There are, of course, exceptions to this rule, but then there are exceptional circumstances, and an institution is to be judged by its norm and not by its exceptions. No one can deny that in large organizations success goes to the bounder, to the man who studies the game rather than the work. Certain of these evils arise from the mere size of such organizations, which by making every individual dependent on his immediate superior tends to give priority to personal considerations. These evils would probably develop, however wise the heads might be, but they are increased a hundredfold by the fact that in all such organizations, whether they be limited liability companies or Government departments, control is from without and authority rests finally in the hands of amateurs.

Certain consequences follow from such an abnormal condition of affairs. Finance having set out to exploit the producer, finds itself nowadays in turn exploited by sharks who prey upon the amateurs. These are the clever men who take the world as they find it. Realizing the stupidity of the men in control, they play upon their vanity and carefully lay traps into which they may fall. In exploiting the exploiters they afford a certain amount of amusement for the exploited, while they perform a useful function in bringing not only the commercial but our legal system into discredit, for it so happens that they are able to pursue their vocation because they are masters of the law.

While on the one hand limited companies have given rise to all manner of legalized fraud, on the other hand they have created widespread disaffection among the workers. The mass of men nowadays do not want to do any work, because they feel that not they but others are going to profit by their labour. So long as competence was rewarded and honour appreciated there was an incentive for men to work. If they became efficient they might get on to their own feet, and the presence of a number of men with such ambitions in industry gave a certain moral tone to it that reacted upon others. But when, owing to the spread of limited companies, all such hopes were definitely removed and the invention of automatic machinery rendered work entirely monotonous, when technical ability, however great, went unrecognized and unrewarded, and proficiency in any department of industry incurred the jealousy of " duds " in high places, demoralization set in. All the old incentives were gone, and no one was left to set a standard. The subconscious instincts of men whose ambitions were thwarted turned into purely destructive channels. Already before the war things had taken this turn, but the wave of patriotism to which the war gave rise led to hopes that a new spirit was to enter industry. But when, through the rapacity of profiteers, it became apparent that such hopes were doomed to disappointment, destructive impulses returned with redoubled energy. That is the secret of the labour unrest. The profiteers have killed the goose that laid the golden eggs.

It was because limited companies sought from the first to secure their position by cornering the market rather than by a regard for their own internal efficiency, that they have for ever been seeking to establish themselves on a larger and larger scale. Consideration of internal efficiency would have urged upon them the advantages of small organizations, which in the nature of things are more manageable, but the policy to which they were committed of maintaining themselves by securing monopolies of the market obliged them to seek to operate on an increasingly larger scale in order that they could more successfully hold their own against competing companies. But the larger the scale they operate upon, the greater becomes their need of capital ; and the greater their need, the more they tended to fall under the control of the banks which monopolized credit. Major C. H. Douglas has given to this new development which has supplanted capitalism the name of Creditism.[1]　Capitalism was essentially private and individual, and because of its private and individual nature a natural boundary was placed to the dimensions of an organization.　But when in order to be successful business had to be started on a big scale, the possibility of the individual capitalist starting any new enterprise became dependent in the vast majority of cases upon being able to get the backing of some bank.　Hence it has come about that while it is an easy matter for a company already established to secure additional capital to extend its business operations, it has become almost impossible for a new man to start ; for a new man is an unknown quantity and is not to be trusted with extensive credit.　It has been thus that the arrival of limited companies has been followed by a centripetal movement in finance which encourages the organization of larger and larger concerns, not because of the needs of efficiency, but because of the exigencies of credit, which in turn still further widens the discrepancy between appearances and reality, between control and potential ability.

In Germany the attempt was made to counteract this centripetal tendency of finance by the institution of credit banks, which it was hoped would restore a distributed initiative by inducing a centrifugal tendency.　It was a proverbial saying in Germany that with the aid of his bank a man builds the first floor of his house by mortgaging the ground floor ; his second by mortgaging the first ; and puts on the roof by the aid of a mortgage upon his second floor.　This is no exaggeration, for the banks were accustomed to advance money to the extent of 90 per cent. to men who desired to set up in business, on a purely speculative goodwill, and to accept as security for the remaining 10 per cent. a valuation of such things as household furniture.　But it all availed nothing.　The widespread distribution of credit increased the efficiency of the industrial machine to such an extent that in fifteen years Germany quadrupled her output, and this led to such an

[1] *Economic Democracy*, by C. H. Douglas (*New Age*, 1919).

intensification of the pace of competition and profits were so reduced that in the years before the war the great mass of German industries were rapidly approaching bankruptcy. The stress of such circumstances doubtless precipitated the war. I have little doubt that England owed her comparative immunity from such trying conditions to her comparative inefficiency.

The failure of limited liability companies as a system of industrial control suggests a comparison with the Mediæval Guild system ; for the difference between them is the difference between the Mediæval and modern worlds. Under the modern system finance plays the all-important part. It comes first and every other consideration plays a quite secondary and unimportant part. As the system develops, technical skill is less and less appreciated, and what naturally follows from it sinks into a lower and lower status. On this side limited companies are living on capital. Their influence tends to undermine all such skill, and as the final test of an organization from the point of view of the public is not the profits it makes but what kind of goods it produces, the limited liability system of control from without stands condemned as the worst system under which industry has ever been organized. The Mediæval Guild system was the exact reverse of this. The technical man or craftsman, who under the limited liability company system is reckoned a man of no account, was in control and he arranged things very differently. Instead of organizing industry for the purpose of extracting profits, he organized it with the aim of producing good work. With this aim in view finance was reduced to the bare minimum by the simple device of fixing prices. In large building works a bookkeeper was employed, but apart from this finance appears to have been entirely absent in production. The financial man confined his attention entirely to distribution, and distribution in those days was a very secondary form of activity. It did not bulk in anything like the proportion it does to-day. The change which has taken the control of industry out of the hands of the technical man and allowed the financier to spread his tentacles over it is due finally to the revival of Roman Law, which broke down barrier after barrier that placed a boundary to financial operations. It began by transforming the Feudal system, based upon the principle of function, into land-lordism. This enabled capitalism to get a foothold in rural areas, to develop domestic industry and undermine the position of the Guilds. But the two things that made the great change were, first, the Industrial Revolution, which undermined the position of the craftsman and gave great opportunities to the financier, and second, the legalization of limited liability, which handed over technical trades entirely to commercial exploitation by divorcing ownership from control and technical ability.

CHAPTER XIX

THE WAR AND THE AFTERMATH

"Commercial intercourse between nations, it was supposed some fifty years ago, would inaugurate an era of peace ; and there appear to be many among you who still cling to this belief. But never was belief more plainly contradicted by the facts. The competition for markets bids fair to be a more fruitful cause of war than was ever in the past the ambition of princes or the bigotry of priests. The peoples of Europe fling themselves, like hungry beasts of prey, on every yet unexploited quarter of the globe. Hitherto they have confined their acts of spoliation to those whom they regard as outside their own pale. But always, while they divide the spoil, they watch one another with a jealous eye ; and sooner or later, when there is nothing left to divide, they will fall upon one another. That is the real meaning of your armaments ; you must devour or be devoured. And it is precisely those trade relations, which it was thought would knit you in the bonds of peace, which, by making every one of you cut-throat rivals of the rest, have brought you within reasonable distance of a general war of extermination " (*Letters from John Chinaman*, by G. LOWES DICKINSON).

IN August, 1914, this prophecy, made some twenty years ago, was fulfilled. The German army entered Belgium, and the long-predicted war broke over Europe. Until the day of its arrival large numbers of people in this country were sceptical as to the reality of the menace. They had been warned too often to believe it. Certain definite actions certainly pointed to the coming of war. But on the other hand certain general considerations weighed heavily against it. The industrial system was a highly complex affair. It could only be maintained by a high degree of reciprocity between the nations. In consequence a European war between nations who had adopted conscription would be a life-and-death struggle which would probably end in the destruction of modern civilization—in a catastrophe in which the victorious as well as the vanquished would be involved. It was difficult to believe that Germany would be oblivious to this fact. There might be Jingoes bent on war in Germany, but then there were Jingoes in England, and it did not necessarily follow that they would get their own way. What reason was there to suppose that difficulties could not be arranged by compromise and moderate opinion prevail ?

In some such way as this the mass of moderately minded people reasoned before the war. That they so entirely misjudged the situation is perhaps finally to be accounted for by the fact that its true inwardness was never written about until after the war had broken out. We were told about the vast preparations that Germany was making for war ; about the growth of armaments in which other European nations followed suit. But we were never told *why* Germany was making such preparations. She had nothing to fear from France—*La revanche* was dead— nor had she anything to fear from England. Why was she arming ? This at the time was an enigma to thinking people who were not carried off their feet by chauvinism. The trade of Germany was advancing by leaps and bounds. To all appearances her prosperity was increasing. Why then did she exhibit this querulous spirit ? No satisfactory answer was forthcoming. Perhaps after all it was only bluff intended to further the ends of her diplomacy. The hazards of a general European war were so incalculable that it was to be supposed that even Germany would not lightly embark upon such an enterprise.

And indeed it is true to say that Germany did not embark lightly on war. That she did eventually declare war was due to the fact that her position had become desperate, and there can be little doubt that a consciousness that it was only a matter of time before such a situation would arise was the motive that all along prompted her to arm. The exhaustion of markets, foreseen by all who ever reflected on the trend of industrialism, had come about at last, and Germany was finding herself in difficulties. The growth of the pressure of competition had indicated for some time that other industrialized nations were beginning to feel the pinch. But they had greater reserves, and their position was far from desperate. England, for example, had a great reserve of wealth in raw materials and colonies which provided an outlet for surplus population and a market for surplus goods. Moreover, there was India, which provided not only a market for goods, but posts for civil servants. But Germany was not so fortunately placed. She was poor in raw materials and had no first-class colonies and no dependencies. So it came about that Germany became accustomed to compare her own position with the more favourable position of England, and to imagine that if only she had colonies and dependencies her economic condition would be different ; the pressure of competition would be relieved and her people would be in a position to pursue their aims unaccompanied by those financial worries which since the opening of the present century had been a constant source of anxiety. This feeling was shared by the whole nation, from capitalists who were eager for concessions to the students of the universities. "Any one," says Mr. de Maeztu, " who has lived in German university circles during the last few years will be able to confirm my statement, that the greatest enthusiasts of colonial expansion in Germany were not the manufacturers, but the students. Their admiration and envy of British power in India were not aroused by commercial prospects, but by the possibility of posts for military and civil bureaucrats. In the future colonial empire of Germany the student dimly discerned billets and pensions for hundreds of thousands of German university graduates." [1] It was the vision of such prospects that induced them to favour a policy of aggression.

The part played by bureaucracies in fomenting racial and international troubles should not be overlooked. The desire of their bureaucracies for expansion was the one bond of common interest between Germany and Austria, offering us some clue as to why the Austrian declaration of war on Serbia was so popular in Vienna. Writing of the Austrian bureaucracy before the war, Mr. Wickham Steed says " the ' race struggle ' in Austria, of which so much has been written, is largely a struggle for bureaucratic appointments. Germans and Czechs have striven for

[1] *Authority, Liberty and Function*, by Raniro de Maeztu, p. 99.

years to increase on the one hand and defend on the other their patrimony of official positions. The essence of the language struggle is that it is a struggle for bureaucratic influence. Similarly, the demand for new Universities or High Schools put forward by Czechs, Ruthenes, Slovenes and Italians but resisted by the Germans, Poles and other nations, as the case may be, are demands for the creation of new machines to turn out potential officials whom the political influence of Parliamentary parties may then be trusted to hoist into bureaucratic appointments. In the Austrian Parliament the Government, which consists mainly of officials, sometimes purchases the support of political leaders by giving State appointments to their kindred or *protégés*, or by promoting *protégés* already appointed. One hand washes the other, and service is rendered for service. On occasion the votes of a whole party can be bought by the appointment of one of its prominent members to a permanent Under-Secretaryship in a Department of State. Once appointed, he is able to facilitate the appointment of other officials of his own race or party. Each position thus conquered forms part of the political patrimony of the race and party by whom it has been secured, and is stoutly defended against attack. Appointments are thus multiplied exceedingly—to the cost of the taxpayer and the complication of public business." ¹

Of course this kind of thing has its limits. A point is reached when the burden of officials becomes so great to the taxpayer and so inimical to the commercial interest of a country that the desire for further expansion on the part of a bureaucracy can only be satisfied by extending their powers over the inhabitants of other countries, and it must be understood that the desire for expansion is inherent in bureaucracies, for expansion provides opportunities for promotion. In a stationary bureaucracy promotion is slow—a matter of waiting for dead men's shoes. "For other classes the national idea of a sovereign State is a disinterested, sentimental, and romantic ideal. For the officials,

¹ *The Hapsburg Monarchy*, by H. Wickham Steed, pp. 77–8. I need scarcely remind my readers that bureaucracies are the consequence of the ideal of the centralized state of Roman Law.

on the other hand, the State is not only an ideal but a source of income. It has been said—by Mr. Norman Angell, I believe—that when the Germans annexed Alsace-Lorraine the rich of Alsace-Lorraine went on being rich, the poor continued to be poor, labourers were still labourers, and that the war had been useless from an economic point of view. And it is quite possible that war may be useless from the point of view of labourers, workmen and masters. But the two thousand French professors in both provinces were replaced by two thousand Germans ; and the same thing happened with the army officers, the judges, the officials of the public health boards, and so on. From the point of view of the bureaucratic interests the war was not merely useless, but positively disastrous for French officialdom and beneficial to the German. A change of flag may not substantially alter the economic regime of a specified district ; but what does undoubtedly change is the bureaucratic personnel. The official follows the flag. The official is therefore the permanent soldier of the flag." [1]

Though bureaucracies have an immediate interest in wars of conquest, they are yet not sufficiently powerful to make wars on their own account. Before a war can be successfully launched the nation as a whole must be brought into line. The terrible financial strain to which Germany had been subjected in the two or three years preceding the war had induced a frame of mind favourable to the war party, and it is conceivable that the war was as much caused by the desire for relief from such trying circumstances as by the warlike proclivities of the German ruling class. Germany was committed to a policy of indefinite industrial expansion, and signs were not wanting that expansion had reached its limit, for the enormous competition in the production of goods had reduced profits to such an extent that it became evident that the German financial system, built upon an inverted pyramid of credit, could not for long bear the strain of such adverse conditions So long as peace continued there was no hope of relief, for the ratio of production due to never slackening energy, technique and scientific development was outstripping the

[1] Maeztu, p. 93.

ratio of demand. " In the fifteen years before the war
Germany had quadrupled her output, and in consequence
a day came when all the world that would take German-
made goods was choked to the lips. Economic difficulties
began to make themselves felt, and then the Prussian
doctrine of force spread with alarming rapidity. War was
decided upon for the purpose of relieving the pressure of
competition by forcing goods upon other markets." [1]   Hence
the demand for colonial expansion, the destruction of the
towns and industries of Belgium and Northern France and
the wholesale destruction of shipping by the submarine
campaign. They had all one object in view—to relieve
the pressure of competition, to get more elbow-room for
German industries. The idea of relieving the pressure of
competition by such commercial sabotage was not a new
one. It had been, as I have pointed out, employed by the
Romans, who destroyed Carthage and the vineyards and
olive-groves of Gaul in order to avoid a damaging competition, but it was a crazy one all the same, for it
embarked Germany upon a policy from which there was
no turning back, and left her no option but to conquer
the world or be annihilated in case of failure. There
was no third alternative, for such action removed the
possibility of a peace by compromise.

It was finally because every other nation in Western
Europe and America was moving into a similar cul-de-sac
that the desperate remedy sought by Germany was no
remedy at all. The reason why all were beginning to find
themselves in difficulties was because each of them had
embarked upor a policy of indefinite economic expansion
on a basis of economic injustice. Each of them had denied
economic justice to the workers and Nemesis was overtaking them all. It is only necessary to reflect on the
general economic situation to realize this. Greed had
blinded them all to the simple economic fact that it is
impossible in the long run to increase production except
on the assumption that consumption be correspondingly
increased. Such an increase of consumption, it is apparent,
could only be permanently secured on an assumption that the

---

[1] *The Coming Trade War*, by Thomas Farrow and Walter Crotch.

workers were allowed to have a proportionate share of the increased wealth which they assisted to produce. But the policy of capitalists all over the world being to secure all the advantages of increased production for themselves, had created great inequalities of wealth, and so it came about that as the people only earned a bare subsistence an increased productivity could only be disposed of finally in two ways : by the increase of luxuries for the wealthy on the one hand— for the increase of consumption had to come entirely from the rich—or by disposing of surplus goods in foreign markets. But such a policy had well-defined limits. No nation could afford to be the consumer of machine-produced goods indefinitely, as in that case the suction would drain its economic resources, and so one nation after another was drawn into the whirlpool of industrial production, until a time came at last when there were no new markets left to exploit. When that point was reached, the fundamental falsity of the whole system revealed itself in the economic paradox that drove Germany into war.

The declaration of war gave the German economic system a new lease of life by the enormous demand it created for munitions, which were sold to the Government at prices which enabled loans and other financial obligations to be met. The money for the payment of these munitions was raised by loans which it was the intention of the German Government to liquidate by means of the huge indemnities which they hoped to get from the Entente. As a measure of temporary economic expediency the war for Germany doubtless served its immediate purpose of setting the financial machine in motion again, but even if Germany had been successful it could not have solved her economic problem when peace returned, because a policy of indefinite industrial expansion, by producing goods in greater quantities than the market could absorb, was bound before long to land her in the same position in which she found herself in 1914. In the event of her being victorious, the most optimistic forecast of her future would place her in the same position as England finds herself in to-day, which is anything but rosy.

The outbreak of war caught England unprepared,

and seriously dislocated the old economic order. Accustomed supplies vanished and exceptional demands immediately sprang up. Into a market of producers competing with each other for a still greater number of consumers, which had kept prices comparatively stationary, though the tendency for prices to rise had been continuous for the twenty previous years, there came an enormous demand for war material of one kind and another, and for this there was only one buyer—the Government, acting at first through the War Office and later through it and the Ministry of Munitions and other Government departments. In the first few months of the war a wave of patriotism passed over the country which apparently was so genuine that it led the Yorkshire woollen manufacturers to offer to supply the Government with khaki at a fixed price, but this offer, which would probably have been followed by other manufacturers, was refused by the War Office, who preferred to continue the system of competitive contracts. The result was disastrous, for it so happened that the needs of the Government were soon to become so great that the large firms found themselves in a position to hold up the State for ransom, and as the patriotic offer of the Yorkshire manufacturers had been refused, they did not scruple to take the fullest advantage of the situation. The unemployed problem to which the war immediately gave rise did not last for long, but was speedily followed by a great demand for labour which in turn was followed by a rise in wages, and from then onwards prices and wages engaged in a neck-and-neck race. Meanwhile, in one way or another, the vast majority of people, either directly or indirectly, were working in the public service, and all this enormous artificial activity was kept in motion and stimulated from above by means of State loans and the wholesale issue of paper money which depreciated the currency to such an extent as still further to inflate the already inflated prices. It was thus that during the war nearly the whole nation came to be living upon borrowed money, and it still continues to do so.

Since the coming of peace the problem has been how to return to the normal. At the close of other wars the

Government have usually disbanded the troops for which they had no further use, exploited the loyalty of the soldiers and then turned them adrift to starve or to make shift as best they could. In spite of public professions, there is no reason to suppose that the Government would not have acted any differently this time, if it had dared to do so. But the scale of the present war made it dangerous for the Government to play the old confidence trick with impunity. The fact that nearly every worker was during the war either directly or indirectly in the public service and the fact that the workers are strongly organized made such a policy unthinkable, and so unemployed allowances are made and the unemployed draw pay until such time as industry can pick itself up again. But a suspicion gains ground that it is no easy matter to get the wheels of industry in motion again. It appears that the problem of reorganizing for peace is going to be a much more difficult matter than organization for war. Consider for a moment what has been taking place. Speculative finance, the motive force of industrialism, has for over four years orientated itself around war production. With peace all this activity has come to an end. Can the old motive and driving force of speculative finance become again operative in the industries it has forsaken? It is questionable. It was an easy matter to transfer the labour of the community from peace production to war production because it was a movement that was in accord with the centrifugal movement in finance. All that was necessary was for the Government to borrow money, place orders for munitions right and left, and the thing was accomplished. To reverse the process will not be such a simple matter, because it involves a centrifugal movement in finance, and this is contrary to the normal trend of things in these days, for whereas the centripetal movement was easy because it could be accomplished by a centralized initiative, a centrifugal movement demands a distributed one, and while our society responds readily to the touch of a centralized initiative, the organs necessary to the exercise of a distributed initiative were in the interests of commercial exploitation destroyed in the past.

It will make the position clearer to say that a distributed initiative exists in any society just to the extent that a man can employ himself. The peasant State enjoys a distributed initiative because, when every man owns his own plot of land or shares in a communal holding, he can set himself to work. This is the reason why peasant nations recuperate so quickly after wars, even under modern conditions. When a war is over, every man can go back to his own plot of land and work away just as he did before the war broke out. But with highly complex industrial communities, whose activities are based upon a highly complex system of finance and which produce largely for distant markets, it is different, because only a small percentage of the activities of such communities have a basis in real human and fundamental needs. Production in such communities comes to depend upon all manner of things, while most members of such communities are dependent upon some one else for employment—ultimately upon the possessors of capital who in such communities monopolize all initiative. Hence it is that so long as present conditions of wealth distribution obtain, if a revival of trade is to take place it must proceed from the initiative of the small group at the top who control the financial situation, and this places a responsibility upon their shoulders heavier than they can bear. Hitherto industrial initiative proceeded from below and was exploited by financiers from above. But now the position is entirely reversed. The short-sighted policy of financiers has gradually taken away initiative from the man below. In seeking to concentrate all wealth in his own hands, the financier has, unfortunately for his own peace of mind, saddled himself with the responsibility of industrial initiative, and I doubt not it will prove to be a burden too heavy for him to support. The man below, so long as he enjoyed autonomy, could exercise initiative, since the range of conditions he had to comprehend was limited and familiar. But as a result of centralization the whole complex economic phenomenon of our society would have to be comprehended intellectually if an initiative such as would set the machinery in motion again is to be exercised, and as the experience

of every man is limited, this becomes an impossible proposition. Industry can no longer be kept going by the
momentum it inherited from the past, and if trade is to
revive it must be galvanized into activity from above, and
that is a different story.

Though I am persuaded that there is finally no escape
from the economic cul-de-sac apart from a return to Mediæval conditions, involving a redistribution of wealth and
initiative, it is yet possible that the crisis may be postponed
a few years by means of financial jugglery. A glimmer
of light comes from America, which, having become the
financial centre of the world, holds the key to the position.
It is proposed that the United States should raise an enormous loan for Europe to enable the War Powers to restore
their industry and credit. The principal means to this
end will be a loan and bond issue such as has never before
been seen, of a nature to secure the necessary funds for
these Powers to buy all they require and to extend their
credit as long as may be necessary—ten, twenty, or thirty
years if requisite, until the time comes when the European
countries no longer need assistance. This proposal is not
a purely philanthropic one. In making it the United
States is just as anxious to solve her own economic problem
as that of the European Powers, for America finds herself
in a position the exact reverse to that in which Germany
found herself before the war. Germany found herself
in financial difficulties because her industries made too
little profit. America is in financial difficulties because
during the war she has made too much profit. The consequence is that while her banks are choked with money
for which investments cannot be found, her industries
are producing a plethora of goods for which markets must
be found. In these difficult circumstances America has
hit upon the cunning device of lending money to the European Powers in order that they may find themselves in
a position to buy the goods which America must produce,
for production in America, as in Germany before the war,
is no longer controlled by demand but by plant. It is a
Gilbertian situation the sequel of which promises to be
interesting. America lends money to the European Powers

in order that they may find themselves in a position to buy American goods. The European Powers lend money to their manufacturers in order that they may be in a position to produce still more goods. But the manufacturers being persuaded that their salvation is to be found in keeping wages down, find that while production increases consumption will not. Hence unemployment and hence unemployed pay, the amount of which is increased from time to time in order that people shall be in a position to buy the goods that must be produced until a point is reached at which a man may be well off if he won't work but only earns a bare subsistence if he does. The period for the repayment of loans is extended from thirty to fifty years, from fifty to a hundred, from a hundred to a thousand years. It is an enchanting prospect to which it is difficult to see the end, for as the tendency of finance is increasingly centripetal it can only be saved from collapse by a centrifugal movement which redistributes the wealth produced. If progress is to be along these lines, a time will come when all Europe will be living upon borrowed money and can keep on borrowing because America fears the collapse of her economic system if she refuses to lend.

Of course things won't work out exactly like that. Human nature would soon come in to upset such a purely economic calculation. But it is as logical and as probable as the deduction from any other economic theory which disregards the moral issue. The really interesting thing about the present situation is that it brings the modern world right up against the problem of wealth distribution. The immediate cause of the war I showed was due to over-production in Germany in the sense that by allowing machinery to proceed unregulated production had got ahead of demand and more goods were produced than the markets would absorb. Ignoring the fact that the war was precipitated because the industrial system before the war had reached its limit of expansion, the Government publicists and others nevertheless advocate a policy of maximum production as the path of economic salvation. They propose, in fact, to reproduce in an intensified form the very conditions that brought the war about.

Meanwhile the manifest fallacy of such a policy becomes apparent from the fact that owing to the flood of profiteering that the war let loose the workers have rebelled. They are refusing to produce merely to make profits for others, and under these changed circumstances a colour is given to the cry for increased production. But it is a false issue, since, low as production has fallen, we produce ten, probably fifty, times as much as is necessary for our needs, considered quantitatively. The present system is not maintained because an enormous output is necessary for our needs, but to effect distribution. We employ people in unnecessary production in order that they may have the money to buy the necessary things of which we produce too little. If any one doubts this, let him answer the question how it came about that in the Middle Ages, when there were no machines, the town worker earned an equivalent of three or four pounds a week and the agricultural worker two-thirds of that amount, taking the value of money as it existed before the war.[1] Of course it cannot be answered. The paradoxical situation in which we find ourselves is due entirely to the fact that since capitalists got the upper hand they have consistently refused to face the problem of distribution. But truth will be out. Nemesis seems to say to the financiers : " If ye will not distribute wealth, neither shall ye distribute goods ; and if ye do not distribute goods, neither shall ye distribute dividends." It is not Socialists who have created this problem, but the financiers themselves. The problem is their own making, due to the avaricious dog-in-the-manger spirit in which they have pursued the accumulation of wealth. While they exerted all their energies towards increasing the volume of production, they entirely lost sight of the fact that a

[1] " The wages of the artisan during the period to which I refer (the fifteenth century) were generally, and through the year, about 6d. per day. Those of the agricultural labourer were about 4d. I am referring to ordinary artisans and ordinary workers. . . . It is plain the day was one of eight hours. . . . Sometimes the labourer is paid for every day in the year, though it is certain he did not work on Sundays and principal holidays. Very often the labourer is fed. In this case, the cost of maintenance is put down at from 6d. to 8d. a week. . . . Food was so abundant and cheap that it was no great matter to throw it in with the wages " (*Six Centuries of Work and Wages*, by J. E. Thorold Rogers, pp. 327–8).

day would come when their position would become perilous unless such increase of production was accompanied by a corresponding increase in consumption. So blind were they to this fact that so far from seeking to increase consumption their constant thought has been how to decrease it by reducing wages. We are up against the logical ending of the Mercantile and Manchester School theory of economics —that the wealth of nations is best secured by increasing production and decreasing consumption. The Nemesis of such a false philosophy has overtaken the world at last.

It is an open question whether a way can be found out of the present impasse and a financial crash such as might precipitate revolution averted. For it is to be feared that the pace at which the crisis is developing is much faster than any possible counter-measures that could be put into operation. But if anything at all can be done it is the wealthy alone who can do it. If they could be induced to face the facts, to realize that the problem is the inevitable consequence of their policy of for ever investing and reinvesting surplus wealth for the purposes of further increase they might be led to see that the spending of their surplus wealth in unremunerative ways would ease the situation if it could not forestall catastrophe. The present impasse could have been predicted by any one who had reflected on the famous arithmetical calculation that shows that a halfpenny put out to 5 per cent. compound interest on the first day of the Christain era would by now amount to more money than the earth could contain. This calculation clearly demonstrates a limit to the possibilities of compound interest, yet it is to such a principle that what we call "sound finance" is committed.

CHAPTER XX

BOLSHEVISM AND THE CLASS WAR

To the average Englishman Bolshevism came like a bolt from the blue. He was sympathetic with the Russian Revolution of March, 1917. He had heard of the Russian bureaucracy, of the secret police, of the transportations to Siberia, etc., and he welcomed the overthrow of the Tsarist regime as the overthrow of an intolerable tyranny. But the Revolution that put the Bolsheviks in power he neither understood nor sympathized with, and why the doctrine of the Class War should have spread with such lightning rapidity over Europe and America he was entirely incapable of comprehending. The Press, to all appearances, found itself in the same dilemma as himself. German gold, Russian gold, Hungarian gold, have in turn been offered as explanations for its conquests, or it is represented as a summer madness incapable of rational explanation.

Yet such is not the case. The rise to power of the Bolsheviks and the subsequent spread of their creed is capable of a perfectly intelligible explanation which would have found its way into all the papers had it been convenient to the Government to admit it. It may be true that the Bolsheviks were at the beginning supplied with German gold. I do not know whether it is true or not. If it were offered them I do not suppose they would have refused it any more than they and other Russian revolutionary anti-war exiles in Switzerland refused to travel through Germany in the train that the Kaiser so kindly placed at their disposal ; and the German Government has proved itself so blind where psychological issues were concerned that it is quite possible it did in the first instance supply the Bolsheviks with the wherewithal to carry on their propaganda. But whether

they did or not does not account for the rise of Bolshevism
or the spread of it in other countries, which is finally to be
accounted for by the fact that capitalists all over the world
have refused for so long to face the facts of modern civilization,
that a point was reached at length when the " evil day," as
it is called, could no longer be postponed. Immediately,
however, it was otherwise. The Bolsheviks rose to power
in Russia because, owing to the incapacity of Kerensky and
his colleagues and the political immaturity of the Russian
people, things had reached such a pass that Russia became
entirely incapable of carrying on the war successfully and
was soon obliged to accept peace on any terms. At the beginning of 1917 Russia had an army which, though no doubt
better equipped than in the first years of the war, was still far
too big. The towns were full of idle soldiery ; the railways
were in imminent peril of breaking down. Some of the
Tsar's ministers came to the conclusion that the best thing
to do was to negotiate a separate peace, but the Tsar, desirous
of honouring his agreement with the Allies, objected, and so
an impasse was reached. These ministers then sought to
force the hand of the Tsar by the provocation of a sham
revolution which they believed they could easily suppress,
but which they could use as an excuse for bringing the war
to an end. But things worked out differently from what
they had expected. The disorder they had provoked turned
against them ; instead of a mock revolution, it proved
a real one. The Provisional Government which came into
power decided to stand by the Allies. At the same time,
however, Soviets of Workmen's and Soldiers' Deputies,
formed after the model of the St. Petersburg Workmen's
Soviet which was in being in the unsuccessful Revolution
of 1905, sprang up in the towns under the leadership and
control of doctrinaire Socialists who, relegating the issue
of the war to a minor position, whole-heartedly set about to
promote the progress of the Revolution. The notorious
" Ordre No. I " of the Petrograd Soviet ruined irretrievably
the discipline of the army. In consequence the great effort
of national regeneration which, many people hoped, might
spring out of the Revolution and pull the country together,
became more and more remote as the first patriotic enthusiasm

of the Revolution died down. Instead, the military and economic muddle gradually increased, until the demand of the anti-war elements for peace negotiations began to be supported on the plea of necessity. The growing unpopularity of Kerensky with all classes led to his downfall in November 1917, and the Bolsheviks, who knew what they wanted and had the energy and the armed backing to force their will on the country, came into power.

Now it is necessary to understand that the Bolsheviks were not supported by the garrisons and the discontented elements generally throughout the country because of any widespread belief in the theories of Marx,[1] but because of the failure of the other political parties to consolidate their authority and pursue an energetic and coherent policy. The Bolsheviks were easily able to paralyse the feeble efforts of the Provisional Government. At the same time they promised to save Russia by making peace with the enemy and declaring an international war upon capitalism. It was natural that their promises of peace, bread and wealth should appeal to large sections of the Russian people at such a time. The people in the towns were hungry. This fact should not be lost sight of. There was plenty of food in Russia, but the peasants refused to part with it for money, because money would not buy any of the things they wanted. It had become impossible, for example, to buy a spade in Russia. Bolshevism gathered strength in the towns because it was only by joining the Bolshevist army that men could get food. These are the root facts of the Russian situation upon which everything else hinges. The later history of the Revolution has been, as might have been expected, a record of ever greater and greater distress ; opinions differ as to the relative blame of the old regime, the Provisional Government and the Bolsheviks for the present chaos in Russia, but this is not a point we need enter into here. Such success as Bolshevism has had in Germany and Austria-Hungary bears an analogy to the success in Russia to the extent that in each case it was due to the combined influence of military defeat, blockade,

---

[1] " Bolshevik " means " majoritaire," and refers to an old split in the Russian Social-Democratic Party in 1903. The " Mensheviks " were the minority on the occasion in question. Both parties accepted the theories of Marx.

hunger in the towns and the intellectual and spiritual bankruptcy of other parties in the State.   Whether it will be
finally victorious remains to be seen.   But it is important
to recognize that *Bolshevism enters to fill a vacuum*.   It will
come here, as to every other country, if ever our bankruptcy
of policy becomes complete.   I do not think we shall suffer
from it, because it so happens that while the governing class
are clearly bankrupt of ideas there are in England other
forces of a constructive nature which gather strength daily.

Now this general bankruptcy of policy and the menace
of Bolshevism are alike due to the fact that the governing
classes in this as of all industrialized nations have consistently
refused to recognize the growth of the social problem.   This
refusal has been a matter of deliberate choice, for they have
been repeatedly warned of the risks they were running,
but they have turned deaf ears to all such counsel.   It
might be urged in extenuation of them that the demand for
reform has invariably been associated with attacks on their
position.   But this cannot be said of Ruskin, who made an
appeal to the governing class which leaves them no possible
excuse.   He warned them in unmistakable language that
industrial civilization was shooting the rapids.

Still nothing was done.   The governing and commercial
class comforted themselves with the assurance that what
Ruskin said might be true but it was not practical.   But
Nemesis has waited upon them.   They refused to listen to
Ruskin ; they are having to listen to Marx.   If Ruskin chas-
tised them with whips, Marx chastises them with scorpions.
It cannot be said that Ruskin has failed, for he has inspired
an enormous number of people, and I firmly believe that he
will be left standing when all the intellectually superior
people who disregard him are dead and forgotten.   For
Ruskin has said more things that are fundamentally and
finally true in economics than any one else.   But Marx was
a realist in a sense that Ruskin was not, and to that extent
was more immediately available for political purposes.
Ruskin appealed to the compassion of the governing class ;
Marx realized they hadn't got any, but that while they
were not to be moved by an appeal to their better nature
they could be moved by fear.   He based his calculations

therefore, upon that assumption. Hence his doctrine of the Class War, by which he hoped to transfer power from the hands of the capitalists to those of the proletariat. While I am of the opinion that as a policy it is finally mistaken, for the result of preaching it has not been to create working-class solidarity but discord everywhere,[1] and while it distorts history to prove that class warfare has always existed, it nevertheless rests on a fact that is undeniably true, namely, that under the existing economic system the interests of capital and labour are irreconcilably opposed—a fact which Ruskin himself admitted when he said, " The art of making yourself rich, in the ordinary mercantile economist's sense, is equally and necessarily the art of keeping your neighbour poor." But while Marx interpreted this fact in the terms of persons as a warfare between classes, Ruskin, on the contrary, saw this conflict of interests as the inevitable accompaniment of a materialist ideal of life which rejects religion and art and their sweetening and refining influences— an interpretation which I am persuaded is the true one. For you can construct on Ruskin's interpretation, but not upon that of Marx, for his materialism and class warfare end finally in producing anarchy and bitterness. They destroy confidence and goodwill, and so finally defeat their own ends. And so it happens that while Marx, by creating a driving force, has forced the issue of social reconstruction to the front, experience will prove that Ruskin laid the foundation that can be built upon, and I am persuaded he will come into favour when reconstruction is taken seriously. For Ruskin by keeping himself clear of class considerations provides a common ground on which all may meet.

It was because the Bolsheviks declared the war to be a capitalist war that their gospel spread so rapidly over Europe. In the immediate sense this charge was untrue except in the case of Germany, who definitely undertook the war to relieve the pressure of competition by forcing German goods on foreign markets. But ultimately it is true, since but for the struggle for markets and concessions that capitalism brought with it there would have been no war. Hence it was the Bolsheviks in declaring war on the capitalists of

[1] See chapter on " The Class War " in my *Guilds and the Social Crisis*.

19

all nations did challenge the reality that lay behind the war, and it was because of this that their propaganda has been followed by such success in other countries. The Bolsheviks touched a subconscious chord of the workers of Europe. Their gospel found a ready response in the democracies of all countries, and would certainly have carried all before it but for the excesses (which there is no reason to doubt) of the Bolshevik regime in Russia. The attempts of the governing class to prevent the spread of its doctrines are the last word in ineptitude, and are more calculated to further them than to destroy them. Instead of asking themselves why Bolshevism has arisen in the world and seeking to remove the evils that are responsible for its outbreak, they still pursue their stupid old policy of sitting on the safety-valve and can think of nothing but repression. Now in the face of any serious social danger, repression of extremists is absolutely necessary in order to gain time to do the things that require to be done, and the sincerest reformer might be driven to employ repression at times, but there is finally no other excuse for its use. Unless repression is accompanied by real reform, it only aggravates the danger. He is a fool who imagines that a menace of world-wide significance such as Bolshevism is can be stamped out merely by repression. It can certainly be eradicated, but only by removing its cause, which is finally to be found in the gross injustices of our social system. Partly as a result of the Socialist agitation, and partly as the result of external causes, of increasing economic pressure, of motor-cars and luxury which were flaunted in the eyes of the people before the war, the people were becoming conscious of the fact that they were the victims of exploitation, while the outbreak of shameless profiteering during the war converted what had hitherto been a special grievance of the working classes into a general grievance affecting every class of the community; for everybody except the few profiteers are affected by the decreasing purchasing power of their earnings. No single thing has so entirely destroyed the confidence of the people in the good faith of the governing class as the way they allowed this abuse to grow up. It has been the last straw that breaks the camel's back. During the last ten years the governing class have entirely bartered away their credit, and it can only be restored by the exercise of a measure of magnanimity equal to their former short-sightedness. There is no reason to suppose that such magnanimity will be exercised. Avarice and stupidity got them into difficulties, and pride prevents them getting out of them. In desperation, they misrepresent and heap abuse on the working man in the hope that public opinion will rally to their support. But such folly only makes matters worse. It goes down less and less with the general public and increases the bitterness of the working class, who have been patient and long-suffering. If they had not been, things could never have reached such a pass. The governing class, to retain power, would need to be born again in order that they might put public interests before private interests. But they are past praying for. There is a Turkish saying that " a herring rots from the head." It is worth remembering when considering the chaotic state of this country. The governing class are responsible, for with them power finally resides. Reform must come not merely because nothing less will satisfy the workers, but because our economic system is rapidly reaching a deadlock. The old political game can't be played much longer.

I said that repression was no remedy for Bolshevism. As a matter of fact it is in one sense the fruit of repression. The foundations of Bolshevism were laid in Russia before the war by the repressive policy of the old regime. Had the Russian Government permitted freedom of discussion on political questions, the country would not, when the Revolution came, have found itself so completely at the mercy of political extremists, for the psychological factor that allowed things in Russia so rapidly to assume an extreme form was that as political discussion was forbidden by the old regime, both the Government and the people lost all sense of political realities, and the overthrow of the old regime was followed by a Babel of political opinion fatal to reasonable judgment. If in England a more conservative spirit prevails, it is entirely due to the fact that on the whole we have enjoyed freedom of discussion. It is insufficiently recognized that such freedom tends towards constitutional methods. On the other hand, while we have enjoyed freedom of speech there have always been reactionary (I use the word in the accepted sense) elements in English life which have been plotting against the people, and it is owing to the gross stupidity of these people that Bolshevism has any foothold at all among us, since apart from their activities the extremists would not have been listened to. I cannot say I am altogether sorry there are a few such stupid people among us, since indirectly they have been the means of waking things up. A Bolshevik government is a thing to be feared as the worst of all tyrannies but it is questionable whether anything at all would get done were the fear of Bolshevism entirely removed. A short account of the rise of Bolshevism in England will make it clear that the " labour unrest " has been deliberately provoked.

" In the summer of 1900 a strike broke out in South Wales on the Taff Vale Railway, in the course of which the Company, naturally enough, suffered a certain amount of injury. They applied to the High Court for an injunction not only against alleged individual wrongdoers, but against the Amalgamated Society of Railway Servants itself, whose agents these wrongdoers were. They also commenced a civil suit for damages against the Union in its corporate capacity. To the surprise of all who were familiar with Trade Union law and practice, and to the consternation of the Labour world, the A.S.R.S. was mulcted, in costs and damages, to the tune of £42,000, and it was decided that a Trade Union could be sued in its collective capacity, and its corporate funds made liable for a tortious act committed by any of its officials or members who could be deemed to be its agents."[1]

It was this judgment which was subsequently upheld by the House of Lords that created the Labour Party. Hitherto it had never occurred to any one to sue a Trade Union for loss of profits in the case of a strike. It was supposed that the Trade Union Act of 1871 afforded absolute protection to Union funds. But this judgment struck a blow at the very existence of Trade Unionism and immediately led to the return of forty Labour members to the House of Commons in 1906, which was speedily

[1] *Trade Unionism*, by C. M. Lloyd, p. 38.

followed by the passing of the Trades Disputes Acts that reversed the decision of the Courts.

It would have been well for the governing class if they could have let matters rest there. Once the Trades Disputes Act was passed the Labour Party rapidly declined in influence, and so things might have remained but for another decision of the Courts. Hitherto the Labour Party had been financed by a levy on the members of affiliated societies, of which the great majority were Trade Unionists. But this did not suit a minority who held other political views. " Mr. W. V. Osborne, the secretary of one of the branches of the Amalgamated Society of Railway Servants, strenuously opposed the right of his Union to levy its members or contribute from its funds in support of the Labour Party. An action in the Chancery Court in 1908 went in favour of the Society; but the judges of the Court of Appeal reversed this decision, and their judgment was finally upheld by the House of Lords." [1] The effect of this decision was doubtless, like the Taff Vale Judgment, very different from what the Lords of Appeal had intended. While on the one hand the Liberal Government found it necessary to come to the rescue of the Labour members by introducing payment of members, on the other it took power out of the hands of the moderate men in the Labour Movement and put it into the hands of extremists by destroying faith in constitutional reform. The Labour Party had secured the support of the Trade Unions by preaching the doctrine that the ends of Labour could be better secured through Labour representation in Parliament than by means of strikes. But after the Osborne Judgment this idea became discredited. It became clear that if Labour devoted its energies to reform by constitutional means it could never be sure of its position and any victories it might win could be snatched from it by decisions of the Courts. Hence the advocates of direct action, who hitherto had scarcely been listened to, became very influential. In less than a twelvemonth after the Osborne Judgment had been upheld in the House of Lords, and as a direct consequence of it, there came in 1911 the great strikes of the dockers, the transport workers and

[1] *Trade Unionism,* by C. M. Lloyd, p. 40.

the railwaymen, to be followed after a few months by the miners. Thus was inaugurated the strike movement which continued until the outbreak of war, when strikes were suspended only to be revived by another piece of stupidity on the part of the powers that be—the Munitions Act, which by penalizing official Trade Unions in the event of a strike led to the unofficial movement known as the Shop Stewards Movement.

Now the effect of these things—the Taff Vale Judgment, the Osborne Judgment and the Munitions Act, combined with the evasive and unsatisfactory policy of the Government in Labour disputes—instead of crushing the Labour Movement, has been to turn what was a comparatively sleepy, lethargic movement into an active fighting force by firmly planting in the mind of Labour the conviction that a conspiracy is abroad to defeat their demands for justice. As one interested in the cause of Labour, I cannot express too highly my appreciation of the services rendered to the Labour Movement by the Courts, since in a few years, through their folly, they have accomplished more in the way of vitalizing the movement than a century of agitators. But the question is now whether the pursuit of such folly can any longer serve a useful purpose, for a suspicion gains ground that if ever confidence is to be restored, action will have to be taken against the lawyers. It is not only through the decisions of the Courts that they create bad blood, but through more direct industrial activity. Since the spread of limited liability companies they have become more closely associated with the administration of industry than was the case before, and they have created endless trouble by pursuing everything in a purely legal spirit. Wherever they make their appearance, good faith can no longer be taken for granted. If an agreement is made with Labour, they do not interpret it in the spirit in which it was intended, but according to the letter. They take their stand on what is written, and set about to discover loopholes, and there are always lawyers ready to place their services at the disposal of any capitalist who wants to evade things. And the Courts back them up in this kind of thing. They do not take their stand on the broad principle, but upon what some phrase can be twisted to mean. No wonder

Labour is suspicious. It has every reason to be. It understands straightforward dealing and can respect an enemy who is open in his dealings, but this kind of twisting and twining is a constant source of irritation and distrust, provocative of trouble. When the Government intervenes in any Labour trouble, it too finds itself at the mercy of these legal influences in the bureaucracy, which, affected only by documents, appears to be mentally incapable of sensing a situation. If the law is being brought into contempt, it is the lawyers who are to blame.

To suspect the lawyers as the *agents provocateurs* of Labour unrest is not unreasonable, for history teaches us that, directly or indirectly, the lawyers have been at the bottom of every rising since Roman Law was revived. Considering that Roman Law corrupted every Mediæval institution and changed government from being an instrument of protection into an instrument of exploitation, it is to be maintained that the growth of class hatred in the deeper and more fundamental sense is finally to be laid to its charge. Mediæval society was organized on a basis of reciprocal rights and duties—a man sacrificed his rights who did not perform his duties. But Roman Law changed all this. It made rights absolute which had been conditional, while it made duties optional. It became the friend of property and the enemy of the people. There are many reasons to suppose that Roman Law as it existed under the Roman Empire was animated by an entirely different spirit from that which animated the lawyers of the revival. Roman Law was not promoted in Rome to further exploitation, but came into existence to hold together a corrupt society which had been rendered unstable by capitalism, and as such its spirit was opportunist. There are strong reasons for supposing that it was in this spirit that the Roman jurists gave legal sanction to private property as the easiest way of avoiding conflict between neighbours, for they did not, like the Mediæval lawyers, seek to enslave the people by the destruction of communal rights. On the contrary, while one of the first measures taken by the Emperors was to place restrictions on the formation of voluntary organizations because under the Republic they had been used as a basis of conspiracy, no obstacle was placed in the path of the formation of such organizations when the danger had passed away. As early as the reign of Antoninus Pius the Collegia which undertook public functions were incorporated by Imperial charter, and the custom of incorporating them was followed by later Emperors. The same thing happened with respect to the treatment of slaves. While the Mediæval jurists were devising means for the reintroduction of slavery, the Roman jurists did their best to humanize the institution. Under the Republic and early Empire, the right of the owner over the slave was absolute, but after the Antonines restrictions were placed on the rights of owners, and provisions made which facilitated the manumission of slaves.

It was not from the spirit of the Roman jurists that the trouble appears to have arisen, but from the fact that the revival of Roman Law was in the first place a revival of the Justinian Code, which rested, on a theory of absolute individual ownership of property. It was this that brought it into collision with the Mediæval usage under which community of ownership, or at any rate community of use, was the prevalent custom. It was because of this that the Roman Law of the revival became individualistic, provocative and corrupt, was promoted as an instrument of oppression and has been used as such ever since. It is the central canker in our society—the active promoter of class hatred, as decisions of the Courts have shown.

This is no idle theory. There is no book that enjoys to-day a greater popularity among the workers than Mr Paul's book *The State*,[1] the whole purpose of which is to show that State Socialists have failed to understand the nature and function of the State, inasmuch as from the earliest times it has been an instrument of capitalist exploitation and cannot therefore be used for the purposes of reconstruction. Though the theory he maintains suffers from exaggeration, it is important to recognize that the central idea of the book has the support of at least one Lord Chancellor, for when Sir Thomas More asked the question,

[1] *The State : its Origin and Function*, by William Paul (Socialist Labour Press).

" What is Government ? " and answered it by saying that it is " a certain conspiracy of rich men procuring their own commodities under the name and title of the Common Wealth," he said precisely the same thing as our Bolsheviks are saying to-day. If I differ from them, it is not in respect to what exists, but as to the remedy to be applied. It is true, as our Bolsheviks maintain, that the State from a very early date has existed as an instrument of exploitation. But it does not follow from this that the evils consequent upon such exploitation are to be remedied by seeking the destruction of the State, for that would be merely to precipitate chaos. Moreover, the State cannot be destroyed, as the Bolsheviks in Russia have found, for in spite of all the abuse of power associated with it, it does perform a function which at all times is indispensable, the function of protection, of maintaining order. Recognizing that to-day this function is exercised in the interests of the wealthy, the problem that presents itself is how the State may be so transformed that it protects the workers against the exploiters instead of, as is the case to-day, the exploiters against the workers. This, I contend, is possible by seeking the abolition of Roman Law, since it was the means of corrupting the State, and replacing it by Mediæval Communal Law. In proportion as this could be done, the spirit of the State would be changed. Instead of usurping all functions, it would delegate them to communal groups of workers organized into Guilds. Instead of being the overwhelming and dominating power it is to-day, it would, stripped of its illegitimate functions, become as it was in the Middle Ages, one power among a plurality of powers. Such a policy, I contend, is more in harmony with the historical law formulated by Marx, " that every new social system develops its embryo within the womb of the old system," than that advocated by his followers. For whereas such a policy would effect a complete transformation of society by action from within, their policy seeks only destruction from without.

CHAPTER XXI

THE PATH TO THE GUILDS

I⊤ is a commonplace of modern thought to say that
" we cannot put the clock back." But if recorded history
has any one single lesson to teach us more than another,
it is precisely, as Mr. Chesterton has said, that we can.
Twice in European history has it been done. The first
time was when Christianity restored the communal basis
of society after it had been destroyed by the capitalism
of Greece and Rome, and the second was when this communal basis of Mediæval society in turn was destroyed
and capitalism re-established by the revival of Roman
Law.[1] The recent admission of the Chancellor of the
Exchequer, that ministers are so overwhelmed with the
details of administration that they have no time to think,
suggests to the student of history that before long the clock
will need to be put back again. For it is manifest that
the process of centralization that has been continuous since
the reign of Henry II has at last reached a point beyond
which it can proceed no farther, since the Government is
confessedly at the mercy of forces it cannot control. In
these circumstances there is but one thing to be done—to
substitute control from without by control from within ;
or, in other words, to restore the communal basis of society
that Roman Law destroyed.

It would be fortunate for us if this simple truth could
become acknowledged, as no single thing would be wrought
with such far-reaching consequences and prevent so much
human suffering. A frank acceptance of the principle of

[1] This fact is hidden from the modern world by current theories of
social evolution which, ignoring the legal origin of economic phenomena,
present the change from feudalism to landlordism and capitalism as the consequence of impersonal economic forces instead of to definite acts of the
human will.

reversion would enable us to arrive at the new social order by means of orderly progression, and would prevent the bloodshed that is the inevitable consequence of a refusal to face the facts. The danger that confronts us is precisely the same as confronted France on the eve of the Revolution. It is the danger that a popular though unconscious movement back to Mediævalism may be frustrated by intellectuals whose eyes are turned in the opposite direction, and revolution be precipitated by the fact that the instinctive impulses of the people, instead of being guided into their proper channels where they would bear fruit a thousandfold, will be brought into collision with doctrinaire idealists who believe in economic evolution as it is not. The average man to-day in his conscious intelligence will subscribe to modernism in some degree, but his instinctive actions are always in the direction of a return to Mediævalism. This fact is illustrated by the arrival of the Trade Union Movement, which was well described by Mr. Chesterton as " a return to the past by men ignorant of the past, like the subconscious action of some man who has lost his memory." The circumstance that the Guild propaganda finds such ready support among Trade Unionists is not due to the economic theories associated with it. Such could not be the case, for not one person in a thousand understands economics. The Guild idea is successful because it is in harmony with the popular psychology. It attacks the wage system and directs attention to the danger of the Servile State—evils with which every working man is familiar—while it presents him with a vision of a new social order in which he may take pleasure in his work. These are the things that have promoted the success of the Guild idea. Approving of such aims, the majority are willing to take its economics for granted as things beyond their understanding. They swallow them without tasting them ; just as a previous generation swallowed Collectivist theories without tasting them because Socialists held out promises of a co-operative commonwealth. Those who deny this contention must explain why, if such was not the case, Socialists rebelled against Collectivism when they discovered where it was leading them. If they had understood its

economic theories they would have known its destination
all along, and would no more have thought about rebelling
against it than does Mr. Sidney Webb. Mr. Webb does not
rebel against it, because he understands it. I am inclined
to think he is the only man who understands Collectivism
and believes in it. At any rate he is the only Collectivist
I ever met who was prepared to accept the deductions from
his premises.

While on the one hand we have in the Trade Union
Movement evidence of an instinctive effort by men to return
to Mediævalism in their capacity as producers, we have in
the present outcry against profiteering and the demand
for a fixed and Just Price evidence of an instinctive effort
of men to return to Mediævalism in their capacity as consumers. It is important that this should be recognized,
for the Trade Union Movement and the movement against
profiteering are the upper and nether millstones between
which capitalism is going to be ground and the Guilds
restored. The movement against profiteering, again, is not
due to any leanings towards Mediæval economics. On
the contrary, it is purely instinctive. Just as the Trade
Union Movement owes its origin to the instinct of self-
preservation of producers, so the demand for the Just Price
owes its origin to the instinct of self-preservation of consumers. Yet both are movements back to Mediævalism.
And so in respect to all of our other ideas of reform : they
all imply reversion to the past. What is democracy but
a form of government that existed among all primitive
peoples ? What is the proposal to nationalize the land
but a reversion to the oldest known form of land tenure ?
What is the demand for a more equitable distribution of
wealth but a reversion to pre-capitalist conditions of society ?
What does the substitution of production for use for production for profit and the abolition of poverty imply but
the reversion to a state of things that existed before such
evils came into existence ? They are all borrowed from
the past, and imply the creation of a social order the exact
antithesis of our present one. But our reformers will not
have it. They do not take the trouble to carry their ideas
to their logical conclusion, and so continue to imagine that

all such ideas may be grafted upon modern industrialism and finance which is built upon their denial and is finally antipathetic to them. The result is as might be expected. Modern attempts at reform invariably produce the opposite effect to that intended, or if they remedy one evil, it is but to create another. Instead of being stepping-stones to the millennium, they prove to be the paved way to the Servile State. The discovery of this leads the workers to rebel; they become suspicious of intellectual leadership, and generally speaking the suspicion is justified, for the intellectuals have misled them. Their prejudice against the past is the root of the whole trouble. If we could get rid of this prejudice it would be easy to bridge the gulf between the workers and intellectuals. They would pull together, and we should get real leadership because we should get understanding. It is easy to understand the modern world if you visualize it from the Mediævalist standpoint, but impossible from the modernist, as the constant change of intellectual fashions clearly demonstrates. Yet though the modernist can find certainty nowhere, he still clings tenaciously to the belief that modernism cannot be entirely wrong.

But even when the modernist is convinced of the truth of Mediæval principles he hesitates to give them his adherence because he experiences a difficulty in basing any practical activity upon them. But that is only a temporary difficulty, and would disappear if Mediæval principles were more generally accepted. Still that is not the issue for which we are immediately contending. The vital issue is not finally whether Mediæval principles can be applied in detail, but that the neglect of them leads modernists to put their trust in measures that are foredoomed to failure, while it blinds them to the significance of movements of popular origin because of false *a priori* ideas. It would be just as unreasonable for an engineer to ignore the laws of physics because he found it difficult to apply them with mathematical precision in a complex structure as it is for Socialists to ignore Mediæval economics because they cannot always be immediately applied. For just as a knowledge of the laws of physics keeps the engineer straight within certain limits by telling him what can and what cannot be done, so a knowledge of Mediæval economics would keep Socialists straight within certain limits, and by relating all their schemes to a central and co-ordinating philosophy prevent them from making fundamental errors. It is precisely because men who become immersed in the details of politics are apt to lose sight of first principles that it is so necessary to keep insisting upon them. Above all, a familiarity with the Mediæval philosophy and point of view would give them some insight into the psychology of the people, who, in spite of all appearances to the contrary, are Mediævalists still.

It is because I feel so much the desirability of a *rapprochement* between intellectuals and the workers that I so strongly urge the importance of Mediæval ideas. The tragedy of the situation is that we live in an age that cries out for leadership and no leaders are forthcoming, nor are there likely to be any so long as the modernist philosophy prevails, since it erects an insurmountable barrier between the workers and their rightful leaders. Here I would observe that my comments are just as true of working-class intellectuals as of those of the middle class, for the working class that reads has been fed on the self-same false philosophies. In so far as working-class culture differs from middle-class culture, it is apt to be harder and narrower ; this is where the real danger lies. When I say that the danger confronting us is precisely the same as that which confronted France on the eve of the Revolution —in that chaos may be precipitated by the fact that the workers and the intellectuals are pulling different ways— it is to working-class rather than middle-class intellectuals that I refer, since the neo-Marxian intellectuals are the only modernists sufficiently convinced of the truth of their creed to be capable of determined action in the event of a crisis. The leadership must fall into their hands, unless in the meantime the Mediævalist position can secure wide acceptance, since apart from such acceptance reformers generally will remain blind to the significance of present-day developments that are finally the result of their teaching, but which do not receive recognition because they come in unexpected forms from unexpected quarters. We look to things coming to us from the east and they come to us from the west. And so the very things which might remove impossible barriers from our path are treated with suspicion and rejected.

The Profiteering Act is a case in point. Owing to the fact that the minds of Socialists are filled with the *a priori* theory of social evolution, which teaches them that industry is to get into fewer and fewer hands until a time comes at length when it will be taken over by the State, they have entirely missed the significance of this Act, which points to a very different conclusion. From the point of view of the average Socialist it is nothing more than a measure of temporary expediency advocated by the Northcliffe Press and adopted by the Government as a means of satisfying popular clamour and of postponing the day of substantial reform. But to the Guildsman it wears a different aspect. While he is not prepared to dispute that such motives led to its enactment, he sees in the effort to fix prices a revival of the central economic idea of the Middle Ages. History teaches him it is an idea with great potentialities and may, if advantage is taken of it by reformers, lead to results very different from those intended. The control of prices, he is persuaded, is a precedent condition of success in any effort to secure economic reform, inasmuch as until prices are fixed it is impossible to plan or arrange anything that may not be subsequently upset by fluctuations of the markets. It is a necessary preliminary to secure the unearned increment for the community, since until prices are fixed it will always be possible for the rich to resist attempts to reduce them by transferring any taxation imposed upon them to the shoulders of other members of the community. Moreover, as the Profiteering Act seeks the co-operation of local authorities, it should operate to promote a revival of local life. Where local authorities have fallen into the hands of shopkeepers, the shopkeepers will be compelled to act in the public interest or be cleared out. Thus the moral issue will become one of paramount importance, and this will pave the way for the arrival of the Just Price, for the people will never be satisfied with a fixed price that is not finally a Just Price. As in the Middle Ages the Guilds owed their existence as economic organizations to the desire for a Just Price, it is reasonable to suppose that once the Government is committed to a policy of regulating prices the restoration of the Guilds can only be a matter of time. Apart from Guilds, it may be possible to fix the prices of a few staple articles of general use, but experience must prove that this is as far as things will go, for there is a limit to the successful application of the principle of control from without. The fixing of prices throughout industry necessitates control from within, and this involves a return to the Guilds.

But the Profiteering Act has other implications. It raises the questions of agriculture, landlordism and Roman Law. It is evident that any fixing of prices throughout industry depends ultimately upon our capacity to fix the price of food, and this must remain impossible so long as we are dependent upon foreign supplies of food. Hence the attempt to fix prices leads to the revival of agriculture. The question as to whether with our large population we shall or shall not ever be able to be entirely independent of such supplies is not the issue. We should aim at being as independent as possible, since the nearer we approach to such a condition, the more stable our economic arrangements will become. The movement towards such a revival should be reinforced by the national urgency of correcting the discrepancy between imports and exports. Before the war, the excess of imports was a matter of no concern, as it represented the returns on our foreign investments and the earnings of our mercantile marine, but nowadays, when our foreign investments have been sold to pay for munitions and our mercantile marine reduced, it is a different matter. It means we are living on capital, that the country is being drained of its economic resources, and that this discrepancy must be corrected if we are to avoid national bankruptcy. The politician and industrialist, looking at this problem, cry aloud for increased production, meaning thereby an increase in the production of industrial wares. But this, as I have shown, is no solution, for the markets of the world cannot absorb an increased production. Yet there is a

sense in which they are right. We do not want an increase
of secondary production such as they urge upon us, but
we do need an increase of primary production. We need
an increase of agricultural produce. This is the one direction
in which an increase of output is immediately practicable,
and it would react to our economic advantage. For not
only would it, by decreasing our imports of food, tend to
correct the balance between imports and exports, but it
would provide an increased home market for our industrial
wares. It would increase our national independence and
lay for us a firm economic base on which we could proceed
to build. . We could then begin to fix prices with some
assurance that what we did would not be upset by the
action of some Food Trust beyond the seas. The fleeting
nature of the prosperity built upon foreign trade is in these
days being brought home to us. The experience of Carthage
and Athens, of Venice and Genoa, of Hanseatic Germany
and of the Dutch, is becoming our experience. A time
came in the life of these States when they found themselves
at the mercy of forces they were powerless to control,
and so it is with us. There is no way out of the impasse
in which we find ourselves but to restore to society the base
that was destroyed by the tyranny of landlordism on the one
hand and the shibboleth of Free Trade on the other. If
a revival of agriculture is to be of real benefit to society,
life in the country must be made attractive again and the
agricultural worker be properly paid, and I would add he
should not be paid less than the equivalent of what he was
able to earn in the Middle Ages, which at the pre-war value
of money would not be less than three pounds a week. No
doubt this will appear entirely impracticable to our
" practical " reformers whose habit of mind it is to put
expediency before principle. But I am assured that the
great increase of demand in the home market created by
such well-paid workers would speedily react to the advantage of the community by relieving the pressure of competition in the towns. We should soon find that a prosperous
peasantry was our greatest economic asset. Raising the
wages of agricultural workers would, moreover, by putting
the labourers on their feet, pave the way for the organization

of agriculture on a Guild basis.   As an intermediate step, however, it would perhaps be necessary to work for small holdings and restored common lands, a combination of which would not unlikely prove to be the most satisfactory form of land-holding.   But in no case should ownership of land be absolute.   On the contrary, land should be held conditionally upon its cultivation and owned by the local authorities, an arrangement I suggest as an alternative to land nationalization because it avoids the evils of bureaucracy.

So self-evident may appear the policy I recommend that the question naturally arises, Why is it not adopted ? The answer is because the revival of agriculture raises the land question, and that touches the governing class in a very tender place.   The outcry that any proposal to tax the land immediately raises is not due to the fact that it touches the wealthy in their economic stronghold, for the money power is in these days infinitely more powerful than the land power, but because it attacks the honour of the governing class.   All the great landowners are in possession of stolen property, and it is said that a great part of such lands have no proper title-deeds.   When Mr. Smillie raised this question at the recent Coal Commission he raised a very pertinent one.   But he neglected a stronger line of attack.   Instead of asking whether the lands held by the dukes had proper title-deeds, he ought to have asked how it came about that any land possessed title-deeds ; whether it was in the interests of the community for men to enjoy privileges without corresponding responsibilities ; and how it came about that landlords found themselves in this irresponsible position to-day.   These questions would have raised the really fundamental issues ;   for no men were in this position before the revival of Roman Law.

It has been the misfortune of the land question that its fundamental importance has been disregarded because it has been associated with moribund solutions of its problems. Every one with a practical knowledge of the circumstances of agriculture and building knew very well that the taxation of land values, though theoretically justifiable, would be followed by consequences very different from those intended.

We are paying in the housing shortage to-day for the Land Campaign of 1909—a fact that has been obscured by the circumstance that the war has rendered cottage-building an uneconomic proposition. If land reformers had been as keen on reviving agriculture, for which they professed concern, as they were for securing the unearned increment of city sites, they would never have fallen into the economic fallacies they did, for in that case they would have begun by enquiring into the circumstances of agriculture, and have made its revival their primary concern. But it has unfortunately happened that while agricultural reformers have shirked the land question, those who have attacked it have had their eyes fixed upon urban values. So land reform has fallen between two stools, and will remain so until the reformers wake up to the fact that the land question is fundamental to all their schemes.

It is a paradox, but I believe it is nevertheless true, that it is this tradition of reformers approaching the problem of reconstruction from the point of view of unearned increment, or surplus value, to use Marxian terminology, that in the past has been their undoing. With their eyes for ever fixed on the money that goes into the pockets of others who have no moral right to it, they incline to approach problems in a ruthless mechanical way that entirely disregards circumstances. These circumstances in turn have a way of defeating them, for problems are to be attacked along the line of their growth and finally in no other way. The root fallacy that leads reformers to be thus for ever attacking problems in the wrong way is that they have fallen into the error of making economics rather than law and morals the starting-point of their enquiries. It is this that has led them to the Collectivist way of thinking, that supposes the solution of the social problem to be nothing more than a matter of detailed arrangements—a way of thinking that has survived the formal rejection of Collectivist theories, and which is still believed in by the neo-Marxians. For their quarrel with the Fabians, as with us, is immediately a quarrel about time. Without any conception of the organic nature of society, they demand an immediate solution of its problems They want the

millennium at once, and have no patience with us because
we do not believe it possible to improvise a new social
system the day after the revolution.   Though they profess
to take their stand upon history, they are strangely oblivious
to its lessons.   For if there is one lesson more than another
that it teaches, it is that organic changes are not brought
about in a catastrophic way.   On the contrary, catastrophes,
in which history abounds, are invariably followed by long
periods of social disorder and chaos, and only indirectly
can be said to lead to any kind of good, in that experience
proves that men will often listen to the voice of truth in
suffering that they scorned in their days of prosperity.
Yet the neo-Marxians are so eager for the millennium that
they seek catastrophe as a means of realizing it.

There is another lesson that history teaches that the
Marxians do not so much ignore as deny—that evils are
never conquered before they are *understood* and faced in
the right spirit.   The history of Greece and Rome abounds
in revolutions, but the revolutionaries were unable to abolish
the evils consequent upon an unregulated currency, because
they did not understand *how* to suppress them.   Plato
might realize that the technical remedy was to be found
in a system of fixed prices, but the moral atmosphere necessary to reduce such an idea to practice was absent in Greek
society, and so his suggestion was ignored.   It was not
until Christianity had entirely transformed the spirit of
society by replacing the individualistic temper of Pagan
society by the spirit of human brotherhood that a solution
was found in the institution of the Just Price as maintained
by the Guilds.   Similarly the transition from Mediæval
to modern society, from communism to individualism, did
not come about owing to some inexorable law of social
evolution, but because the moral sanction of Mediæval
society was gradually undermined by the lawyers and
their Roman Law.   They undermined the communal spirit
that sustained the Guilds by affirming the right of every
man to buy in the cheapest market and to sell in the dearest,
while they transformed Feudalism into landlordism by
denying the Mediæval theory of reciprocal rights and duties,
and exalting the rights of the individual at the expense

of those of the community. What Marxians call social evolution is nothing more or less than the social and economic consequences of such teaching—a truth which even they instinctively recognize, for they are not content to leave the coming of the millennium to the blind workings of the historic process about which they are so eloquent, but seek to promote it by inculcating the doctrines of class-consciousness into the minds of the workers. There is nothing inevitable about social changes. The direction can at any time be changed where there is the will and the understanding. But for the revival of Roman Law and the immoral teachings associated with it, European society would have continued to develop on Mediæval lines to this day as indeed it continued to develop in Asia and remained until European capitalism began to undermine it.

Recognizing, then, that all societies are finally the expression or materialization of their dominant philosophy, and that when in the Middle Ages communal relationships obtained they were sustained by the teachings of Christianity, the question may reasonably be asked whether the policy we advocate does not imply a return to Christianity ; must not reformers return to the churches ? The answer is that this would be the case if the churches taught Christianity as it was understood by the Early Christians. But such is not the case. The churches in the past made terms with the mammon of unrighteousness, and though it is true that they are changing, we have to recognize that they are changing in response to the rebellion against capitalism from without rather than from any movement from within—at any rate in so far as their attitude towards social questions is concerned. If the churches had taken the lead in attacking capitalism, there would be a case for joining them, but considering that they did not, and are so much bound up with the existing order, to advocate such a policy would not only lead to endless misunderstanding, but would hamper us in the immediate work that requires to be done. Hitherto Guildsmen have approached the problem from one particular angle. They have sought to transform the Trade Unions into Guilds by urging upon the latter a policy of encroaching control

This policy is good as far as it goes. But it is not the only thing that requires to be done. It is not only necessary to approach the problem of establishing Guilds from the point of view of the producer ; it is equally necessary to approach it from the point of view of the consumer. For this reason I would urge that we should not neglect the new weapon that the Profiteering Act has placed in our hands. Let us recognize the significance of this Act as giving legal sanction to the central economic idea of the Middle Ages. Let us study its implications and make the working of the Act the basis of activities that will lead step by step on the one hand to the revival of agriculture and the abolition of landlordism, and on the other to the return of the Guilds. For if the public can be persuaded of the desirability of Guilds from the point of view of consumers, half our battle would be won. The movement from above would join hands with the movement from below and Guilds arise naturally from the union.

Meanwhile those whom personal bias leads to a consideration of the more fundamental propositions underlying the problem of reconstruction should be urged to concentrate their energies upon the abolition of Roman Law. Such an attack would tend to create the kind of intellectual background of which the Reform Movement stands so much in need. It would in the first place prevent the Guild Movement from getting side-tracked by counteracting the pernicious influence of the Marxian interpretation of history. In the next it would impress upon the minds of people the idea that social and economic changes are preceded by changes in ideas. Then it would demonstrate the primacy of law over economics ; and lastly it would bring Mediæval ideas into a direct relationship with the modern thought, because it so happens that it is impossible to attack Roman Law without at the same time affirming Mediæval principles.[1]

---

[1] In *Authority, Liberty and Function*, by Ramiro de Maeztu (Allen & Unwin) the antithesis between Roman and Mediæval Law is carried further by showing that whereas Roman Law is subjective in conception, Mediæval Law is objective, and the issue is widened by showing that all our ideas from Renaissance times onward have become increasingly subjective. It is a book which I cannot too strongly recommend to my readers, as it is one to which I feel I owe much.

Law is the link between morals and economics as it is between philosophy and politics and between industrialism and militarism. To attack Roman Law is therefore to attack the modern system at a very vital and strategic point. It would create a force that would restore the communal spirit of the Middle Ages. For after all there are only two types of society that have existed since currency was introduced—the capitalist civilizations of Greece and Rome and of modern Europe and America that did not control currency, and the communal societies of Mediæval Europe and Asia that did. There is, finally, no third type of society, inasmuch as all societies conform to one or other of these types, differing only to the extent that in different societies emphasis is given to different aspects of them. Hence it is reasonable to suppose that as the capitalist civilization of Rome was followed by the communal civilization of Mediævalism, the reaction against capitalism to-day will carry us along to a future where the promise of the Middle Ages will be fulfilled.

PRINCIPAL BOOKS CONSULTED

CHAPTER I

FOWLER, W. WARDE . . Rome
JONES, H. STUART . . . The Roman Empire
LIDDELL, HENRY S. . . History of Rome
NITTI, FRANCESCO S. . . Catholic Socialism
SCHMITZ, LEONHARD . . History of Greece
ZIMMERN, ALFRED E. . . . The Greek Commonwealth

CHAPTER II

ASHLEY, W. J. . . . . . An Introduction to English Economic History
and Theory
BRENTANO, L. . . . . . History and Development of Gilds
LAMBERT, J. M. . . . . . Two Thousand Years of Guild Life
LIPSON, E. . . . . . . An Introduction to the Economic History of
England
NOEL, CONRAD . . . . Socialism in Church History

CHAPTER III

ASHLEY, W. J. . . . . . An Introduction to English Economic History
and Theory
GIERKE, OTTO . . . . Political Theories of the Middle Ages
JANSSEN, JOHANNES E. . History of the German People at the Close
of the Middle Ages
O'NEILL, H. C. . . . . New Things and Old in St. Thomas Aquinas
Cambridge Modern History

CHAPTER IV

JANSSEN, JOHANNES E. . History of the German People at the Close
of the Middle Ages
JENKS, EDWARD . . . Law and Politics in the Middle Ages
MAEZTU, RAMIRO DE . . Authority, Liberty and Function
MAINE, SIR HENRY . . Ancient Law
MAITLAND, F. W. . . . Introduction to Gierke's Political Theories of
the Middle Ages
RASHDALL, HASTINGS . . The Universities of Europe in the Middle Ages
VINOGRADOFF, SIR PAUL . Roman Law in Mediæval Europe

CHAPTER V

ASHLEY, W. J.	An Introduction to English Economic History and Theory
GOOCH, G. P.	Political Thought in England from Bacon to Halifax
GREEN, J. R.	History of the English People
JARRETT, BEDE	Mediæval Socialism
VINOGRADOFF, SIR PAUL .	Roman Law in Mediæval Europe

CHAPTER VI

BUSSELL, F. W. . . .	Religious Thought and Heresy in the Middle Ages
	The Cambridge Mediæval History
GIBBON, EDWARD . . .	Decline and Fall of the Roman Empire
NITTI, FRANCESCO S. . .	Catholic Socialism
PAULI, REINHOLD . . .	Pictures of Old England

CHAPTER VII

JANSSEN, JOHANNES E. .	History of the German People at the Close of the Middle Ages
PAULI, REINHOLD . . .	Pictures of Old England
RASHDALL, HASTINGS . .	The Universities of Europe in the Middle Ages
WALSH, J. J.	The Popes and Science

CHAPTER VIII

LETHABY, W. R. . . .	Mediæval Art
MORRIS, WILLIAM . . .	Gothic Architecture
	Architecture, Industry and Wealth
RUSKIN, JOHN	The Stones of Venice
	Seven Lamps of Architecture

CHAPTER IX

ANDERSON, W. J. . . .	The Architecture of the Renaissance in Italy
BLOMFIELD, R. T. . . .	A History of Renaissance Architecture in England
	The Cambridge Modern History, vol. i.
GOTCH, J. A.	Early Renaissance Architecture in England
PATER, WALTER . . .	The Renaissance
RUSKIN, JOHN	Stones of Venice
SABATIER, PAUL . . .	Life of St. Francis of Assisi
SYMONDS, J. A.	Renaissance in Italy

CHAPTER X

AGATE, LEONARD D. . . . Luther and the Reformation
The Cambridge Modern History
JANSSEN, JOHANNES E. . . . History of the German People at the Close
of the Middle Ages

CHAPTERS XI AND XII

COBBETT, WILLIAM . . . . A History of the Protestant Reformation
CUNNINGHAM, W. . . . . The Growth of English Industry and Com-
merce
LINGARD, JOHN . . . . . The History of England
TAWNEY, R. H. . . . . . The Agrarian Problem in the Sixteenth
Century
The Cambridge Modern History

CHAPTER XIII

KROPOTKIN, P. A. . . The Great French Revolution
BELLOC, HILAIRE . . . The French Revolution
BON, GUSTAVE LE . . . Psychology of Revolution
The Cambridge Modern History
MIGNET, F. A. . . . . History of the French Revolution
THIERS, L. A. . . . . The History of the French Revolution
TOZER, HENRY J. . . . Translation of Rousseau's Social Contract,
with Introduction

CHAPTER XIV

ASHLEY, W. J. . . . . An Introduction to English Economic History
and Theory
BRENTANO, L. . . . . History and Development of Gilds
CUNNINGHAM, W. . . . The Growth of English Industry and Commerce

CHAPTER XV

CUNNINGHAM, W. . . . The Growth of English Industry and Com-
merce
GOOCH, G. P. . . . . Political Thought in England from Bacon to
Halifax
HAMMOND, J. L. and B. . The Town Labourer, 1760–1832
The Cambridge Modern History, vol. ii.
PRICE, L. L. . . . . A Short History of Political Economy in
England

CHAPTER XVI

CUNNINGHAM, W. . . . The Growth of English Industry and Commerce
HAMMOND, J. L. and B. . The Town Labourer, 1760–1832
PERRIS, G. H. . . . . The Industrial History of Modern England

CHAPTER XVII

CARLYLE, THOMAS . . . Past and Present
                       Latter Day Pamphlets
CHESTERTON, G. K. . . The Victorian Age in Literature
COBBETT, WILLIAM . . . Rural Rides, etc.
HAMMOND, J. L. and B. . The Town Labourer, 1760–1832
MORLEY, JOHN . . . . Life of Richard Cobden
SEIGNOBOS, CHARLES . . A Political History of Europe since 1814
WEBB, S. and B. . . . History of Trade Unionism

CHAPTER XVIII

NAPIER, T. B. . . . . Essay in " A Century of Law Reform "
POWELL, ELLIS T. . . The Evolution of the Money Market

CHAPTER XIX

CHESTERTON, CECIL . . The Prussian hath Said in his Heart
FARROW, T., and CROTCH, W. The Coming Trade War
HUEFFER, F. M. . . . When Blood was their Argument
MAEZTU, RAMIRO DE . . Authority, Liberty and Function in the Light of the War
LAUGHLIN, J. L. . . The Credit of the Nations
STEED, WICKHAM . . The Hapsburg Monarchy
TAYLOR, G. R. S. . . . Psychology of the Great War

CHAPTER XX

ANET, CLAUDE . . . . La Revolution Russé (vol. i. translated into English)
KEELING, H. V. . . . Bolshevism
KERENSKY, A. F. . . The Prelude to Bolshevism
LLOYD, C. M. . . . . Trade Unionism
PAUL, W. . . . . . The State : its Origin and Function
RANSOME, ARTHUR . . . Six Weeks in Russia in 1919
SACKS, A. J. . . . . The Dawn of the Russian Revolution
STARR, MARK . . . . A Worker Looks at History
TROTSKY, LEON . . . The Russian Revolution

INDEX

Aachen, 118
Abbas, 106
Abbasid dynasty, 106
Act of Six Articles, 171
Advancement of Learning, 116
Æneid, the, 27, 130
Agriculture : rural depopulation, 19, 21, 168, 255 ; Guilds of, 51, 79 ; evictions, 70, 77, 174, 175 ; sheep-farming, 78, 173, 174, 215 ; under Canon Law, 224; encouragement of by Cecil, 227 ; destruction of by Free Trade, 255 ; limited liability company in, 262; need of revival of, 306, 307, 310. *See also* Land-holding
Agrippa, 29
Aix-la-Chapelle, 118
Albert IV, Duke of Bavaria, 52
Albertus Magnus, 109, 111, 112, 131
Albigenses, 96-8
Alchemy, 103, 108
Alcuin of York, 93
Alexander the Great, 18
Alexander, the Nuncio, 143
Alexander III, Pope, 65
Alexander VI, Pope, 133
Alexandria, 87
Ali, 106
Almansur, 106
Alsace-Lorraine, 8, 275
America, 228, 240, 281, 311
Angell, Norman, 275
Anti-Corn Law League, 254
Antoninus Pius, Emperor of Rome, 31, 296.
Antony, 29
Apprenticeship, under Guilds, 40, 123 ; Act of Henry IV, 215 ; Statute of, 219, 226 ; repeal of, 200
Apulia, 24

Aquinas. *See* St. Thomas Aquinas
Arabic, 106
Architecture, 92, 109, 112, 134, 246 ; Greek, 119-121 ; Roman, 118-121, 133, 135, 136 ; Byzantine, 89, 90 ; Gothic, 102, 117 *seq.*, 113, 165 ; French Gothic, 125 ; English Gothic, 125 ; Norman, 123 ; Tudor, 124 ; Italian Gothic, 125, 134 ; Flemish Gothic, 125 ; Renaissance, 112, 125, 134 *seq.* ; Vernacular Renaissance, Elizabethan, Jacobean, Queen Anne, Georgian, 135
Armada, Spanish, 227
Armaments, 272
Armies : of Rome, 28 ; mercenary, 176 ; of French Revolution, 204, 208
Aristocracy, Revival of, 187
Aristotle, 5, 15, 37, 105 *seq.*, 128, 130, 131, 153, 156, 230, 256
Arthur, Prince, 160
Arts of the Middle Ages, 117 *seq.*
Asceticism, 107
Ashley, W. J., quoted, 74, 77, 155, 218, 219
Ashton, 241
Asia, 309, 311
Astrology, 108
Athens, 16, 18, 19, 305
Attica, 16
Augustus, 28-32, 211
Austria, 273, 287
Authority, 122, 172, 187
Averroes, 106, 107, 113
Azo, 76

Bacon, Lord, 80, 83, 114
Bacon, Roger, 111
Baedeker's Guides, 125
Bagdad, 106
Bankers, 22, 154
Barbarians, 25, 89

Basle, 110. *See* Universities
Bavaria, 151.
Beauvais, Synod of, 96
Bede, 92
Belgium, 24, 271, 276
Belloc, Hilaire, quoted, 170
Benedict XIV, Pope, 104
Benedictines, 92, 129, 130
Berg, 67
Bible, 34, 35, 113, 114, 184
Billaud-Varennes, 206
Bill of Rights, 82
Black Death, 78
Bohemia, 129
Boleyn, Anne, 159
Bologna, 61, 105, 109. *See* Universities
Bolsheviks, Bolshevism, 285 *seq. See also* Marx, Class War, and Materialist Conception of History
Bon, Gustave le, quoted, 209
Boniface VIII, Pope, 65, 104
Borgia, Cæsar, 133
Boritzer, Matthew, 135
Bracton, 73, 75, 76
Brentano, L., quoted, 37, 38, 220, 221
Britain, 88, 91
Bruges, the belfry at, 125
Bruno, 113
Brutus, 88
Bubble Act, 260; repeal of, 261
Buddhism, 35, 36
Bulgaria, 86
Bullion, 228-30
Bureaucracy, 28, 86, 211, 212, 273, 274, 275, 295
Bussell, F. W., quoted, 107

Cabul, 18
Cæsar, 28, 118, 130
Caliphate, 106
Calvin, Calvinism, 155, 171, 182, 192
Cambridge, King's College Chapel, 124; Trinity College, 135
Cambridge Modern History, quoted, 130, 131, 143, 168, 177
Canon Law, 59, 62, 63, 65, 67, 224
Capitalism follows introduction of currency and growth of foreign trade in Greece, 13 *seq.*; follows militarism in Rome, 19 *seq.*; joint-stock companies in Rome, 21, 22; destruction of rivals by Romans, 24;
creates social disorders, 23; paralyses government, 27; Augustus curbs power of capitalists, 29; Roman Law a product of capitalism, 32; suppressed in Middle Ages, 39; reappears after revival of Roman Law, 70, 83; in Germany in Middle Ages, 147; in England, 215; capitalists invest in land, 173; promote sheep-farming, 173; exploit "domestic industry," 215; undermine the Guilds, 215-18; triumphs with Reformation, 156; prosperity restored by capitalists after suppression of monasteries, 226; growth of belief in, 228; mercantilism, 229 *seq.*; Manchester School, 233 *seq.*; Industrial Revolution, 237 *seq.*; Free Trade, 255-6; Limited Liability Companies, 259 *seq.*; a cause of the war, 275; the economic cul-de-sac, 281; leads to Bolshevism, 286
Carpenter, E., quoted, 115
Carrier, 206
Carthage, 24, 85, 276, 305
Catastrophism, 249, 308
Catharists, 96, 100
Cathedrals of Amiens, Bourges, Chartres, Paris, Rheims, Rouen, Milan, Orvieto, 125
Catherine of Arragon, 158
Catholics, 171 *seq.*
Cecil, W., Lord Burghley, 227
Chambers of Commerce, 219
Chantries Bill, 219
Charlemagne, Emperor, 55, 56, 118
Charles I, 184, 185, 239, 240
Charles IV, Emperor, 67
Charles V, Emperor, 151, 160
Chartists, 252-4
Chaucer, 129
Chemistry, 102, 103, 111
Chesterton, G. K., quoted, 45, 83, 125, 189, 298, 299
Chivalry, 49, 71
Christian Admonition, 224
Christian Fathers, 29, 88, 129, 130
Christianity, communal basis of, 34, 35, 298; introduces a new moral principle, 35; sustained the communal spirit of Middle Ages, 36; and the Guilds, 37; made possible

the Just Price, 39 ; Greek philosophy incorporated in Christian dogmas, 88 ; need of dogmas, 88 ; Gothic architecture, expression of, 120-1 ; Renaissance not originally a reaction against Christianity, but against Franciscan Gospel of Poverty, 127 *seq.* ; Reformation an attempt to return to discipline of Early Church, 152 ; Puritanism a perversion of Christianity, 139-40, 184-5, 308-9

Church and State, 54 *seq.*, 65 *seq.*, 98, 160, 171, 178, 193, 244. *See also* Holy Roman Empire

Church, Eastern, 89, 91, 106

Church of England, 174

Church, Western or Roman : civilized the barbarians, 91 ; preserved learning through the Dark Ages, 92, 130 ; opposed to heresy, 94 *seq.* ; encouraged science, 105 *seq.* ; attempted to suppress revival of Roman Law, 65 ; *Unam Sanctum*, 66 ; established the Inquisition, 98 ; corrupted by Renaissance, 57, 133, 142-3 ; wealth of, 27, 37, 60, 92, 166, 170 ; attitude towards property, 27, 156 ; towards usury, 153 ; reason for post-Reformation policy, 177-8

Cicero, 24, 88, 120

Cistercians, 98, 129

Civil War, the, 186, 240

Class War, 18, 19, 24, 84, 150, 174-5, 236, 246, 285 *seq.*

Clement V, Pope, 99

Clement VII, Pope, 159

Cleopatra, 29

Coal Commission, 306

Cobbett, Wm., quoted, 86, 102, 162, 163, 183, 184, 250, 251

Coke, Edward, 82

Collectivism, 299, 307

Collegia, Roman, 30, 31, 38

Combination Laws, 222 ; repeal of, 222.

Commentators, 64, 98

Committee of Public Safety, 207

Communal art, 119, 137 ; culture, 137 ; law, *see* Mediæval Law ; property, *see* Land-holding ; basis of Christianity, *see* Christianity

Conrad II, Emperor, 60

Conservatives, 299

Constantine the Great, 31, 96

Constantinople, 89, 91, 107, 131 ; Council of, 36

Constituent Assembly, 204. *See* French Revolution

Convention, the, 205. *See* French Revolution

Coomaraswamy, A. K., quoted, 242

Corinth, 24, 85, 276

Corn Laws, 254, 255

Cortes, 163

Coutances, Bishop of, 60

Coventry, 221

Cowley, E., quoted, 248

Craft culture, 112, 137

Credit, Creditism, 268, 275

Cromwell, Oliver, 83 ; Thomas, 161 *seq.*

Crown, the, 158, 260, 261

Cuba, 50

Cunningham, E., quoted, 166, 167, 170, 215

Currency, 13 *seq.*, 19, 20, 22, 32, 34, 51, 79, 199, 200, 201, 208, 213, 214, 217, 230, 278, 308

Czechs, 273

Dante, 130

Danton, 206

Dark Ages, 89, 91, 92, 93. *See also* Learning

Davanent, Chas., 232

Decretum, the, 65

Defender of the Faith, 158

Deloume, A., quoted, 88

Depopulation. *See* Agriculture

Dickinson, J. Lowes, 271

Diocletian, Emperor of Rome, 31

Directory, the, 208-10. *See* French Revolution

Disraeli, Benjamin, 250, 257

Disraeli, Isaac, quoted, 186

Discourses on the Commonweal, 175

Dissection, 102, 103, 104

Divina Commedia, 130

Divine Right of Kings, 51, 64, 81, 82, 195

Division of Labour. *See* Industrial Revolution

Dogmas, 88, 122

Domesday Book, 49

Dominicans, 109, 111, 117, 126

Douglas, C. H., 268
Dover, 184
Dutch, the, 229, 305
Dutch War, the, 229

Early Christians, 35, 36, 96, 152
Early Church, 34, 87, 88, 96, 142, 152-3
East India Company, 232, 259
Economic cul-de-sac, 276, 281
Education system, 169
Edward VI, 164, 171 *seq.*, 219, 226, 239
Elective priesthood, 145, 153
Elizabeth, Queen, 80, 165, 181 *seq.*, 226, 239, 259
Empire, Eastern, 89, 118 ; Western, 89, 130
Enclosures, 77, 174, 175. *See* Landholding and Agriculture
England, 65, 126, 158 *seq.*, 272, 291
Entente, the 277
Epicureanism, 132
Epitadeus, Ephor, 16
Equality, 195-7   *See* French Revolution
Erasmus, 145, 146
Etruria, 25
Eupatrid, 14
Evictions. *See* Agriculture

Fabians, 45, 307
Factory Acts, 241, system, *see* Industrial Revolution
Farrow, Thos., and Crotch, W., quoted, 276
Fawkes, Guy, 183
Feudalism, Feudal System, 25, 48-51, 74, 75, 77, 78, 84, 148, 173, 192, 202, 214
Ficino, Marsilio, 131
Finance, after-war problems of, 279 *seq.*
Fire Insurance Co.'s of London, 220
Fisher, John, Bishop of Rochester, 160
Flanders, Hotels de Ville of, 124
Flemings, 41
Florence, 105, 154
Foreign Trade, 18, 19, 127, 147, 226, 230, 231, 239, 271, 272, 277, 305
Fouché, 206
Fowler, W. Warde, quoted, 25, 30

France, 65, 96, 97, 126, 189 *seq.*, 272, 299, 302
France, Northern, 24, 276
Franciscans, 93, 109, 111, 112, 117, 126, 128, 129, 132, 154, 161
Frederick Barbarossa, Emperor, 65, 98
Frederick II, Emperor, 98, 99
Free Trade, Free Traders, 229, 232, 233, 254-6
French Revolution, 33, 189 *seq.*, 247 ; inspired by Rousseau, 191 ; a frustrated movement back to Mediævalism, 190 ; a consequence of the policy of Louis XVI, 190 ; limitations of Rousseau, 191 ; the *Social Contract*, explanation of, 193 *seq.* ; not understood by his followers, 203 ; the Constituent Assembly, 204 ; the Girondins, 205 ; the Convention, 205 ; the Jacobins, 205 ; the Terror, 206 ; Robespierre, 206 ; Committee of Public Safety, 207 ; corruption of the Assemblies, 207 ; the counter-Revolution, 208 ; the Directory, 208 ; the Catholic revival, 208 ; the *coup d'état* of Napoleon, 209 ; his policy, 210 ; why the Revolution failed, 211
French Revolution of 1848, 252
Fronde, 190
Fuero Juzgo, 32

Galileo, 113
Gaul, 24, 85
Gelasius, Pope, 56
General Will, 202.   *See Social Contract*
Geneva, 192
German Empire, 64, 72, 93
Germans, 23, 24, 85, 273-5
Germany, 19, 64, 67, 68, 70, 96, 97, 126, 139 *seq.*, 158, 161, 191, 268, 270, 271, 273, 275, 276, 287
Gierke, Otto, quoted, 53
Girondins, 205, 210. *See also* French Revolution
Gladstone, 257
Glasgow, 261
Glossators, 62, 64
Gloucester, Humphrey, Duke of, 164
Gnostics, 97
Gooch, G. P., quoted, 81, 232

Gothic architecture, 118 *seq.*
Gothic Revivalists, 102
Gracchi, the, 20, 26-8
Gracchus, Tiberius, 25-27 ; Caius, 26
Gratian, 59, 65
Great Schism, 57, 143
Greece, 13 *seq.*, 192, 198, 199, 298, 308, 311
Greece, City States of, 198. *See Social Contract*
Greek culture. *See* Learning
Gregory the Great, Pope, 91
Gregory VII, Pope, 60
Gregory IX, Pope, 65, 98, 99, 100, 107
Guild idea, the, 299, 300
Guilds, the Guild System, 15, 30, 31, 37, 38 *seq.*, 47, 79, 84, 86, 122, 123, 147, 199, 200, 214 *seq.*, 222, 224, 229, 238, 240, 250, 269, 270, 304, 308, 310 ; rise of, 37 ; religious Guilds, 37 ; Frith Guilds, 38 ; economic Guilds, 39 ; communist spirit of, 37, 39 ; to enforce Just Price, 39, 40 ; Guilds Merchant, 40-2, 44, 146-7, 260 ; Craft Guilds, 41-3, 123 ; Merchant Adventurers, 42 ; Journeymen Fraternities, 42 ; taxation of, 215 ; decline of, 215 *seq.* ; tyranny of, 44-5, 216 ; attempted reorganization of, 217 ; defeat of, 218 ; confiscation of property of, 219 ; survival of, 219 ; fixed prices leads to a revival of, 304-8, 310
Guildsman, 303, 309
Gunpowder Plot, 183

Haingerichte, 150
Hales, John, 175
Hanseatic League, 147, 305 ; steelyard in London, 147
Hammond, J. L. and B., quoted, 238
Hampden, John, 186
Heine, 32, 33
Henry I, 74
Henry II, 74, 160, 298
Henry IV, Emperor, 61
Henry VII, 217
Henry VIII, 158 *seq.*, 171, 174, 175, 217, 224, 228
Heresy, 93 *seq.*, 103, 107, 108, 109, 112, 113, 171, 248 ; Manichean, 66,

95, 96, 97, 132 ; Arian, 95 ; Nestorian, 95
Heretics, 95, 100, 171, 183
History of the Reformation, 251
Hohenstaufen family, 65, 98
Holy Roman Empire, theory of, 54 ; centre of European life, 55 ; quarrel over Right of Investiture, 56, 60 ; undermined by revival of Roman Law, 61 *seq.* ; impotence of, in fifteen century, 71 ; destruction of by armies of Napoleon, 55
Honorius III, Pope, 65
Horace, 130
House of Commons. *See* Parliament
House of Lords, 292-3
Housing shortage, 307
Hudson Bay Company, 260
Hugh of St. Victor, 66
Hungary, 65
Humanists, 129 *seq.*, 131, 132, 146
Huss, Hussite movement, 129, 158
Huxley, J. H., quoted, 113

India, 273
Indulgences, 141 *seq.*
Industrial movement, 258
Industrial Revolution, years of dramatic change, 237 ; invention of machinery made possible by division of labour, 238 ; workers dislike of, 238 ; built upon a slave class, 239 ; opposition of Tudors and Stuarts to mechanical invention, 239-40 ; dominated by Puritan spirit, 240-1 ; cruelty of the system, 241 ; in Germany, America and India, 241-2 ; has industrialism come to stay, 242 ; reared on a base of social injustice, 242 ; imminence of economic breakdown, 243 ; every popular demand incompatible with industrialism, 243 ; workers seek its destruction, 244 ; division of labour must be challenged, 245 ; only small machines permitted in the future, 245
Industry, domestic system of, 215
Innocent III, Pope, 66, 98
Innocent IV, Pope, 65
Inquisition, 98 *seq.*
Investiture, Right of, 57, 60
Ireland, 239

21

Irnerius, 61, 62
Isocrates, 18
Italy, 29, 68, 89, 96, 126 *seq.*, 146, 161

Jacks, I. P., quoted, 123
Jacobins, 194, 201, 203-6, 210
James I, 51, 81, 165, 183, 230, 239, 260
Janiculum, 20
Janssen, Johannes, quoted, 47, 52, 56, 70, 72, 110, 135, 145, 146, 147, 149, 225
Jarrett, Bede, quoted, 128, 154
Jerome, 158
Jews, 100
John of Gaunt, 78, 140, 156
John of Salisbury, 53
John XXII, Pope, 103, 110
Joint-Stock Companies, in Rome, 21, 22; in England, 260 *seq. See also* Limited Liability Companies
Jones, H. Stuart, quoted, 31
Joshua, 114
Julick, 67
Junkerdom, 85
Jurists, Roman, 59, 199, 295, 296; Mediæval, 61 *seq.*, 73, 75, 76, 295, 296
Justinian Code, 61, 64-5, 75, 80, 89, 218, 296

Kepler, 113
Kerensky, 286, 287
Knights, robber, 48; chivalrous, 49
Knox, John, 182
Kropotkin, P., quoted, 190

Labour Party, 258, 292, 293
Lacher, Lawrence, 135
Laissez-faire, 233-4
Lancashire, 239, 241
Land-holding, communal system of land-holding, broken up by currency and private property established, in Greece, 13 *seq.*; in Rome, 19 *seq.*; Christianity preserves communal land system of barbarian tribes, 37; Church property, 37, 60, 92, 166; land under feudal system, 50; revival of Roman Law transforms feudalism into landlordism, 76-7; provokes Peasants' Revolt of 1381,

78-9; provokes Peasants' War in Germany, 150; suppression of monasteries results in land-grabbing, 161 *seq.*; Reformation a victory for landlordism, 156, 170, 182; changed attitude towards property of new landlords, 173; Peasants' Revolt of 1549, 173 *seq.*; the Civil War a triumph of landlordism, 185-6; relations of property and currency, 208; French Revolution creates new landlords, 208; suggested system of land-holding, 305-6; land and title deeds, 306. *See also* Agriculture
Langenstein, Heinrich von, 47
Lambert, J. M., 31
Lateran Council (1179), 98
Law Courts, 292, 293, 294, 296
Lawyers, 66, 67, 70, 73, 74, 75, 76, 78, 80, 82, 153, 156, 167, 173, 204, 210, 226, 294, 295, 308. *See also* Roman Law
League of Nations, 55
Learning, traditions of, preserved through the Dark Ages at Constantinople, 89; knowledge of Greek faded from the West, 130; Latin Classics preserved by the Benedictines, 92, 93, 130; re-discovery of Aristotle, 106-7; emigration of Greek scholars to Italy after fall of Constantinople, 89, 131; Revival of Learning, 130 *seq.*, 168. *See also* Heresy, Science and Renaissance
Legislator, the, 196. *See Social Contract*
Leith, 182
Leitzkau, 144
Leo III, Pope, 55
Leo X, Pope, 141
Lethaby, W. R., quoted, 90, 119, 123
Letters of John Chinaman, 271
Levant, 68, 146
Liberals, 45, 205, 252
Libraries, destruction of at Reformation, 164
Licinian Law, 25
Limited Liability Companies, 259 *seq.*; Acts of, 1855, 1856 and 1862, 261-2; Board of Trade returns of, 262; corrupting influence of, 262 *seq.*;

create labour troubles, 294. *See also* Joint-Stock Companies
Lingard, John, quoted, 171
Lipson, E., quoted, 38, 40, 42, 43
Lloyd, C. M., quoted, 292, 293
Lodge, Sir Oliver, 115
Lollards, 158
Lombards, 56, 118
London, 136, 171, 186, 219
Louis XIV, 190
Louis XVI, 191
Louis XVIII, 209
Lowell, 120
Lucian, 130
Ludovici, A. M., 186-7
Luther, 114, 141 *seq.*, 151, 156, 158
Lutherans, 152, 171
Lycurgus, 15, 16, 17

Macaulay, 114
Macclesfield, 221
Machiavelli, 133, 161
Machinery, hypnotic influence of, 247, 248, 250, 256. *See* Industrial Revolution
Maeztu, Ramiro de, quoted, 45, 187, 203, 273, 275, 277, 310
Magic, 97, 108
Mahomet, 105
Maine, Sir Henry, quoted, 22
Maitland, F. W., quoted, 65
Malynes, Gerard, 230
Manchester School, 233 *seq.*, 252, 259, 260, 284
Manegold, of Lautenbach, 53
Manichean Heresy. *See* Heresy
Marat, 201
Marcus Aurelins, 94
Marius, 27, 28
Markets, exhaustion of, 271, 272, 275, 277
Marston, Chas., quoted, 36
Martial, 130
Marx, Marxians, 8, 9, 10, 45, 46, 86, 87, 88, 155, 174, 175, 194, 212, 235, 287, 288, 289, 297, 302, 307, 308, 309, 310. *See also* Bolshevists, Class War, Materialist Conception of History
Mary, Queen of England, 179 *seq.*
Mary, Queen of Scots, 182
Materialist conception of history, 8, 9, 10

Matilda, Countess of Tuscany, 61
Maximilian, Emperor, 143
Maximum Production, 275, 277, 281, 282
Mediæval law, communal law, customary law, 32, 51, 58, 68, 69, 73, 75, 192, 194, 297
Mediævalist position, 298 *seq.*
Medical schools in the Middle Ages, 105
Medici, Giovanni de, 132
Medici, Giuliano de, 133
Medici, Lorenzo de, 132
Mediterranean, 13, 105
Melanchthon, 114, 156
Mercantilism, 229 *seq.*, 232
Mercenaries, 176
Merchants, middlemen, 14, 18, 22, 41, 147, 214, 225, 255, 256, 260
Merton, Statute of, 77
Metric System, 211
Mexico, 50
Michelangelo, 133, 134
Mill, John Stuart, 235
Milman, quoted, 66
Mirandola, Pico della, 131
Mivart, Professor, 113
Modernism, 248
Monarchy, 51, 52, 53, 80, 81, 84, 195
Monasteries, 86, 130 ; suppression of, 152, 157, 158 *seq.*
Monastic arts, 168
Monastic orders, 91, 92, 93, 108 *seq.*
Montes Pietatis, 154
Montford, Simon de, 93
More, Sir Thomas, 160, 174, 236
Mountain, the, 205. *See* French Revolution
Mun, Thomas, 230-3
Munitions Act, 294
Munitions, Ministry of, 278
Music, 92, 94, 109

Napoleon, 55, 189, 209 *seq.*
Napoleonic Wars, 246, 249, 254
Navigation Act, 229, 230
Neo-Platonism, 87-88
Nero, 21
Nestorians, 95, 105
Netherlands, 173, 191, 227
Nevers, Bishop of, 60
Newton, 113
Nineteenth Century, 246 *seq.*

Noel, Conrad, quoted, 36
Norman Conquest, 49
North Dudley, 232
Northcliffe Press, 303
Northumberland, Duke of, 176
Novum Organum, 114
Nuneaton, 221
Nuremberg, 67, 151

Oligarchy, 18, 29, 246
O'Neill, H. C., quoted, 52, 53
Ommiades, 106
Orleans, 70
Osborne Judgment, 293-4
Otto II, Emperor, 60
Ovid, 130
Oxford. *See* Universities

Paganism, 29, 34, 35, 36, 87, 88, 122,
    126, 131, 132, 146, 192, 193
Painting, 109, 134, 135
Pantheism, 107, 117
Papacy, 56, 57, 59, 65, 66, 91, 98 *seq.*,
    102 *seq.*, 128, 132, 133, 141-3, 159,
    180
Papal Medical School, 105
Paris : Church of St. Denis, 124;
    Treaty of (1229), 98. *See* Universities
Paris, commune of, 204, 205, 206;
    Council of, 107
Parliament, 80, 82, 83, 98, 161, 171,
    175, 180, 185, 186, 220, 221, 250,
    257, 260
Party System, 257
Patricians (Patrons), 19, 20, 22
Paul, W., quoted, 244, 296
Pauli, Reinhold, quoted, 92, 93, 111,
    147
Payment of members, 293
Peasants' Revolt (1381), 43, 79, 80,
    156, 217
Peasants' Revolt (1549), 173-6
Peasants' War in Germany, 150-1
Peel, Sir Robert, 254
Peloponnesian War, 15-18
Peru, Conquest of, 163
Petrarch, 130
Petronius, 132
Philip of Spain, 182
Pisistratus, 17
Pitt, William, 221
Pius II, Pope, 110

Pizarro, 163
Place, Francis, 232
Plain, the, 205. *See* French Revolution
Plato, 15, 88, 93, 94, 131, 308
Pliny, 21
Poland, 68, 146
Pole, Cardinal, 180
Poles, the, 274
Poor Law, Elizabethan, 167, 168
Popanilla, 257
Poverty, Gospel of, 127, 128
Price, Just or Fixed, 15, 39, 40, 45, 47,
    79, 190, 193, 199, 200, 201, 212, 218,
    233, 300, 303, 304. *See also* Guilds
Printing, 142, 145, 168, 171
Profiteering, 15, 18, 39, 147, 177, 201,
    207, 212, 218, 267, 278, 282, 283,
    290
Profiteering Act, 303, 310
Property. *See* Land-holding
Protection, 255
Protestantism, 81, 82, 110, 114, 139
    seq., 158 *seq.*, 170 *seq.*
Publicani, 22, 88
Punic Wars, 20, 21
Puritans, 82, 140, 184, 185, 186, 240,
    241

Quick, O. C., quoted, 88, 97
Quintessence of Ibsenism, 248
Quintilian, 130

Radicals, 247, 250, 251, 252, 257
Railway boom, collapse of, 261
Railway Servants, Amalgamated Society of, 292, 293
Railways, building of, 189, 249, 255
Rashdall, Hastings, quoted, 62, 106,
    107, 110
Rationalism, 107, 117, 138
Ratisbon, Council of, 147
Ravenna, 61
Reform Bill (1832), 252
Reformation, 57, 114, 139 *seq.*, 158
    seq., 170 *seq.*
Regulated companies, 260
Reichskammergericht, 67
Reims, Synod of, 60
Renaissance, the, 112, 126 *seq.*, 139,
    146, 161, 192; a reaction against
    Franciscan Gospel of Poverty, 126-
    131; attempts at reconciliation of

Plato with Christianity, 131 ; Paganism of later Renaissance, 131 ; corruption which followed Pagan ideal 132 ; its reaction on the Papacy, 133 ; destroyed the arts, 133-136 ; bad influence of Michelangelo, 134 ; destroyed communal culture, 137 ; led to Reformation, 139 ; and French Revolution, 192

Renaissance Popes, 57, 133, 142, 143

Repgow, Eike von, 69

Resurrection of the Body, 97, 103, 132

Ricardo, 235

Richard II, 158

Richmond, Duke of, 159

Robespierre, 206-7

Rogers, Thorold, quoted, 220, 283

Roman Law, 26, 32-3, 37, 51, 56, 58, seq., 72 seq., 89, 98, 101, 144, 146, 148, 150, 156, 170, 175, 177, 190, 192, 194, 199, 210, 214, 222, 251, 269, 274, 295-8, 304, 306, 310, 311 ; origins of, 32 ; Heine on, 32-3 ; after decline of Empire, 58 ; Visigothic compilation, 59 ; superseded by Canon law, 59 ; revival follows quarrel over Investiture, 60 ; Irnerius revives Justinian Code, 61 ; Glossators infatuated by it, 62 ; how it differs from Mediæval law, 63 ; adopted by Emperors, 64 ; sows discord between Church and State, 66 ; reception in Germany, 67-68 ; supersedes customary law, 69 ; Sir Paul Vinogradoff on reasons for reception, 69 ; breaks up the Mediæval Empire, 71 ; English law Roman in principle, 73 ; Henry II and Royal Courts of Justice, 74 ; attempt to transform feudalism into slavery, 75 ; transforms feudalism into landlordism, 77 ; Statute of Merton, 77 ; lawyers become stewards of feudal lords, 77 ; provokes Peasants' Revolt of 1381, 78-9 ; lawyers capture Parliament, 80 ; undermine the Monarchy, 81 ; paralyses government, 83 ; lawyers transform odium to Mediæval institutions, 84 ; need of its abolition, 310-11. *See also* Lawyers

Rome, 17 seq., 101, 105, 132, 192, 199, 295, 298, 308, 311 ; under the Republic, 52, 88, 296 ; under the Empire, 27 seq., 38, 48, 58, 88, 211, 296 ; generals, 27, 28 ; bureaucracy, 28, 86 ; proletariat, 27 ; taxation, 22, 29 ; unemployed, 21, 30 ; governors of provinces, 23

Rome, St. Peter's at, 141

Roper, Sir Anthony, 186

Rousseau, 189, 191 seq. *See Social Contract* and French Revolution

Royalists, French, 209-10. *See also* French Revolution

Royal African Company, 260

Royal Courts of Justice, 74, 76

Ruskin, John, 102, 234-5, 251, 257, 288, 289

Russell, Lord, 176

Russia, 68, 146, 286, 291

Russian Revolution, 201, 285 seq

Ruthenes, 274

St. Antonino, 128, 154, 155

St. Augustine, 91, 130

St. Bernard, 66

St. Dominic, 108, 109

St. Francis, 93, 108, 126, 127, 128, 129, 133, 134

St. Thomas Aquinas, 37, 51, 53, 66, 109, 111, 112, 128, 131, 156, 218, 225

Sachenspiegel, the, 67, 69

Sallust, 130

Salvation Army, 108

Saracens, 86, 105, 107, 118

Savonarola, 131

Saxony, Courts of, 69

Scandinavian North, 68, 146

Scholars at Oxford and Cambridge, 168

Science, 92, 102 seq., 118

Scipio, 28

Scotland, 65, 182, 183

Scott, Sir Walter, 102

Scottish Revolt, 182

Scriptures, interpretation of, 113, 140, 145, 153, 171, 186

Sculpture, 134, 135

Senate, Roman, 23, 24, 26, 27, 28 ; Senators, 24 ; Senatorial families, 21, 23

Seneca, 88

Serbia, 273

Serfs, 48, 49, 50

Serlio, 134
Servile State, 8, 30, 299, 301
Seutonius, 130
Sevèrus Alexander, Emperor of Rome, 31
Seymour, Jane, 159, 160
Shaw, G. Bernard, 248
Sheep-farming. See Agriculture
Sheffield, 223
Shop Stewards' Movement, 294
Sixtus IV, Pope, 100, 133
Slave Wars, 25, 121
Slavery, 16, 17, 24, 25, 75, 121, 199, 241, 296
Slovenes, 274
Smiles, Samuel, 241
Smillie, R., 306
Smith, Adam, 229, 232-5, 247, 251, 252, 263.
Social Contract, 193; key to, 193; Church and State, 193; morality and law, 194; republicanism and monarchy, 195; doctrine of equality, 195; the problem of the legislator, 196; advocacy of small states and small property, 197; City States of Greece as model, 198; influence of Roman Law, 199; relationship of property and currency, 200; the doctrine of the General Will, 202; Rousseau's reservations disregarded, 203. See also French Revolution
Socialism, Socialists, 33, 106, 178, 198, 212, 213, 299, 301, 303
Socrates, 93
Soissons, Bishop of, 96
Solon, 15-18
Somerset, Duke of, 171 seq.
South Sea Bubble, 261
South Sea Company, 260
Soviets, 286
Spain, 65, 96, 97, 99, 100, 106, 118, 178
Sparta, 15, 16, 18
Spartacus, 25
Spitalfields Acts, 221
Starr, Mark, 87
Statius, 130
Steed, Wickham, quoted, 273-4
Stoic philosophy, 25
Stuarts, the, 82, 183-187, 239, 240
Succession Act, 159
Sulla, 28

Sumptuary Laws, 17, 148, 231
Sunday Observance Laws, 185
Switzerland, 285
Sybil, 257

Taff Vale Judgment, 292, 293, 294
Tallien, 206
Tawney, R. H., quoted, 173-4
Taxation of Land Values, 306
Terence, 130
Terror, the, 206. See also French Revolution
Theory of Moral Sentiments, 234
Théot, Catherine, 206
Toleration, 171-2
Tories, 252
Torquemada, 99
Torture, 99
Trade Routes, change of, 228
Trade Unions, 222, 252, 292, 293, 294; Act of, 1871, 222, 292; functions of, 223; a basis for restored Guilds, 223, 299, 300, 309
Trades Disputes Act, 293
Tribune, 25, 26
Trinity, Doctrine of, 88
Trithemius, 225
Tsar, the, 286
Tudor Monarchy, 74; 159 seq., 215, 217-9, 224 seq., 230
Turks, 143

Unam Sanctum, 66
Unemployment, 18, 21, 30, 210, 227, 240, 278
Uniformity, Acts of, 179
Universities, Mediæval, 110, 111; Basle, 110; Bologna, 109; Cambridge, 168; Paris, 106-9; Oxford, 109, 164, 168; German, 67
Unto this Last, 235
Usury, 17, 20, 70, 88, 150, 153-5
Utopia, 174

Vendée, 205
Venice, 89, 105, 305
Verres, 88
Vienna, 273
Villains, 49, 75, 76
Vincent of Beauvais, 111
Vinogradoff, Sir Paul, quoted, 59, 67, 69, 75, 76
Virgil, 29, 130

Vitruvius, 134
Voltaire, 198

Wage system, 299
Wages, assessment of, 219, 220 ; in fifteenth century, 283 ; iron law of, 235
Walpole, Sir Robert, 260
Walsh, J. J., quoted, 103, 104
War, the Great European, 271 *seq.*
War Office, 278
Wars of the Roses, 159, 160
Warwick, Earl of, 176
Wealth, concentration of, 246, 249; problem of distribution of, 282 ; Gospel of, 226, 228, 229
Wealth of Nations, 231, 248, 263
Webb, Sidney, 300
Welfare Work, 29
Westminster Abbey, 124

Wharton, Thos., quoted, 164
William I, 49
William II, 60
William of Malmesbury, 90
Wimpheling, 149
Witchcraft, 97, 108
Wittenberg Castle, 141
Wolsey, Cardinal, 161, 174
Wool, export of, 173
Worms, Diet of (1122), 61 ; (1521), 145
Wren, Sir Christopher, 135
Wycliffe, 139-141, 156, 158

York, 184
Yorkshire Woollen Manufacturers, 278

Zimmern, Alf., quoted, 14, 15, 18
Zwinglians, 171

BOOKS RELATING TO NATIONAL GUILDS

NATIONAL GUILDS, by S. G. Hobson, edited by A. R. Orage (Bell & Sons, 6s.)
AN ALPHABET OF ECONOMICS, by A. R. Orage (T. Fisher Unwin, 4s. 6d.)
GUILD PRINCIPLES IN PEACE AND WAR, by S. G. Hobson (Bell, 2s. 6d.)

> *These books approach the subject primarily from the point of view of the Wage System*

THE WORLD OF LABOUR, by G. D. H. Cole (Bell, 4s. 6d.)
SELF-GOVERNMENT IN INDUSTRY, by G. D. H. Cole (Bell, 4s. 6d.)
LABOUR IN THE COMMONWEALTH, by G. D. H. Cole (Headley, 5s. 6d.)
THE MEANING OF NATIONAL GUILDS, by M. B. Reckitt and C. E. Bechhofer (Palmer & Hayward, 7s. 6d.)

> *These books approach the subject primarily from the point of view of Trade Unionism*

AUTHORITY, LIBERTY AND FUNCTION, by Ramiro de Maeztu (Allen & Unwin, 4s. 6d.)

> *This book, which I referred to in a footnote (page 310 and elsewhere), is concerned with the philosophy underlying a Guild revival. It approaches the subject from a mediævalist standpoint*

THE RESTORATION OF THE GUILD SYSTEM, by A. J. Penty (out of print)
OLD WORLDS FOR NEW, by A. J. Penty (Allen & Unwin, 3s. 6d.)
GUILDS AND THE SOCIAL CRISIS, by A. J. Penty (Allen & Unwin, 2s. 6d.)
THE GUILD STATE, by G. R. S. Taylor (Allen & Unwin, 3s. 6d.)

> *These books approach the subject from the point of view of mediæval economics*

www.ingramcontent.com/pod-product-compliance
Lightning Source LLC
La Vergne TN
LVHW091213080426
835509LV00009B/976